Manchester

WHAT'S NEW | WHAT'S ON | WHAT'S BEST

www.timeout.com/manchester

Contents

Don't Miss

Itineraries

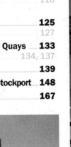

Published by Time (
Universal House
251 Tottenham Cou
London W1T 7AB
Tel: + 44 (0)20 781
Fax: + 44 (0)20 78:
Email: guides@time
www.timeout.com

Managing Director |
Editorial Director R
Deputy Series Edit
Financial Director Gareth Garner
Editorial Manager Holly Pick
Accountant Kemi Olufuwa

Time Out Guides is a wholly owned subsidiary of Time Out Group Ltd.

© Time Out Group Ltd
Chairman Tony Elliott
Financial Director Richard Waterlow
Time Out Magazine Ltd MD David Pepper
Group General Manager/Director Nichola Coulthard
Managing Director, Time Out International Cathy Runciman
Time Out Communications Ltd MD David Pepper
Group Marketing Director John Luck
Group Art Director John Oakey
Group IT Director Simon Chappell

Time Out and the Time Out logo are trademarks of Time Out Group Ltd.

This edition first published in Great Britain in 2007 by Ebury Publishing

Ebury Publishing is a division of The Random House Group Ltd
Company information can be found on www.randomhouse.co.uk
10 9 8 7 6 5 4 3 2 1

Distributed in USA by Publishers Group West (www.pgw.com)
Distributed in Canada by Publishers Group Canada (www.pgcbooks.ca)
For further distribution details, see www.timeout.com

ISBN 10: 1-84670-038-8
ISBN 13: 978184670-0385

A CIP catalogue record for this book is available from the British Library

Colour reprographics by Wyndeham Icon, 3 & 4 Maverton Road, London E3 2JE

Printed and bound by Firmengruppe APPL, aprinta druck, Wemding, Germany

Papers used by Ebury Publishing are natural, recyclable products made from wood
grown in sustainable forests

Manchester Shortlist

The **Time Out Manchester Shortlist** is one of a new series of guides that draws on Time Out's background as a magazine publisher to keep you current with everything that's going on in town. As well as Manchester's classic sights and the best of its eating, drinking and entertainment, the guide picks out the most exciting venues to have recently opened, and gives a full calendar of annual events. It also includes features on the important news, trends and openings, all compiled by locally based editors and writers. Whether you're visiting for the first time in your life or the fourth time this year, you'll find the *Time Out Manchester Shortlist* contains everything you need to know, in a portable and easy-to-use format.

The guide divides central Manchester into seven areas, each of which contains listings for Sights & museums, Eating & drinking, Shopping, Nightlife and Arts & leisure, along with maps pinpointing all their locations. At the front of the book are chapters rounding up each of these scenes city-wide, and giving a Shortlist of our overall picks in a variety of categories. We also include itineraries for days out, as well as essentials including transport information and hotels.

Our listings use phone numbers as dialled from within Manchester. From outside the city, dial 0161 (the area code – drop the '0' if calling from abroad) and the number given. We have noted price categories by using one to four pound signs (£-££££), representing budget, moderate, expensive and luxury. Major credit cards are accepted unless otherwise stated. We also indicate when a venue is NEW .

All our listings are double-checked but businesses do sometimes close or change their hours or prices, so it's a good idea to call a venue before visiting. While every effort has been made to ensure accuracy, the publishers cannot accept responsibility for any errors that this guide may contain.

Venues are marked on the maps using symbols numbered according to their order within the chapter and colour-coded according to the type of venue they represent:

- ❶ Sights & museums
- ❶ Eating & drinking
- ❶ Shopping
- ❶ Nightlife
- ❶ Arts & leisure

SHORTLIST
Online

The *Time Out Manchester Shortlist* is as up to date as it is possible for a printed guidebook to be. And to keep it completely current, it has a regularly updated online companion, at **www. timeout.com/manchester**. Here you'll find the latest news of the latest openings and exhibitions, as well as picks from visitors and residents – ideal for planning a trip. Time Out is the city specialist, so you'll also find travel information for more than 100 cities worldwide on our site, at www.timeout.com/travel.

Time Out Manchester Shortlist

EDITORIAL

Section Editors
  Sights & Museums Rob Haynes
  Eating & Drinking Andrew Shanahan
  (eating), Vida Bromby-Tavenner (drinking)
  Shopping Flic Everett
  Nightlife Alex Eyre
  Arts & Leisure Susie Stubbs
  Hotels Caroline Shaw
Consultant Editor Mark Hillsdon
Listings Editor Caroline Shaw
Commissioning Editor Ruth Jarvis
London Editor Anna Norman
Proofreader Nick Rider
Indexer Amy Simmons

STUDIO

Art Director Scott Moore
Art Editor Pinelope Kourmouzoglou
Senior Designer Josephine Spencer

Graphic Designer Henry Elphick
Digital Imaging Simon Foster
Ad Make-up Jenni Prichard
Picture Editor Jael Marschner
Deputy Picture Editor Tracey Kerrigan
Picture Researcher Helen McFarland

ADVERTISING

Sales Director/Sponsorship Mark Phillips
Sales Manager Alison Wallen
Advertising Sales Andrew Haworth
Advertising Assistant Kate Staddon
Copy Controller Baris Tosun

MARKETING

Marketing Manager Yvonne Poon
Marketing Designer Anthony Huggins

PRODUCTION

Production Manager Brendan McKeown
Production Co-ordinator Caroline Bradford

PHOTOGRAPHY

Photography by: pages 2 (bottom right), 13, 21, 22, 24, 44, 50, 53, 60, 63, 74, 76, 78, 88, 94, 95, 130, 139, 140, 145, 155, 175, 178, 180 Simon Buckley; pages 2, 7, 20, 25, 26, 29, 33, 34, 58, 65, 68, 70, 84, 86, 93, 98, 101, 110, 143, 147 Tim Otley; pages 2 (top left),15, 60, 66, 129, 148, 153 Mark Reeves; pages 8, 43, 46, 47, 49, 56, 61, 62 (right), 63, 64, 72, 73, 80, 81, 82, 103, 106, 107, 113, 114, 123, 125, 126, 131, 133, 138 John Oakey; page 35 Daniel Parker; page 36 Royal Horticultural Society; page 39 Jamie Hewlett/Manchester International Festival 2007; page 42 Jason Lock; page 55 David Oakey; page 90 Karina Lax; pages 97, 104 NEEMO; page 146 Larry Hickmott; page 152 Ben Blackall; page 167 NTPL/Ian Shaw; page 168 Joanne Moyes/Alamy; pages 171, 176 Nick Smith/Staying Cool. Cover photograph: B of the Bang by Thomas Hetherwick. Robert Harding Picture Library Ltd/Alamy.

The following images were provided by the featured establishments/artists: pages 3, 59, 62, 120, 149, 151, 172.

MAPS

Maps by: JS Graphics (john@jsgraphics.co.uk). Maps are based on material supplied by Lovell Johns Ltd, except maps on pages 116 and 137 which are supplied by Netmaps.

Thanks to Bill Borrows, Bruce O'Brien, Christine Cort, Simon Platt, Stephen Poole, Drew Stokes and all the writers of the *Time Out Manchester* preview magazine.

About Time Out

Founded in 1968, Time Out has expanded from humble London beginnings into the leading resource for those wanting to know what's happening in the world's greatest cities. As well as our influential what's-on weeklies in London, New York and Chicago, we publish more than a dozen other listings magazines in cities as varied as Beijing, Beirut and Mumbai. The magazines established Time Out's trademark style: sharp writing, informed reviewing and bang up-to-date inside knowledge of every scene.

Time Out made the natural leap into travel guides in the 1980s with the City Guide series, which now extends to over 50 destinations around the world. Written and researched by expert local writers and generously illustrated with original photography, the full-size guides cover a larger area than our Shortlist guides and include many more venue reviews, along with additional background features and a full set of maps.

Throughout this rapid growth, the company has remained proudly independent, still owned by Tony Elliott nearly four decades after he started Time Out London as a single fold-out sheet of A5 paper. This independence extends to the editorial content of all our publications, this Shortlist included. No establishment has been featured because it has advertised, and no payment has influenced any of our reviews. And, for our critics, there's definitely no such thing as a free lunch: all restaurants and bars are visited and reviewed anonymously, and Time Out always picks up the bill. For more about the company, see www.timeout.com.

Don't Miss

St Ann's Square p11

Sights & Museums

The blending of history and heritage in Manchester is a constant, highly active and very visible process. Driven by the 1996 IRA bomb and the staging of 2002's Commonwealth Games, the last decade has seen as furious a programme of rebuilding as the city has experienced since the cotton mills and their attendant slums sprang up in 19th-century Cottonopolis. Today, any exhaustive city guide would be made redundant within days, as new building conversions spring up citywide like stop-motion footage of fungus on a nature documentary.

The anchor of history, though, holds steady. Manchester is no stranger to upheaval, having witnessed and absorbed abrupt incursions of interlopers from Roman legions to Bonnie Prince Charlie's Jacobite rebellion and late 20th-century Irish republicanism.

At the end of it all, the Manchester of today is a far brasher place, for which much of the credit, if that's the appropriate word, must go to the 1996 explosion. The largest bomb to be detonated in mainland Britain, it took no lives but did ultimately provide the impetus for a regeneration that has left areas of the centre unrecognisable to anyone who last saw them a decade earlier. This allows the city to present itself as a living, vibrant and developing location, but has itself come at a cost, as much of the character of the old city is being subsumed under pricey new accommodation, while old-fashioned pubs are fast being replaced by rapacious wine bars.

Still, the enviable sweep of history represented across the city remains intact, albeit often buried beneath indifferent promotion. Manchester's museums have all benefited from the financial quantum leap in the wake of the bomb and the Commonwealth Games; the council have faced up to the fact that talking the city up as an international player means actually having to make it look like an international city. In many ways Manchester still lags behind in this sense, but old favourites such as the Manchester Art Gallery (p61) and Manchester Museum (p115) have had major refits, while entirely new attractions such as the Lowry (p138), Imperial War Museum North (p137), Urbis (p65) and Sportcity (p139) have arrived in very modern architectural forms and wrenched the city into the 21st century.

New public spaces

The arrival of self-explanatory New Cathedral Street nicely connects old and new Manchester, and opens up the old sightline between the cathedral and St Ann's church (now bordered by glossy new shops). In the background, Beetham Tower looms iconically. The new public spaces of Cathedral Gardens (p60) and Exchange Square (p60) have added some much needed air amid an oppressively claustrophobic mania for development, although decent green space still comes at a premium, and generally every demolished building is immediately replaced with another taller one. A near-psychotic drive to turn the City Centre into a residential area sometimes creates the feeling that the population is being replaced by an invisible army of subletters. Affordable housing remains a mostly notional concept.

DON'T MISS

SHORTLIST

Best new
- Imperial War Museum North (p137)
- The Lowry (p138)
- Urbis (p65)

Best restoration projects
- Gorton Monastery (p141)
- Victoria Baths (p153)

Best people watching
- Cathedral Gardens (p60)
- Exchange Square (p60)

Best-kept secrets
- Gaskell House (p150)
- Greater Manchester Police Museum (p88)
- St Mary's (The Hidden Gem) (p63)

Most impressive history
- Chetham's Library (p60)
- Manchester Cathedral (p62)
- St Ann's Church (p63)
- Town Hall (p63)

Best sculpture
- B of the Bang (p141)

Boldest new statement
- Beetham Tower (p127)
- Urbis (p65)

Most beautiful stained-glass
- Manchester Jewish Museum (p143)
- Manchester Cathedral (p62)

Best museum revamps
- John Rylands Library (p61)
- Manchester Art Gallery (p61)
- Manchester Museum (p115)

Most emblematic
- Salford Lad's Club (p134)
- Strangeways (p143)

Most impressive views
- Imperial War Museum North tower (p137)

Manchester
The Card

Packed with the latest special offers
and discounts, Manchester – The Card is
a must-have for the best value short break.

To receive your FREE card, apply now at
www.visitmanchester.com/freecard

Unsung treasures

A conurbation of this size can only support so much new activity, and the dramatic burst of new attractions which arrived just in time to flutter the city's eyelashes towards the gaze of the world for the Commonwealth Games has inevitably calmed down. With no further new major attractions planned, locals await instead the relaunch of Elizabeth Gaskell's House, John Rylands Library, Gorton Monastery and Victoria Baths.

When all this finally occurs it would be nice to see the city blow its trumpet a little more about its lesser known exhibition spaces. Chetham's Library (p60) is still more likely to receive visits from touring Chinese communists than Manchester's own citizens, while museums dedicated to police, transport or the city's Jewish community remain quietly unsung.

A city that can boast a significant hand in communism, computers, atomic theory and splitting the atom and that's given us so many era-defining moments, from inflatable bananas on the football terraces to scallies skanking in flares, really shouldn't be boasting so many hidden treasures and best-kept secrets. Much of greater Manchester currently resides on the 'tentative' list of UNESCO world heritage sites. Perhaps the future will be a little less provisory.

And with such an incredible musical heritage – Oasis, Joy Division and New Order, Morrissey and the Smiths, Buzzcocks, the Hollies, the Stone Roses, Bee Gees, Happy Mondays, Simply Red, M People, Badly Drawn Boy – even rock deity Lemmy used to live in Stockport – visitors on a musical heritage trail will find much to occupy them. Current hot hopes like the Longcut or the Answering

Machine might perhaps be spoken of in the same revered tones by the next edition of this guide. Or perhaps it will be one of a hundred others currently honing their craft in the city's rehearsal rooms.

We've drawn attention to a handful of sites (the Haçienda, Salford Lad's Club, Strangeways), but there are so many more skulking away. Granted, their narky mind-yer-own-business attitude is all part of the allure – sentimentality plays little part in the Mancunian psyche and most bands are too busy getting on with things to stop and celebrate the past – but is it beyond the bounds of reasonable imagination to picture a centre (dare one say museum?) commemorating Manchester's formidable musical pedigree?

A final note for the thousands who arrive here every year tickled by the notion of spending a few minutes on Coronation Street. The most famous set on television is not open to the public, and hasn't been since the closure of the Granada Studios tour in 1999. Indeed, at the time of writing, the 'Street' may not even remain in its current location at all. But this is all part of the mercurial pattern of heritage and change in Manchester. You may not be able to see the Websters, Duckworths et al enacting their daily lives, but for pretty much everything else, welcome to our city.

Neighbourhoods

Much of the centre is heavily commercial, the Northern Quarter strenuously fashionable while Chinatown is great for eating out.

The medieval quarter, from St Ann's Square to the cathedral, boasts the city's most pleasing architecture. Castlefield is where epochs collide most impressively, from the Roman settlement where Manchester began, to the canals

one **DaySaver**

DaySaver

Time out in Manchester?

Get unlimited travel on any bus, train
or tram with a System One DaySaver

system(one)**travelcards**.co.uk

traveline
public transport info
0870 608 2 608

Buy from the bus driver, at tram
stops or train stations

Heaton Hall

DON'T MISS

that are the enduring fingerprints of the Industrial Revolution.

Salford Quays is far more visitable now than a decade ago, when it was a museum-less concept waiting to spark. North Manchester is mainly residential, but offers much impressive parkland – including Heaton Park, the jewel in the city's green crown, containing Grade I-listed Heaton Hall, and other less heralded gems like Boggart Hole Clough – while beyond affluent South Manchester and Stockport the path heads towards Cheshire and fertile National Trust territory.

Manchester, as already observed, doesn't usually go out of its way to proclaim its greatness. The interested visitor can consequently experience an element of discovery in the simplest journey. The compact centre makes walking an attractive option.

A much-underrated activity in Manchester, as in many UK cities, is walking and observing the upper levels of buildings; once the gaze rises above the drearily repetitive chain-store fronts, unexpected architectural delights are often revealed. Try the old warehouses around Balloon Street, or the grandeur of King Street. Guided walks from the Visitor Centre (p65) can add context and historical facts.

Otherwise, the established attractions are uniformly good. Even those that divide opinion, like Urbis, are fascinating buildings, and a large part of the city's sightseeing can be done for free. The good folk of Manchester tend to ignore most of the treasures on their doorstep, so you're unlikely to suffer the crowds that can blight some of London's attractions.

River Restaurant p17

Eating & Drinking

As is so often the case, it was Morrissey who got it right. Although he probably wasn't thinking of Manchester when he sang that it was the bomb that would bring us together, it's certainly an apposite comment for a city that has seen itself reborn in the light of the 1996 IRA attack. The much-discussed city regeneration has seen an exponential increase in urban dwellings, and swathes of the landscape redesigned. Add to this the rise and rise of the remortgaged middle-classes, who are now splashing more cash around, and you've got a hugely generalised theory as to why Manchester's food and drink scene has changed so much in the last decade.

The lure of the local

Along with an explosion in the sheer number of restaurants (it's official: every old bank in the city is now an eaterie) there has also been a gradual culinary shift towards the realisation that if your restaurant is described as Modern British then that needn't be an insult. Manchester chefs are shrugging off the overbearing influences of other cuisines and beginning to take a fresh look at what English food, and more specifically North Western food, is all about. Isinglass (p154), Olive Lounge & Bistro (p144), Establishment (p66), Le Mont (p68) and many more are indicative of a new wave of restaurants that cook familiar

Art reviews, festivals, fairs & sales, exhibitions, tours, walks. Time In plugged in, TV listings, film of the day, terrestrial choice, digital choice, radio, podcast of the week. Nightlife night pass, house, electro & techno, social club, after-dark diary, compilation corner. Food & Drink reviews, food & drink 50, what to drink this weekend. Around Town previews, events, museums. Music gigs, listings, critics' choice, jazz, folk, latin, rock, pop, dance, on the up, classical, it happened here, booking ahead, booking of the week, opera. Theatre musicals, west end, fringe, plays, show of the week, openings. Books reviews, how I write, book of the week. Comedy listings, venues, critics' choice. Dance shows, bookings, critics' choice. Film reviews, close-up, film of the week, critics' choice, the directors, film listings, festivals & seasons, other cinema, DVD of the week, box office top ten. Gay & Lesbian listings, critics' choice. Kids events, weekend choice, outings, shows. Sport things to watch, sportsboard, things to do, touchlines. Consume london lives, check out, streets of London, travel solutions. Health & Fitness clubs & classes.

For the Londoner and the visitor

The best of London every week

Online
timeout.com/london

To your door
timeout.com/subscribe
0800 068 0050

In Store
at shops across London

dishes but that also never stop questioning how things can be done better.

That's not to say the scene is xenophobic; more that we're finally remembering who we are and, of course, part of our identity comes from the fact that Manchester is home to people from all around the globe. Visitors should note that our restaurant scene seems to take in every country in the world, and that the 'ethnic' places provide some of the best dining opportunities. From Dimitris to Koreana to Jai Kathmandu, to the whistle stop tour of the Far East that is Tampopo – this level of diversity is not widely found in the UK outside London.

Manchester can hold its head up high when it comes to sourcing fresh ingredients and using local produce; some of the country's best products are grown a short drive away. Choice (p131) recently planned a menu containing only ingredients grown, caught or produced within 20 miles of the city; it even featured a breast of wild mallard with a Vimto glaze (bonus point if you knew that Vimto was invented around where the old UMIST campus stands).

The Michelin curse

The long-mourned absence of Michelin stars from Manchester's eateries – despite the arrival of talented chefs such as the River Restaurant's (p135) Eyck Zimmer – still rankles. There is concern among local food-connoisseurs that, due to the exorbitant city centre rents, restaurateurs are reluctant to experiment with cuisine. As Juniper's Paul Kitching notes: 'Manchester people get what they want; I just can't imagine that if they wanted five or six Michelin-starred restaurants then that's what they would get.' Echoing

SHORTLIST

Best new
- Barburrito (p104)
- Cloud 23 (p131)
- Luso (p69)
- Olive Lounge & Bistro (p144)

What the…?
- Lounge Ten (p68)
- Temple of Convenience (p119)
- That Café (p158)
- This & That (p92)

Classic Manchester
- Briton's Protection (p66)
- Dry Bar (p91)
- Juniper (p157)
- Peveril of the Peak (p119)
- Sam's Chop House (p69)

Cocktail time
- Cloud 23 (p131)
- Grill on the Alley (p67)
- Obsidian (p69)

Late-night snacking
- Cord (p91)
- EastZEast (p105)
- Hunter's BBQ (p91)
- Pacific (p106)

Hangover hunger
- Abergeldie Café (p90)
- Bluu (p91)
- Metropolitan (p157)
- Trof (p158)

Most awe-inspiring
- Establishment (p66)
- French (p67)
- Great John Street Hotel bar (p173)
- Teppanyaki (p106)

Best rainy day option
- Isinglass (p154)
- Soup Kitchen (p92)

Best food-bars
- Bluu (p91)
- Northern Quarter Restaurant & Bar (p92)
- Obsidian (p69)

timeout.com

Over 50 of the world's greatest
cities reviewed in one site.

his comments, Paul Heathcote recently noted that although the city is well-stocked with mid-range eateries, there are sizeable gaps at the top end. Clearly, the city would be indebted to either Paul if they would have a crack at breaking Manchester's Michelin curse.

Pubs and bars

It's a conundrum that, for all its mid-range glory, Manchester is woefully short on gastropubs. For every Sam's Chop House, Ox or Lass O'Gowrie there are pubs who consider a prawn and Marie-rose baguette the zenith of culinary sophistication. Our prediction is that, with the smoking ban looming, the city's pubs are, however, getting set to diversify, and that the city will subsequently get gastropubitis. Quite frankly, we can't wait.

For all the scarcity of good pub-grub, Manchester must be the world's capital for food-bars. These establishments would love to have you believe that eating dinner in the middle of a nightclub is the most desirable thing in the world. They're wrong – although there are examples of places that manage to do both eating and drinking well (Obsidian, Northern Quarter Restaurant & Bar, Bluu), these are exceptions, and it is generally still better to visit bars or pubs for drinks and restaurants and cafés for food.

On that note, Manchester still does cool bars better than almost anywhere else in the UK. Both the quirky, lovable bars with diehard customers – like Dry Bar, Odd, A Place Called Common, Night & Day and Swish – and well-heeled bars like the cocktail-dispensing Socio Rehab or the altitudinous Cloud 23 are well worth checking out, and a bar crawl across Manchester would be time and

money well spent. Although you'll always find innovative bars in the city, the region's pubs are also in fine fettle and, as usual, Manchester is well-represented in the *Good Beer Guide*. Classic venues like Peveril of the Peak (p119), whiskey specialists Briton's Protection (p66) and the canal-side Dukes 92 (p131) are all well rated.

The whirlwind of hype is still focused on the Northern Quarter. The area has developed a very individual atmosphere deserving of preservation; the task is to prevent the district from becoming a victim of its own success. There's little new to speak of in Chinatown – but then, there's no need for it to change. It continues to set benchmarks for consistency and quality, and you'd be hard pushed to get a bad meal here (although, as with everywhere, buffets are best avoided). Yang Sing, Teppanyaki, Pacific and Red Chilli are four restaurants of real quality in this area. These are harder times for Rusholme's Curry Mile: with EastZEast seeing off all-comers there's no reason these days to visit the neon strip unless you want a sari or some traditional Indian sweets. Something serious needs to happen to lift its standards before it's too late.

Branching out

The real key to getting the most out of Manchester's food scene is to investigate the suburbs. For the cost of a bus ticket you can get down to Altrincham to look in at Michelin-starred Juniper (p157 and box p152), whiz across to Whalley Range for dinner at Palmiro (p157) or just get off at Manchester's best food suburb – West Didsbury, a 25-minute bus ride from the city centre – where you can enjoy the Metropolitan, Greens and the Lime Tree.

Although Salford Quays is currently a no-go zone restaurant-wise (unless you're keen on bad chains), a five-minute tram-, bus- or car-ride will get you in striking distance of a good eaterie.

The next few years promise to bring more culinary excitement to the city. We're eagerly awaiting the arrival, in 2007, of student-chic heroes Trof to the Northern Quarter, and once Steve McLoughlin really gets his hands on the menu at the Podium then the Hilton should have a restaurant to brag about. We also can't wait for Choice's second venture 'somewhere in South Manchester', and 2007 should see the arrival of Michael Caines when the Rossetti (p177) is converted into an Abode hotel. It will also be interesting to see how the city's restaurants participate in Manchester's International Festival (p39) in the summer and what inspiration Manchester's Food & Drink Festival will bring in the next few years. Finally, don't forget Eyck Zimmer is in peak form, after being crowned Knorr National Chef of the Year and Manchester's Food & Drink Festival chef of the year in 2006. It seems that satiating times may well be on the horizon.

Peveril of the Peak p19

Rags to Bitches p23

Shopping

The last decade has seen Manchester ascend from high street mediocrity to a retail playground worth at least twice Philip Green's personal pension fund. It would be absurd to deny the role that the IRA bomb, planted right outside the moribund Marks & Spencer, played in ushering in this new era of shopping. Yet the bomb wasn't the only catalyst for change; the relatively recent focus by urban designers nationwide on regenerating city centres, the rise of the pink pound and the UK's new-found love affair with the credit card over the last few years can also be identified as contributing factors.

Perhaps due to its industrial, muck-and-brass past, Manchester subsequently went a bit flash.

Subtlety is a gradual learning curve, and a delicately logo-ed jacket lining still isn't serious competition for a full-on label-flash and a gleaming Range Rover stuffed with Louis Vuitton bags. Designer shops aren't in short supply, from the opulent intimacy of Vivienne Westwood to the crashing timpani of tills that is Harvey Nichols. Buyers for the pricier stores know that anything too high-necked, eccentric or baggy won't sell. Manchester likes to see and be seen, and for girls, that means plenty of tanned, toned flesh, with a shiny leather bag the size of an elephant's bladder to set it all off. Boys, too, like to stand out – and that means the right jeans, the

DON'T MISS

best jackets and distressed T-shirts that cost the best part of £100.

Of course, it's not all WAGs and their wannabes. Manchester is also home to one of the biggest (if not *the* biggest) student populations in Europe, whose voracious appetite for cool clothes, music and books has contributed significantly to the expansion of the city's hippest area, the Northern Quarter. Bound by Oldham Street and High Street, the rabbit warren of roads in what used to be a grim, run-down garment district is now spangled with independent boutiques such as Wood, Westworld and Rags to Bitches (p99), second-hand bookshops, and an ever-growing collection of record stores. It's also home to Afflecks Palace, four storeys of shops selling everything required to turn a teenage country bumpkin into a hip young gunslinger, from battered trilbies and witty T-shirts to stripey tights, kitsch posters and psychedelic bongs. The Northern Quarter still has some way to go before it's a tourist experience as cute and comfortable as, say, the Lanes in Brighton – but it offers an eclectic shopping experience light years away from the ubiquity of the high street.

If the high street's calling, though, there are few shopping areas in Britain that can beat the combined forces of the Arndale (p72), with its fancy new extension, and Market Street, which looks much as it always has, but still pulls weekend crowds like a cup final at Old Trafford. All the big boys – M&S, Boots, Primark, HMV, Adidas – are joined by the usual parade of fashion stores, including a few edgier newcomers like Urban Outfitters.

Those who prefer to shop in spacious comfort, however, will bypass the heaving fleshpots of the Arndale and head directly to the serious shopper's axis of Exchange

SHORTLIST

Best new
- Arndale Market (p73)
- Co Cu (p75)
- Vox Pop Music (p100)

Best department stores
- Harvey Nichols (p76)
- Selfridges (p79)

Best for culture vultures
- Fopp (p75)
- Magma (p96)
- Mortens (p161)

Best for street-style
- Aspecto (p73)
- McQueen (p161)

Heaven for foodies
- Love Saves the Day (p132)
- Selfridges food department (p79)
- Unicorn Grocery (p161)

Most innovative
- Beatin' Rhythm (p94)
- Rags To Bitches (p99)
- Rockers (p99)

Best for kids
- Oilily (p79)
- Pixie (p161)

Great fun
- Fred Aldous (p95)
- Oklahoma (p96)
- Pop (p99)

Goods most coveted by WAGs
- Flannels (p75)
- Hermès (p77)
- Vivienne Westwood (p81)

Best for gifts
- Agent Provocateur (p73)
- C Aston (p73)
- Hotel Chocolat (p77)
- Penhaligons (p79)

Best bargains
- Fopp (p75)
- Office Sale Shop (p77)
- TK Maxx (p80)

Square, St Ann's Square and King Street, where shops whose wares feature regularly in glossy magazines proliferate. Selfridges (p79) and Harvey Nichols (p76) between them take care of everyone who understands the difference between Marni and McCartney, while the glossy sweep of high-end fashion stores that line New Exchange street offers a series of clearly defined – and desirable – looks for the less sartorially certain.

If Manchester is fast becoming a retail tale of two cities, with the creative independents providing the flip side to the designer dream, nobody actually seems to mind. Rather than sticking to their designated patch, Manchester shoppers are happy to wander between the two extremes, with wannabe WAGs and businessmen popping into the craft market or strolling down Oldham Street to Magma (p96), perhaps, for a quirky gift, and the skint but savvy youngsters playing dress-up in Selfridges all afternoon, then

spending £2 on a coffee at the end of it. The intimate scale of the City Centre – which can be crossed easily within 15 minutes – means that everyone feels they can go anywhere. Even King Street, with its patrician airs, happily devotes space to *Big Issue* sellers, mobile phone shops and high street chains, while Deansgate's newsagents and scruffy record shops lead on to the art deco splendour of House of Fraser, topped by the eye-wateringly pricey Bauer Millet car showroom at the Castlefield end. Whatever you want is available within a couple of square miles. Ten years ago, it wasn't possible to find half of it within 100 miles.

And if the City Centre's too much hassle, the suburbs are striving to compete. Chorlton's Beech Road, home to a stretch of imaginative, affordable boutiques, galleries and gift shops, draws loyal customers from all over South Manchester, while Didsbury offers a chance to cherry-pick from a selection of interesting delis, book traders and fashion shops. The outlying towns to the North and East – Stockport, Bury, Prestwich – offer solid high street shopping opportunities and great markets, while Salford is home to the Lowry Outlet Mall (p138), where several members of the city's great and good have been spotted taking advantage of the up to 75 per cent discounts at Whistles, Flannels, Karen Millen and the like.

Mancunians love to shop. The new-found popularity of retail therapy can be explained partly as a response to the city being continuously labelled as that place where it always rains and where everyone looks like Liam Gallagher. It could also be because locals are lucky enough to have access to the best spectrum of shops outside the capital. Mostly, though, it's down to one simple fact: that they simply can.

Selfridges

Manchester 235 p28

Nightlife

Despite the apparent desire of developers to change the city by burying it in high-rise residential accommodation, one area of Manchester is standing firm: its legendary nightlife scene. Since the era of 1960s rock 'n' roll band Freddie and the Dreamers, Manchester's independent music tradition has defined the city; noise complaints from new neighbours and a lack of top-class venues aren't going to stop promoters carrying on the party. With the Northern Quarter radiating creative vibrancy, new musicians making their mark and genre-bending club promoters running riot, the variety, quality and energy of the after-dark scene in 2007 is on trademark roof-raising, trainer-wrecking form.

Clubs

The creativity and diversity that made Manchester the clubbing capital of Europe remains evident today, 20 years after the acid house revolution. But beware the promises of generic, money-for-old-rope-style indie promotions, which are legion.

Instead, find the rock 'n' roll spirit of Madchester alive and scissor-kicking at Clint Boon's brilliant Disco Rescue at South (p85), or turn your attention to a new breed of club night – champions of your next favourite band like Blowout, Tramp! and High Voltage, who've spent the past year or so creating a different kind of mayhem in the pubs and clubs around Piccadilly, fusing bleeding-edge live acts with DJs to keep the indie faithful happy.

If esoteric beats are more your thing, check out Music Box (p122) on Oxford Street for flagship underground electronic music shindigs Keep it Unreal and Electric Chair. For underground techno, house and breaks venture into Ancoats, where Sankeys (p146) has emerged from its latest refurb looking fresher than ever, with its infamous Friday nighter Tribal Sessions still drawing the crowds.

Manchester has its share of identikit chain bars. For something different to kick off a night out, head to the finally up-and-come Northern Quarter where (mostly) independent bars often offer quirky aural entertainment as well as decent drinks. The perfect warm-up for the area's favourite nightclub, former burlesque bar Mint Lounge (p100 and box p97), has found rude form over the past 12 months as home to numerous quality club nights, and is a safe bet for getting your groove on any weekend. Settling into a new residency at Mint is Friends and Family, run by the Fat City label. The night is champion of local and stateside underground hip hop, and one of the original catalysts of Manchester's now world-class hip hop scene. Other hip hop-tions include C'mon Feet and Ape; the latter celebrated its first birthday in 2006 by organising a piss-up in a brewery – or more accurately, an insanely successful danceathon featuring a jaw-dropping line-up of talent at the former Boddington's Brewery, just north of the city centre. In the lead up to Christmas 2006, a team of promoters struck a deal to strip out the brewery warehouses and host a series of club nights in the massive industrial space. If the project works, it's hard to imagine that this'll be the last party we'll see there.

Back to regular events, and for those into filthy bassline breaks,

Fuse at the Roadhouse (p102) is well worth checking out and Metropolis at Music Box ably flies the flag for the largely under-represented drum 'n' bass scene.

Across town, the scene is less vintage Adidas, more hairdressers, handbags and honeydew Martinis. Drinking on Deansgate and Deansgate Locks is a self-consciously glamorous affair that normally starts in cocktail bars (like footballers' former favourites Cocoa Rooms and Sugar Lounge) and leads on to dressier dance clubs like Emporia (p131), Ampersand (p82) in the City Centre, and Paparazzi (p85). Proceed only with designer labels present, correct and obviously displayed.

Music

Manchester today is a melting pot of influences, which means era-defining, city-wide soundscapes like Madchester are unlikely to happen

Ampersand

again. But given the vibrancy of the current scene that's no bad thing. As well as stadium-filling, festival-headlining acts like New Order, Doves and Elbow, Manchester has electronic-influenced innovators Polytechnic and the Longcut, the spine-tinglingly brilliant singer/songwriter Liam Frost, new grunge from Nine Black Alps and, coming up behind them, a wealth of excellent unsigned acts plying their trade all over town in a bewildering array of genres from folk to metal, indie to hip hop and beyond.

To catch a lot of talent in a short space of time, visit the city during August or October when two musical showcases bring it all together for easy consumption. Launched as a show of resilience a year after the IRA bombing in 1996, Dpercussion (p37) turns Castlefield into a booty-shaking carnival of civic pride at the end of each summer, with its organisers roping in the city's best artists and promoters to boost the fun.

If you can hack the pace, test yourself further at In the City (p42), a festival of new music that was founded in 1992 and that makes Manchester its own over five frantic days each autumn. As well as giving the music industry a chance to congregate outside the big smoke, ITC also gives music lovers the chance to take in an unprecedented amount of tunes from hundreds of unsigned artists in every available venue in town. It's worth showing up; if you're in the right place at the right time, you'll be the first to see tomorrow's big stars: Oasis and Coldplay both played ITC on their way to becoming rock royalty. See if you can spot who's next.

Another essential diary date is relative newcomer Manchester vs Cancer (p120). Launched in 2006, this charity gig brought together 14 Mancunian artists for

SHORTLIST

Best for underground sounds
- Attic (p121)
- Music Box (p122)
- Sankeys (p146)

Best for gigs
- Manchester Apollo (p62)
- Manchester Academy (p122)
- Night & Day (p100)
- Roadhouse (p102)

Best for rockers
- Jilly's Rockworld (p122)

Best for cocktails
- Manchester 235 (p83)
- One Central Street (p85)

Most glamorous
- Ampersand (p82)
- Paparrazzi (p85)

None more Manchester
- Big Hands (p121)
- Cord (p91)
- Night & Day (p100)
- South (p85)

Best for gay clubbers
- Club Alter Ego (p111)
- Essential (p112)

Best place to play dress up
- Tiger Lounge (p85)
- Whim Wham club at Charlie's Karaoke Bar (p111)

Best for dancing
- Mint Lounge (p100)

Best for laughs
- Comedy Store (p131)
- Opus (p83)

Best for sound systems
- Pure (p85)
- Sankeys (p146)

Best for Sunday sessions
- Mint Lounge (p100)
- Tribeca (p109)

Best for food with your grooves
- Matt & Phred's (p100)

an historically great performance. Run by ex-Smiths bassist Andy Rourke, MvC has awesome credentials and generates universal goodwill; future MvC festivals promise to be memorable events.

The venues hosting all of this great music range from the very large (Manchester Arena; p83) to the tiny (Retro; p112), each with their own charms. For a quintessentially Mancunian gig experience, try heart-of-the-local-scene venues Night & Day (p100) and the Roadhouse, or drop into intimate live jazz music bar Matt & Phred's (p100) – but make sure you book ahead for the latter: weekends get very busy. For something a touch more upmarket (but still with a rock 'n' roll soul), try the gorgeous Manchester 235 (p83). With beautiful, '40s-inspired decor, a casino, bar and two restaurants as well as a live music space to call its own, this £13million venture has finally dragged the Great Northern leisure development out of mediocrity. If it continues to deliver on its promises, it'll be an essential port of call.

Gay & lesbian

Previously in a perennial state of flux, the Gay Village seems to have hit a plateau of late with all its available bar space taken up, bedded in and running smoothly. Canal Street being what it is, however, you can guarantee that there's drama and intrigue just around the corner. And so it is that the latest problem on the horizon isn't *Queer as Folk*-inspired tourism or fear of commercialisation but pesky developers queuing up to construct yet more flats – this time right in the heart of Manchester's second most famous street.

Not that that's bothering the drinkers. As the planning battles

continue, in the pedestrianised road by the canal it's business as usual: alfresco beers by day, karaoke crooning and high-tempo hedonism by night. But then if Canal Street can see off the marauding hen parties, maybe these Village people are right not to be too worried about the team of men in fluorescent waistcoats and hard hats. Hang on, we feel a song coming on...

Comedy

Manchester's comedy scene is currently enjoying a resurgence with the arrival of some of the UK's leading independent TV production outfits. Baby Cow, run by Henry Normal, has an office in Manchester; as does Hat Trick North, the northern arm of the London production company responsible for *Have I Got News For You*. And then there's BBC North, which has a thriving comedy unit at the Beeb's Oxford Road HQ.

That energy is mirrored on the stand-up scene, which revolves around three central locations: the flagship Comedy Store (p131), old favourite the Frog & Bucket (p100) and accomplished newcomer Opus (p83), with a weekly trip out of town to Toby Hadoke's XS Malarky in Fallowfield, long considered essential for serious scenesters. Comedy City, a new night launched in September 2006 at the City of Manchester Stadium (p147), may soon be joining this holy quadrangle; promoter Ashley Boroda got the Friday night gig off to a bright start with some high-profile bookings (the likes of Jason Manford).

Elsewhere in the city, Dancehouse (p124) and the Lowry (p138) act as receiving houses for some of the bigger names in comedy, as well as television/radio show filmings, while smaller venues like Iguana offer laughs with your lager on a standard night out.

Bridgewater Hall p34

Arts & Leisure

Manchester is emerging from a decade's worth of cultural construction. The magnificent Bridgewater Hall (p123) was among the first of the new-builds, followed by Salford's Lowry centre (p138) and the museum of urban culture, Urbis (p65). Other already-standing centres have meanwhile been undergoing renovation – Manchester Art Gallery (p62) recently benefitted from a £35million spit-and-polish – while the increasing numbers of luxury hotels and spas (such as the Sienna Spa; p87) are an indication of the city's renewed fortunes.

But building and rebuilding is only half the story. Alongside the shiny new arts complexes, Manchester has shored up its cultural confidence, and nowhere is this more evident than in the city's burgeoning festivals scene. Autumn has now become the unofficial start of the festival season, although there are now so many events that activity is pretty much year-round. Leading the pack is the new and ambitious Manchester International Festival (p39), followed up by food and drink, comedy and literature festivals. Music festivals now abound in Manchester, with Dpercussion, In The City and Futuresonic all regular fixtures.

Venues have also upped the ante, with many now offering so much under one roof that it's easy to lose whole days sampling their individual cultural wares. Add-ons

include the Royal Exchange's (p87) book and craft shops and Cornerhouse's café-bar (one of the best coffee spots in the city for quality beverages and atmosphere).

But it's the unmistakable infusion of Mancunian flavour that makes downtime here so good. Whether it's the laid-back vibe of the King's Arms (p135), with its theatre space, Studio Salford (p138), upstairs, or the edginess of Contact Theatre (p124), you'll never forget where you are. The industrial heritage settings – the neo-classical grandeur of the Portico (p87), the glass-roofed atrium of the Craft & Design Centre (p95) – are unique. If it sometimes feels you can't move for exposed brick and restored ironwork, that's no bad thing, for, while the city may have its feet firmly planted in historical soil, its face is definately turned to a bright future.

Sport & leisure

This city of sporting prowess seamlessly produces world-class athletes and puts on international events. The two football clubs, City and United (p147 and p64), ignite passionate debate wherever you go, and the city boasts four rugby league clubs, one of rugby union's top teams (Sale Sharks, currently Champions of England) and Lancashire Cricket Club, based at Old Trafford. But there's also room for more specialist events. Manchester Velodrome (p147) houses a 3,500-seat track for what might be considered a minority sport (track cycling) – and yet the venue's winter season events regularly pull in 3,000 punters. The World Track Cycling Championships to be held here in Easter 2008 are sure to sell out – and these are not the only international championships the city is hosting in the near future. Look out for the Paralympic World

S H O R T L I S T

Most anticipated event
- Manchester International Festival (p39)

Best new festival
- Manchester Literature Festival (p42)

Best new film festival
- Family Friendly Film Festival (p41)
- Manchester International Film Festival (p42)

Grand dame of classical music
- The Hallé, which is 150 in 2008 (p123)

Best for cutting-edge dance and theatre
- Contact Theatre (p124)

Champion of new playwriting
- Royal Exchange (p87)

Best eclectic arts centre
- The King's Arms (p135)

Best cinema
- Cornerhouse (p124)

Loveliest hidden gems
- Chetham's Library & School of Music (p60)
- Portico Library (p87)
- Victoria Baths (p153)

Best participant sport
- Great Manchester Run (p41)

Best spectator sport
- World Track Cycling Championships (p35)

Best chill-out spa
- Inner Sanctuary Spa (p102)

Best spiritual retreat
- Manchester Buddhist Centre (p102)

Lushest park
- Fletcher Moss Gardens (p150)

DON'T MISS

Cup, Salford Triathlon World Cup and the EHF European Hockey Championships in 2007.

Another draw for Manchester is the ease with which visitors can indulge in healthy pursuits. The ten-year-old Buddhist Centre (p102) offers drop-in meditation and yoga classes, and has recently added pain management classes and Alexander Technique sessions to its list of services. And if trekking through the urban landscape leaves you yearning for space and fresh air, then head out to Heaton Hall (p140). This 18th-century house, with its impressive grounds, is coming towards the end of a decade-long restoration project.

Film

There's great enthusiasm for film in this city, with independent festivals including Kino's biennial Manchester International Film Festival and the Family Friendly Film Festival (set up in 2006). The only one of its kind in the UK, the latter is a rare chance to expand the young uns' experience of film – through workshops, interesting venues and a film choice that hits higher than the usual kiddies cartoon fare.

When it comes to venues, Cornerhouse (p124) is king. Its refurbished screens show the widest selection of arthouse, independent and foreign language films in town, while visits from international directors add an extra dimension for cinephiles. Regular festivals – Spanish & Latin American, Exposures – are a chance to get under the skin of cinematic developments. Also check out the Manchester International Festival – the 2007 2007 commissions include a new film by British film director Greg Hall called *Kapital*, which was shot on the streets of Manchester.

Theatre

With its 30th anniversary season playing to packed houses, it's surprising to learn that the Royal Exchange (p87) has found time to nurture new talent. But it's done exactly that, with the results of the 2005 Playwriting Competition performed as part of Manchester International Festival. A writer-in-residence and the National Playwriting Conference (July 2007) reveal a dedication to developing new work that's being replicated across the city, most notably at Contact Theatre (who hold 'pitch parties' to uncover new talent) and the University's little-known Martin Harris Centre.

Other highlights include Pete Postlethwaite playing Prospero in the Exchange's production of *The Tempest* and Bolton Octagon's 40th anniversary season – which includes five world premières.

Studio Salford p31

Dance

The best classical dance
performances come courtesy of
the Lowry, Palace Theatre and
Opera House. The latter two,
sister venues run by the same
organisation, put on reliable
touring shows from the English
National Ballet, with *The Three
Musketeers* (May 2007) typical
of their performances. The Lowry,
meanwhile, excels at contemporary
dance, and brings the likes of
Eclipse (billed as the UK's first
circus musical) to Manchester
in 2007, plus works by the
Birmingham Royal Ballet and
contemporary European and
international touring companies.
For edgier work head to Contact
Theatre or Greenroom, whose
intimate spaces mean you can
get up close and personal to the
newest moves in contemporary
and urban dance.

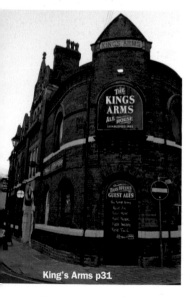

King's Arms p31

Classical music

The Hallé celebrates its 150th
anniversary in 2008, at a time
when classical music in the city
has never looked in better shape.
Under Mark Elder, who has
committed himself to the orchestra
until the end of the decade, the
Hallé is enjoying the kind of
critical and popular success
unseen since its 1960s Sir John
Barbirolli heyday. While its
anniversary season promises
outstanding performances, other
highlights include a weekend in
2007 to mark Edward Elgar's
150th birthday.

Bridgewater Hall, performing
home of both the Hallé and BBC
Philharmonic, recently celebrated
its first decade, its success no
doubt helped by the friendly
rivalry between Mark Elder and
the equally charismatic head
of the Phil, Gianandrea Noseda.
Noseda's artistic direction is
formidable: when he led the Phil
through its first complete cycle
of the Beethoven symphonies in
30 years, the performances were
uploaded onto the BBC's website.
1.4m quick-fire downloads later,
the Phil realised it had someone
rather special fronting its orchestra.

The public profile of the Royal
Northern College of Music (RNCM;
p124) has just got better, with
the opening of a new wing on
Oxford Road, while the University
of Manchester's Quatuor Danel
Quartet – arguably one of the
best quartets in Europe – regularly
plays just up the road at the
Martin Harris Centre. Manchester
International Festival is also
having a positive impact on
classical music, with Manchester
Camerata and a new organisation,
the Exodus Live International
Orchestra, both busily working on
their contributions to the festival.

Calendar

Manchester Jazz Festival p37

The following are the pick of the annual events that happen in Manchester, as well as the major forthcoming one-off events. Further information and exact dates can be found nearer the time from flyers and seasonal guides available from tourist information centres (p188). For gay and lesbian events, look out for *Out Northwest* magazine.

January

Mid Jan **National Winter Ales Festival**
New Central Hall, Corporation Street
www.winterales.uku.co.uk
A selection of over 200 brews, with a good range of winter warmers.

February

Jan/Feb (date varies)
Chinese New Year
Chinatown
www.manchesterlive.co.uk

Fireworks and the Golden Dragon Parade in the city's Chinatown.

March

Early-mid Mar **Manchester Irish Festival**
Various locations
www.manchesteririshfestival.co.uk
A two-week festival culminating in one of the UK's largest St Patrick's Day parades.

Mid Mar **¡Viva! Spanish & Latin American Film Festival**
Cornerhouse, p124
www.vivafilmfestival.co.uk
Ten days of Hispanic film screenings, with a healthy selection of premières and previews.

27-30 (2008) **UCI World Track Cycling Championships**
Manchester Velodrome, p144
www.britishcycling.org.uk
Faster, faster – watch the world's best cyclists get in a spin, at the velodrome.

RHS Flower Show at Tatton Park

April

9-13 (2008) **9th FINA World Swimming Championships**
MEN Arena, p83
www.mancheseter2008.org
The UK hosts its first FINA World Championships – in Manchester.

May

7-13 (2007) **Visa Paralympic World Cup**
Manchester Velodrome, p144
www.visaparalympicworldcup.com
350 athletes from 49 countries take part in this high-profile annual competition.

14 (2008) **UEFA Cup Final**
City of Manchester Stadium, p146
www.uefa.com
Club teams compete for Europe's second major football trophy.

Mid May **Futuresonic**
Various locations
www.futuresonic.com
Electronic, experimental music and arts, with international and local artists.

Late May **BUPA Great Manchester Run**
City Centre
www.greatrun.org
See box p41.

June

2-3 (2007) **Elgar in his Kingdom**
Bridgewater Hall, p123
www.halle.co.uk
A weekend of performances celebrating Elgar's 150th birthday.

Mid June **Salford Mini Soccer Festival**
Salford Sports Village, Kersal
www.salfordminisoccerfestival.co.uk
300 teams of under-12s battle it out in the nation's biggest event of its kind.

Mid June **British Open Athletics Championships**
Sportcity
www.disabilitysport.org.uk
International, multi-disability annual athletics event.

Mid-late June **Exodus Outdoor Festival**
Platt Fields
www.can.uk.com/exodus
World music and dance from refugee communities, at this one-day festival.

Late June-mid July **Manchester International Festival (MIF)**
Various locations
www.manchesterinternational festival.com
See box p39.

July

Ongoing Manchester International Festival (see June)

5 (2007) **Imperial War Museum North's Fifth Anniversary**
Imperial War Museum North
http://north.iwm.org.uk

Mid-late July **Rusholme Project**
Curry Mile
www.shisha.net
Celebrating multicultural Rusholme through installation art. Launches at the end of MIF 2007 (see box p39).

Late July **RHS Flower Show at Tatton Park**
Tatton Park
www.rhs.org.uk/tatton
Horticultural heaven, over ten days.

Late July **Manchester Jazz Festival**
Various locations
www.manchesterjazz.com
Popular festival featuring around 50 bands in indoor and outdoor venues, over a period of one to two weeks.

Late July **Salford BG Triathlon World Cup**
Salford Quays
www.trisalford.info
Elite swims cycle and run in the only leg of this supreme test of fitness to be held in the UK.

July/Aug **Dragon Boat Race**
Salford Quays
www.dragonboatfestivals.co.uk
30 teams take to the water for a one-day battle of the oars.

THE SHORTLIST

WHAT'S NEW | WHAT'S ON | WHAT'S BEST

Barcelona
WHAT'S NEW | WHAT'S ON | WHAT'S NEXT

Berlin
WHAT'S NEW | WHAT'S ON | WHAT'S NEXT

London
WHAT'S NEW | WHAT'S ON | WHAT'S NEXT

Manchester
WHAT'S NEW | WHAT'S ON | WHAT'S NEXT

New York
WHAT'S NEW | WHAT'S ON | WHAT'S NEXT

Paris
WHAT'S NEW | WHAT'S ON | WHAT'S NEXT

Prague
WHAT'S NEW | WHAT'S ON | WHAT'S NEXT

Rome
WHAT'S NEW | WHAT'S ON | WHAT'S NEXT

Coming soon…

Amsterdam
2008
WHAT'S NEW | WHAT'S ON | WHAT'S NEXT

Dubrovnik
WHAT'S NEW | WHAT'S ON | WHAT'S NEXT

Las Vegas
WHAT'S NEW | WHAT'S ON | WHAT'S NEXT

Tokyo
WHAT'S NEW | WHAT'S ON | WHAT'S NEXT

Venice
WHAT'S NEW | WHAT'S ON | WHAT'S NEXT

- **POCKET–SIZE GUIDES**
- **WRITTEN BY LOCAL EXPERTS**
- **KEY VENUES PINPOINTED ON MAPS**

Available at all major bookshops at only
£6.99 and from timeout.com/shop

Time Out
SHORTLIST

The big one

Manchester International Festival (MIF) is nothing if not ambitious. This new biennial arts bonanza was kick-started in 2005 by a riotous 'preview' gig from Damon Albarn's virtual band Gorillaz. Pop and hip hop luminaries Shaun Ryder, Neneh Cherry and De La Soul joined Albarn in a concert signalling the festival's boisterous intention to become one of the brightest events on the global calendar.

With the nearby Liverpool Biennial emphasising the visual arts, Manchester wisely took a different tack in developing its own festival, creating the world's only showcase of entirely new, commissioned work. There's nothing second-hand playing here, with the number of world premières in double digits in 2007. And although there's a distinctly musical flavour to the programme, the inaugural festival presents a marvellous mishmash of music, film, visual and digital art, debates, circus and theatre.

The 2005 Gorillaz concert was just the start of an ongoing contribution from musical polymath Damon Albarn. His *Monkey: Journey to the West* – a circus-inspired operatic take on an ancient Chinese tale (logo pictured) – is the centrepiece of

the 2007 festival and premières in Manchester before moving on to Paris and Berlin.

Also in 2007, Hans Ulrich Obrist of London's Serpentine Gallery directs *Il Tempo del Postino*, an exhibition-cum-performance from a group of international visual artists. *The Pianist* brings together a concert-pianist and theatre director for an unusual performance of the story of survival in Nazi-occupied Warsaw. And award-winning filmmaker Greg Hall premières *Kapital*, a film that sets traditional fairytales on the wet and windy streets of Manchester. The city's other arts organisations, meanwhile, step up to the mark with Manchester Firsts, a collection of performances and exhibitions that include an orchestra made up of musicians from local refugee communities, a film and music installation at Cornerhouse (p124) and a large-scale outdoor artwork slap-bang in the middle of Curry Mile. Pre-festival events include artist Steve McQueen's creative response to the Iraq War, shown at the Central Library (until July '07). With the whole city engaged in the festival, the event is one of Manchester's must-dos.

■ www.manchesterinternational festival.com

MANCHESTER INTERNATIONAL FESTIVAL

First for Manchester

28 June - 15 July 2007

'A festival like you've never seen before...
it will be entirely devoted to newly
commissioned work. This makes it unique -
certainly in this country, probably in the world.'

Daily Telegraph, January 2007

To find out more, visit:
www.manchesterinternationalfestival.com

August

Early Aug Dpercussion
Castlefield, various locations
www.dpercussion.com
One-day music festival celebrating over ten years of post-bomb partying.

Mid-late Aug Family Friendly Film Festival
Various locations
www.familyfriendly.org.uk
Ten days of U-rated film and workshops.

Mid-late Aug Manchester Pride
Gay Village
www.manchesterpride.com
Ten days of floats, parades and parties.

18-26 (2007) EuroHockey Nations Championships, Women & Men
Belle Vue
www.eurohockeymanchester2007.com
The biggest hockey event staged in England since the 1986 World Cup.

September

Sept-Oct Viva La Muralists! Festival of Illustrative Street Art
Various locations
www.myspace.com/vivalamuralists
Graffiti, stencilling and outdoor scribblings, in this two-month festival.

Sept 2007-July 2008 Bolton Octagon's 40th anniversary celebrations
Octagon Theatre, p146
www.octagonbolton.co.uk

October

Ongoing Viva La Muralists! (see Sept), Bolton Octagon's 40th anniversary celebrations (see Sept)

Early Oct Dashehra Diwali Mela
Platt Fields Park, Fallowfield
www.indianassociation.org.uk
Bhangra, Bollywood, Indian brass bands, live dance, food and fireworks.

Early-mid Oct Manchester Food & Drink Festival
Various locations
www.foodanddrinkfestival.com

On your marks…

Get set for the Great Manchester Run.

Set up in the afterglow of the Commonwealth Games, this 25,000-strong race, held in May, has quickly become one of the most popular events in the British running calendar. Organised by the brains behind the Great North Run, Manchester was the natural choice to host a new 10k: the city renowned for football also excels in cricket, cycling, rugby – and running. And with a route taking in Manchester United's ground, fleet-of-foot football fans get the best of both worlds.

Even for the less energetic, the setting makes for a good day out. Runners and spectators alike can enjoy the views: Salford Quays, Imperial War Museum North, Albert Square and the Town Hall. The Hallé Orchestra always exert themselves to bring the 'sporting proms' to the Bridgewater Hall (p123) the night before the main race, and those wanting to make a weekend of it can watch their kids participate in the Junior Run at Sportcity on the Saturday, before making for the finish line themselves on the Sunday.

The only downside is the inevitable road chaos. If you're planning on racing, ditch the car and take the tram, train or bus. And to make sure your foot gets a place at the starting line sign up for email reminders as early as possible before the race, at www.greatrun.org – the run will sell out faster than you can say 'Paula Radcliffe'. Tickets go on sale in mid January.

Ten days of gourmet activity, with food stalls, celebrated chefs, and special initiatives from the city's restaurants.

Mid Oct **Manchester Literature Festival**
Various locations
www.mlfestival.co.uk
Ten days of literary delights.

Mid Oct **In The City**
Various locations
www.inthecity.co.uk
Mix with the pros for three days, as they try to spot the next big thing in music.

Late Oct **Manchester Comedy Festival**
Various locations
www.manchestercomedyfestival.com
12 days of up-and-coming stand-ups, as well as big-hitters.

Late Oct **Mind Body Spirit**
Manchester Central, p62
www.mindbodyspirit.co.uk
Re-align your chakras at this three-day show dedicated to alternative therapies.

Late Oct-early Nov **Manchester International Film Festival**
Various venues
www.kinofilm.org.uk

A new biennial festival of independent film, which launches in 2007.

November

Ongoing Bolton Octagon's 40th anniversary celebrations (see Sept); Kino Manchester International Film Festival (see Oct)

Mid Nov **Christmas Lights Switch On**
Albert Square, City Centre
www.manchester.gov.uk

Mid Nov-Late Dec **Manchester Christmas Markets**
Albert Square and St Ann's Square
www.manchester.gov.uk/markets
Stocking fillers, Glühwein and festive food in the North West's biggest, oldest and best markets.

December

Early Dec **Exposures UK Student Film Festival**
Cornerhouse, p124
www.exposuresfilmfestival.co.uk
Four days of screenings by the UK's very best graduate filmmakers.

Paul Heathcote at Manchester Food & Drink Festival p41

Itineraries

The pillar box that survived the blast

Manchester: A Secret History

Is it a characteristic defiance, a certain insecurity or just sloppiness which leads to Manchester being so coy about its astonishing past? The city has been midwife to the Industrial Revolution, to the Football League and to communism. The first TUC congress was held here, Ernest Rutherford split the atom and Alan Turing oversaw the beginnings of the computer age in the city. And yet these gems are largely overlooked in its history. A little craning of the neck and a certain amount of initiative is needed, but in a city centre as compact as Manchester's, the past can be explored with minimal effort.

It should take about an hour to complete this walk, which goes from one side of the city centre to the other, and across 2,000 years of history.

Start at Miller Street car park, in the shadow of the CIS tower (now the site of the largest solar-panelled project in the UK), at the junction of Rochdale Road and Miller Street. It may take a heroic feat of imagination to picture it now, but this is where modern Manchester – indeed, it could be argued, the modern world – was born in 1780 when Richard Arkwright built his first cotton mill, thus kickstarting the Industrial Revolution.

Perhaps somewhat symbolic of the unsentimental greed of the capitalist revolution that it inspired, the site lies unrecorded, literally buried beneath a scruffy concrete car park, but it was latterly drawn attention to when Channel 4's *Time Team* programme excavated the site in 2005. Over to the north, the rising towers of what is now called the Green Quarter loom up above the old slum district of Red Bank. Friedrich Engels – himself the beneficiary of his family's cotton wealth – paid several visits to this area (as well as to Little Ireland, behind Oxford Road station) to document the appallingly filthy living conditions. His observations led to the writing of his *Conditions of the Working Classes in England* in 1844.

Walk downhill from here and turn left onto Corporation Street. Soon you will see Victoria Station on the right with **Balloon Street** on the left. If you're curious about that street's name, then a small blue plaque above your head records that the pioneering aeronaut James Sadler made the city's first balloon ascent near here in 1785. The derelict block on the right – City Buildings – was the site of the home of Ann Lee, who would go on to establish the utopian Shaker movement in late 18th-century America. In her day the road was called Toad Lane; today it is **Todd Lane**, but this row of buildings facing Urbis is

now not even dignified with a road sign. Continue along Corporation Street underneath the striking new glass **Arndale Bridge**, and notice the **red pillar box** on the right. This is the pillar box that was somehow left standing when the IRA bomb exploded a few feet away from here in 1996. Take the next left turn now, where the garish experience of Market Street will drive away all thought of history for five gaudy minutes (less, if you run). Just past Market Street Metrolink stop you will reach the corner of **Piccadilly Gardens**. Look up to your right. Now home to the Abbey Bank, this building was the Royal Hotel in 1888, and an innocuous plaque records that the Football League was officially formed here in the April of that year. It seems appropriate that the city should go on to such a distinguished footballing history.

Walk down **Mosley Street** now, past Manchester Art Gallery and across **Princess Street**. Immediately to your right is the former site of John Dalton's laboratory, where Dalton helped establish the principles of modern atomic theory. Carry on to the end of **St Peter's Square** – the central cenotaph garden marks the site of the demolished St Peter's Church – and turn right a short way along **Peter Street** to reach what is now the **Radisson Edwardian** (p177), one of the city's plusher new hotels. This was formerly the **Free Trade Hall**, one of the numerous reminders of the city's radical past that has been transformed into a distinctly more capitalist present. Around this site, back in 1819, a public protest for parliamentary reform degenerated into bloodshed – the infamous Peterloo Massacre – when sabre-wielding troops galloped into a crowd of around 60,000, killing

11 and injuring 400 (the blue plaque now on the wall rather charitably refers to this as being the crowd's 'subsequent dispersal'). Various musical anecdotes can be relayed about the Free Trade Hall. From 1858 to 1996 the spot was home to the Hallé Orchestra, Britain's longest-established symphony orchestra, now situated five minutes away in the Bridgewater Hall (p123). Bob Dylan received his infamous 'Judas' heckle here shortly after going electric in 1966, while in the upstairs Lesser Free Trade Hall, in 1976, the Sex Pistols played two momentous gigs. The show's promoters, Howard Devoto and Pete Shelley, would go on to form Buzzcocks, while also in attendance were future members of Joy Division, Simply Red, the Fall and the Smiths.

The former Haçienda club

Turn back the way you came and take one of the next two right turns, either of which will lead you straight to the newly named **Manchester Central Convention Complex** (p62; previously called G-Mex), which was formerly the Victorian-era Central railway station. Bear right and follow Lower Mosley Street, with the Bridgewater Hall passing on your left, then cross the road at the traffic lights, and note the housing development on your left at the next crossroads. Another example of Manchester's viciously unsentimental attitude towards its heritage means that the site of the **Haçienda** – in its day perhaps the most famous club in the world – now resides beneath the block of flats that today bears the former club's name. To be fair, when open, the club would go out of its way not to advertise its presence; at the height of the 1990s Madchester rave scene it was identified merely by a small brass plaque.

From here go right down **Whitworth Street West** towards Deansgate for the short walk to Castlefield. The best route is to turn right at the Deansgate traffic lights, walk beneath the railway bridge and go left down **Liverpool Road**. Note the signs to your left pointing out the remains of Roman Manchester. Here lie the disappointingly scarce remnants of the four **Roman forts** built between the first and fifth centuries; most of the remains were destroyed during the Industrial Revolution, as the Rochdale canal and the still-standing railway viaducts were ploughed unsentimentally through.

In AD 79 Julius Agricola's wooden fort established the community of *Mancunium* here. The **Beetham Tower** (p127) looms close over the site now, an imposing reminder of the distance travelled in the two millennia since.

St Ann's Passage

Manchester in...

...one hour

Sixty minutes isn't very long, so we'll give you a choice. One option is to indulge yourself in **Exchange Square**: the city's retail-cum-cultural epicentre is a fantastic public space that was designed in the wake of the 1996 IRA bombing. Here, you'll find the **Triangle**, a state-of-the-art shopping mall located in the former Corn Exchange, as well as **Selfridges**. And in the distance looms the hulk of the **Arndale Shopping Centre** and the **Printworks** entertainment complex. If you've got time for a museum, try **Urbis** (p65).

Alternatively, if you leave Exchange Square via Shambles Square, you'll pass two of the city's oldest public houses – the **Old Wellington Inn** and **Sinclair's Oyster Bar** (both p69). Incredibly, this is the third home for both places:

they were moved here in 1971 to make way for redevelopment, and then shifted again following the post-bomb rebuild. Manchester's often overlooked 600-year-old **Cathedral** (p62) is next door on Cateaton Street; beyond it is **Chetham's Library & School of Music** (p60). The library's ancient texts should hold the interest of any bibliophiles for a little while. Enjoy a browse in the reading room, a former haunt of a certain K Marx. The School of Music puts on free lunchtime concerts. If, after all that, you've still a few minutes to spare, hot-foot it up Corporation Street and on to Cross Street, where you can fall into **Mr Thomas's Chop House** (832 2245,www. tomschophouse.com) for some bubble-and-squeak soup and another crafty pint.

...an afternoon

It's always edifying to combine a cuppa with culture, so kick off at **Suburb** (63 Deansgate, 832 3642) with a cup of herbal, green or berry-flavoured Teany tea. It's also a sandwich bar: grab a pre-walk snack and browse the small art and photo exhibitions while you munch.

Deansgate itself is a major stretch of listed Mancunian real estate, central to the city's emergence as a railway and canal capital, that links the northern and southern neighbourhoods. There are dozens of drinking dens dotted along this key artery: if you're in need of further refreshment, try **Atlas** (376 Deansgate, 834 2124), which has outlived lesser attempts at the 'cool' lounge-bar concept.

Halfway up the old thoroughfare sits **St Ann's Square**, an elegant civic space created in the 18th century. The square and its surrounding streets and passages were designated a Conservation Area by Manchester City Council in the 1970s. If you're not grabbed by the neo-classical **St Ann's Church** (p63), which sometimes stages music recitals, you may be more inspired by the big-brand stores here, such as Habitat and Gap. Wander up and down the Barton Arcade and visit former **Kendal's** department store. Now a House of Fraser after a recent refit, the shop is still referred to locally by its old name. **King Street**, parallel to St Ann Street, offers higher-end retail options, with the likes of Armani, Joseph and Vivienne Westwood.

As afternoon turns to evening, a couple of nearby cultural options slide into focus: the **Opera House** and the **Royal Exchange** theatre (both p97). Before a performance at either place, head into **Harvey Nichols** for a long cocktail, as the sun (if you're lucky) begins to dip.

...24 hours

Mornings in Manchester are usually relatively calm: even Market Street and the Arndale Centre are quiet before lunch. However, there's more interesting shopping and streetlife elsewhere: have a roam around the **Northern Quarter's** offbeat fashion outlets, the shops of **Afflecks Palace**, and the commercial and artistic studios of the **Craft & Design Centre**, formerly Smithfield Fish Market.

Wandering back into the city centre, a couple of cultural spaces beckon. The striking **Bridgewater Hall** (p123) stages lunchtime concerts a couple of times a week, and dishes up sandwiches and snacks daily in its Stalls Café Bar. There's also a café at **Cornerhouse** (p124), home to a gallery and cinema. If you're here on a Sunday, try the Breakfast Club deal – a full English with a classic film screening.

To balance the modern with the ancient, trip along to Deansgate and visit the excellent **People's History Museum** (p63), which dispenses a history lesson as seen through Mancunian eyes. Even if you're not hungry yet, it's worth crossing the River Irwell, a short walk from the Museum, and nibbling at the **Lowry Hotel's** (p179) afternoon tea. The **River Restaurant** (p135) offers gliding waiters, exquisite cakes and champagne to wash it all down.

If you're quick, there'll be enough time for a little fresh air and green grass. Head for **Fletcher Moss Gardens** (p150) in Didsbury, before an early-evening pint at one of the nearby countrified inns and an aesthetically pleasing vegetarian meal at Simon Rimmer's **Greens** restaurant (p154). No need for a late-night taxi, at least not if you're sleeping at the **Didsbury House Hotel** (p181), a vivacious little Victorian boutique conversion.

Printworks p47

Salford Lads Club

Music Tour

Music is in Manchester's genetic makeup. From the jazz and folk explosion of the 1950s to Northern Soul, the Haçienda, Madchester, Grand Central and the current crop of Mancunian musicians like Elbow, Doves and Badly Drawn Boy, the city has been at the heart of some of the most important musical movements the UK has seen. There are enough stories to fill a book on Manchester music; here we've tried to cram in as many musical facts and landmarks as possible. Inevitably we have had to leave some things out, but the following tour should fill an afternoon (and, if you want, evening) and offers a sample of the places that make up Manchester's musical DNA.

A good place to start is at the foot of the **Duke of Wellington Statue** on the far side of **Piccadilly Gardens** (p104), the monument that featured on the cover of Buzzcocks' 1977 *Spiral Scratch* EP – the record credited as being the first independent, DIY punk record. From here, head to the collection of bus stops on the opposite side of the gardens and catch the 33 bus to Salford from stand P. Buses leave every 30 minutes, so you shouldn't have to wait too long, and a ticket will cost not much more than £3.

Once on the bus, you'll travel from Piccadilly down Portland Street, on to Chepstow Street and then Bridgewater Street. As you reach the lights here cast your eyes to the right, where you should be able to make out **Bridgewater Hall** (p123), the city's celebrated state-of-the-art classical music venue (and performing home of the Hallé) and **Manchester Central Convention Complex** (p62), formerly **G-Mex**, the scene of countless gigs, from New Order to Take That via Oasis. Morrissey was the final artist to play at G-Mex before the place was rebranded and transformed into an international conference and convention centre in January 2007.

The bus will then head down Whitworth Street and briefly on to Deansgate, crossing the canal before heading out down Liverpool Road. Sit back for a few minutes as you make your way towards Salford. The journey should take about ten minutes in total. Get off the bus at the Oldfield/Regent Road stop just after the Sainsbury's supermarket on the right. Walk up the road, from the bus stop, and take the first left down Gloucester Street, before turning immediately right down **Coronation Street**. This is the original Coronation Street – the place that spawned a soap opera and also a pop star, as Peter Noone first appeared in the show before going on to form Mancunian beat combo Herman's Hermits.

Continue past the red brick terraces, passing Regent Square on your left, until you reach what initially may appear to be a deserted building. But continue to the far side of the premises and you'll find the main entrance to the **Salford Lads Club** (p134). The iconic doorway, with its sign above, is exactly as it appeared in the famous photograph of the Smiths, taken by Stephen Wright, that was published on the inside of *The Queen is Dead* cover. The spot is a mecca for all Smiths fans, who pose for their own versions of the shot outside. There are more Morrissey moments to be had inside the Lads club, as the venue has recently opened a room dedicated to the Smiths. Also check out the sports hall, where Joy Division's Peter Hook played football as a youngster, and, if you

ask nicely, they might even let you look in the room that the Hollies used to rehearse in upstairs.

From the *Queen is Dead* entrance head back out onto the main road. Before crossing, take a moment and look above the roofs of the not very impressive trading estate buildings opposite and you should be able to make out the top of the **Salford Gasworks**. This is the image that inspired the song 'Dirty Old Town' by Ewan McColl.

Jump back on the 33 and into Manchester, alighting on Liverpool Road, just after the Museum of Science & Industry. From here turn right on to Deansgate and immediately left on to Whitworth Street before crossing and heading down the pedestrianised street opposite. Pass **Love Saves the Day** (p132), Manchester's favourite coffee shop – and a good place for a break if you're in need of one – and take the second left down **Little Peter Street**. Prizes go to those who can find the small blue plaque that is the only indication of the **Boardwalk**'s previous existence. The club and rehearsal rooms were a breeding ground for all things Madchester and showcased local legends like James, the Happy Mondays and the Charlatans. Follow this road up to the main thoroughfare and turn left to join the junction, where the imposing new apartments on the opposite corner mark the place where the infamous **Haçienda** club once stood. Opened by Tony Wilson, Rob Gretton and New Order in 1982, the venue was the home of house music and popularised the hippy Madchester indie sound. It was also where Madonna gave her first UK performance.

From here follow Whitworth Street up to the **Ritz** on the left, the longest running club in Manchester. Originally a jazz ballroom, and later a disco venue, it is here that the Smiths performed their first concert in 1982; the place is still going strong today.

Turning left onto Oxford Street, wander down past local institution **Jilly's Rockworld** (p122) on the right, where rock fans have flocked for over 20 years. The affiliated Music Box, on the same spot, hosts club nights like Mr Scruff's Keep it Unreal. This is also the original site of Rafters, where Warsaw (who later became Joy Division) made some of their first appearances.

Continue on (looking left down Bridgewater Street as you go, to get the full effect of the Bridgewater Hall and Manchester Central) until you reach the old **Free Trade Hall** on Peter Street. Now the Radisson Edwardian hotel (p177), the venue was the place where Bob Dylan famously suffered the 'Judas' heckle, and where the Sex Pistols performed their seminal 1976 gig, organised by Howard Devoto and Peter Shelley of the soon-to-be-formed Buzzcocks. It is said that one Mark E Smith (the Fall), Morrissey and Ian Curtis (Joy Division) were all present in the crowd, and toddled off to start their own bands not long after.

Continue down Peter Street and then right back onto Deansgate. Follow the road past the end of Lloyd Street, on the right – the location of the **Oasis club/coffee bar**, a lesser-known but equally important piece of the Northern Soul puzzle as the infamous **Twisted Wheel Club**, which was originally located on parallel Brazenose Street (Queen Street is in-between), before it moved to Whitworth Street. Head up Brazenose Street and imagine what it would have been like in the '60s when the road was packed with scooters and suited mods who flocked to the soul music mecca.

Continue straight down Brazenose Street and you will find yourself opposite the **Town Hall** on Albert Square. It was here that Take That made their final farewells after announcing their split in 1996. Turn left and make your way along **Cross Street**. You may well be ready for a drink and a sit-down by this stage; if so, turn right up St Ann Street and take an immediate left down Pall Mall to stop at **Corbieres** (p66) on Half Moon Street. This little-known bar is a favourite with local bands like Elbow. If there are no musicians to be spotted then make your own fun and select some songs from the brilliantly stocked jukebox.

After suitable refreshment follow Pall Mall out onto pedestrianised Market Street, and turn right. While the masses of shoppers might be a bit off-putting, there is a strong chance that you may see some buskers. Talented Royal Northern College of Music students regularly pitch themselves up near Boots.

Once at the top of Market Street, turn left down Tib Street and into the creative heart of Manchester, the Northern Quarter. **Affleck's Palace** (p94) on the corner of Tib Street and Church Street is a local landmark. Wander around the exterior and find some of the trademark mosaic artwork by Mark Kennedy depicting Manchester's musical heroes.

Take a bit of time out here to explore the many and hugely varied record shops the area has to offer. Everything from world and roots to nosebleed techno can be found in the superfluous independent record stores on Thomas Street, Tib Street and Oldham Street. **Piccadilly Records**, on Oldham Street, is the best place for young blood

ITINERARIES

The former Free Trade Hall

and indie pressings, while hip hop fanatics will love **Fat City** across the road. The shop was once managed by Mark Rae (Grand Central Records) and was the place where he first met man from the Hinterland, Aim (aka Andy Turner), who's critically acclaimed *Cold Water Music* added fuel to the strong local hip hop and breakbeat scene.

If you're looking to continue the musical theme into the evening then head to the legendary **Dry Bar** (p91) on Oldham Street. Established by Factory Records in the mid 1980s, this was the original Haçienda pre-club bar, and former hangout of bands like the Happy Mondays and New Order. The scenesters have

moved on, but the place still holds a certain charm. **Night & Day** (p100) next door is also a good bet, with live music most nights. Legend has it that it was outside this venue that Mark E Smith hailed what he thought was a taxi, but which turned out to be Damon Gough's (aka Badly Drawn Boy) car. The be-hatted one agreed to give the Fall frontman a lift to Stockport on the condition that he record one of Gough's songs in return. (Smith is said to have left his false teeth in the car – maybe as a tip!). If guitar music isn't your thing, though, then pop round to **Matt & Phred's** (p100) on Tib Street for the evening, and enjoy some live jazz, and pizza.

what a wonderful world

Rags *to* **Bitches**

MANCHESTER'S MOST BEATUIFUL BOUTIQUE
vintage clothes, jewellery and homeware
60 Tib St, Northern Quarter, Manchester M4 1LG
0161 835 9265

www.rags-to-bitches.co.uk

Manchester
by Area

Urbis p65

City Centre

The 1996 IRA bomb is credited with kick-starting Manchester's City Centre regeneration. Work had in fact been underway for some years, but the blast that ripped the heart out of the city, injuring over 200 people, did provide an unprecedented opportunity to remodel it. The Corn Exchange became the swish **Triangle** arcade. The **Royal Exchange** got a £30-million facelift. New public squares were unveiled. **Exchange Square**'s concentric benches now provide a stopping point for weary shoppers, while **Cathedral Gardens** are a skater-kid hangout. Manchester got its own 'museum of the city', **Urbis**, while the much-maligned **Arndale Centre** was extended.

A glass twist of a footbridge connects **Selfridges** to the Arndale, and just below it sits the postbox that became a symbol of the city's determination to recover from the IRA blast. Despite being within a few feet of the biggest explosion, it survived intact. It stood proud when all around was shattered and broken, and it's the perfect place now to post your postcards.

Slotted between Victoria Station and the Triangle, a corner of medieval Manchester lives on. **Chetham's Library**, with 15th-century library and baronial hall, sits above the confluence of the rivers Irk and Irwell. Not far away squats **Manchester Cathedral**, close by Hanging Ditch. Local folklore has it that the ditch refers to the practice of tying a noose around the neck of miscreants and kicking them off the bridge. In truth, Hanging Ditch marks the

course of the River Irk, where 12th-century fullers (cloth cleaners) would hang their cloth to dry.

Chetham's played a pivotal role during the Industrial Revolution. Manchester became the world's largest centre of manufacturing (nicknamed 'Cottonopolis'), and was rammed with impoverished mill workers. Friedrich Engels and Karl Marx used to meet at Chetham's to discuss what they saw. Between them they penned two central socialist texts: *The Condition of the Working Classes in England* and the Communist Manifesto.

Further south, Alfred Waterhouse's **Town Hall** is a reminder of Manchester's industrial ambition and is one of its most important buildings. Ford Madox Ford's wall murals are particularly notable, but even the corridors, with mosaic floors and decorative vaulted ceilings, are remarkable. Look out for the bee motif, an emblem of Manchester's industriousness.

Chetham's isn't the only atmospheric library. The **John Rylands Library** is a neo-Gothic masterpiece, while the **Portico** leans to the neo-Classic. Further down the road is the **Central Library**. This relative newcomer (1934) was once the largest public library in the UK.

Sights & museums

Abraham Lincoln Statue

Lincoln Square, Brazenose Street, M2. Metrolink St Peter's Square/City Centre buses/Deansgate or Oxford Road rail. **Map** p58 C4 ❶

An imposing if slightly incongruous presence amid the City Centre office blocks, this statue was given to the city in 1919 in recognition of the support that Lincoln received from the citizens of Manchester in his campaign against slavery. It was moved into the City Centre for the first time in 1986, from its original location in Platt Fields Park.

Literary treasures

Five millennia of human literary endeavour will be accessible by all once again from spring 2007, when Deansgate's **John Rylands Library** (p61) reopens its doors. The library is a prime contender for Manchester's most overlooked treasure, considering the wealth of genuinely astonishing material that lies in its vaults, including the world's oldest surviving fragment of the New Testament, 4,000 year-old Sumerian clay tablets from the dawn of human writing and a selection of William Caxton's books from the 15th-century revolution in printing.

The building has been closed since 2003 while undergoing an extensive programme of renovation; the project was near to completion at the time of writing, bringing the building (just over a hundred years old, despite giving the impression of near-medieval antiquity) up to 21st-century standards of access. A new audio guide will lead visitors around the library's architectural treasures.

The old building was a rather imposing fixture. Despite sitting on a busy City Centre traffic corridor and always being open and free to the public, it seemed to intimidate the casual visitor. The brand new entrance wing, composed of a glass rectangle alongside the sandstone original, may sit a little uneasily in terms of style, but it's far more welcoming and obvious, and the previously inadequate disabled access has now been fully upgraded.

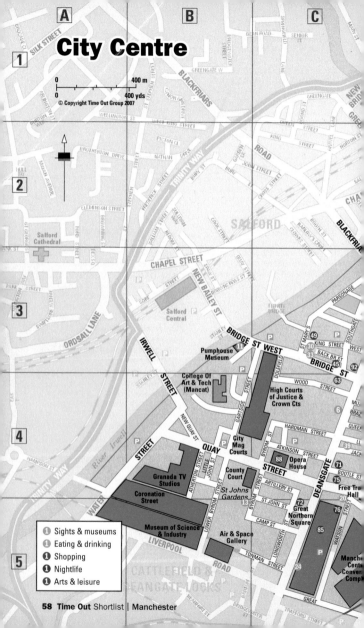

City Centre

Cathedral Gardens

M4. Metrolink Victoria/City Centre buses/Victoria rail. **Map** p59 D2 ❷

A pleasing post-bomb open space that nestles between Urbis (p65), Chetham's Library and School (see below), Victoria Station (p65) and the Triangle shopping centre (p80). The gracefully undulating grass slopes and layered water features are colonised every Saturday by a sociologist's paradise – hordes of teenage alt-rock tribes and pockets of clattering skateboarders, putting the space to a vibrant if unpredicted use.

Central Library

St Peter's Square, M2 5PD (234 1900/ www.manchester.gov.uk). Metrolink St Peter's Square/City Centre buses/ Oxford Road rail. **Open** 9am-8pm Mon-Thur; 9am-5pm Fri, Sat. Specific department times may vary. **Admission** free. **Map** p59 D4 ❸

The library's classical revival style disguises the fact that it was only built in 1934, since when it has become one of the city's most recognisable landmarks. Simply browse, chill in the café or emit coughs to check for the echo in the great domed central hall. Outside, the building's graceful exterior arc makes a photogenic match with the neighbouring sweep of the Town Hall extension.

Chetham's Library & School of Music

Long Millgate, M3 1SB (834 7961/ www.chethams.org.uk). Metrolink Victoria/City Centre buses/Victoria rail. **Open** 9am-12.30pm, 1.30-4.30pm Mon-Fri. **Admission** free. **Map** p59 D2 ❹

Chetham's Library is a stunning piece of the 15th century that has survived more or less intact to the present day. The library itself and its surrounding cloisters exude an almost tangible sense of history. Within its impressive walls, Karl Marx and adopted Mancunian Friedrich Engels met in the reading room to research the birth of Communist theory. Reading bays with lockable iron gates (a novel security measure introduced in 1740) are a feature. This is a functioning library (the oldest in the English-speaking world), so always ring ahead to check all rooms are available to visit. Weekly guided tours take in further buildings – booking well in advance is recommended. The adjoining school of music is the largest of its kind in the UK and puts on 100 public performances a year, plus free lunchtime concerts every weekday.

Exchange Square

M4. Metrolink Victoria/City Centre buses/Victoria rail. **Map** p59 D2 ❺

Manchester Central Convention Complex p62

Exchange Square

MANCHESTER BY AREA

Another of the new spaces afforded by the bomb, Exchange Square has rows of amphitheatre seating (complete with decorative metal bars to spoil the fun of more adventurous skateboarders) arranged, like living room furniture around a television, to face the Triangle's big screen. A playful water feature is occasionally given the washing-up liquid treatment by mischievous youths. Surrounded by enormo-shopping centres (the new wing of the Arndale, M&S, the Triangle), there's no danger of anyone using the square to get a rest, but it's an inventive communal space.

John Rylands Library
150 Deansgate, M3 3EH (834 5343). Metrolink St Peter's Square/City Centre buses/Deansgate Rail. **Map** p58 C4 ❻
Despite giving the impression of near-medieval antiquity, this glorious building is in fact just over a century old. First opened in 1900, among its astonishing treasures are the world's oldest surviving fragment of the New Testament. The guided tours are highly recommended, and there is also a changing programme of exhibitions. Three years of renovation and rebuilding has left the library with an entire new entrance wing. See box p57.

Manchester Art Gallery
Mosley Street, M2 3JL (235 8888/ www.manchestergalleries.org). Metrolink Mosley Street/City Centre buses/ Piccadilly rail. **Open** 10am-5pm Tue-Sun. **Admission** free. **Map** p59 E4 ❼
A noted home to some stunning Pre-Raphaelite art. Highlights of the three floors of the permanent collection include Rossetti's *Astarte Syriaca* as well as notable pieces by both Turner and Modigliani and a superb collection of impressionist paintings of early 20th-century Manchester by the underrated Adolph Valette, Lowry's early art teacher. There's also a changing programme of prestigious exhibitions on the top floor. The building itself, designed by Charles Barry in 1824, had an extensive £35 million extension and refit in 2002, letting in more light, opening a new wing and installing an interactive children's gallery.

Manchester Cathedral

Manchester Art Gallery p61

Manchester Cathedral

Cathedral Yard, M3 1SX (835 4030/
www.manchestercathedral.org).
Metrolink Victoria/City Centre buses/
Victoria rail. **Open** 8am-7pm Mon-
Fri; 8am-5pm Sat; 8.30am-7.30pm Sun.
Times may vary Aug, Easter, Christmas.
Admission free. **Map** p59 D2

A church building of some description
has existed on this site since the first mil-
lennium, and the present cathedral has
adapted to structural damage inflicted
variously during the Civil War, from a
direct hit from German bombers in 1941
and by the IRA bomb of 1996. Of particular note is the beautiful wooden roof,
the Anglo-Saxon Angel Stone (possibly
a survival from an earlier church on the
site) and the stained glass Fire Window,
which evocatively bleeds flame-coloured
light into the Regimental chapel.

Manchester Central Convention Complex

Off Lower Mosley Street, M2 3GX (834
2700/www.manchestercentral.co.uk).
Metrolink G-Mex/City Centre buses/
Deansgate rail. **Map** p59 D5

The site of the city's third main station
(Central Station) in the late 19th century, which closed shortly after the railway line became obsolete in 1969. In
1986 the building was resurrected as G-
Mex (Greater Manchester Exhibition
centre) hosting sports and trade events.
It was also used as a concert venue – the
Smiths and Oasis played here – before
the MEN Arena usurped that role. Now
with a new attached conference centre
(previously a seperate entity, as
Manchester International Convention
Centre), the place has been rebranded,
and opened as Manchester Central in
January 2007. It hosted, as G-Mex, the
2006 Labour Party Conference.

Peace Garden

St Peter's Square, M2. Metrolink St
Peter's Square/City Centre buses/
Oxford Road rail. **Map** p59 D4

Manchester became a the world's first
nuclear-free city in 1980 at the height
of world nuclear paranoia. Today the
world is no more safe and the garden
isn't especially peaceful, bordered as it
is by the busy Princess Street and a

tramline. Still, centred around the Messenger of Peace statue and sheltered by the Town Hall, it offers a lunchtime refuge for City Centre office staff.

People's History Museum

Bridge Street, M3 3ER (228 7212/ http://82.71.77.169). Metrolink St Peter's Square/City Centre buses. **Open** 11am-4.30pm Tue-Sun, bank hols. **Admission** free. **Map** p58 B3 ⑪

The region's estimable industrial and trade union heritage is celebrated in this museum. A potentially dry subject matter is enlivened by an imaginative layout and some surprising artefacts, including a truncheon wrenched from a policeman during the Peterloo Massacre and a lock of Tom Paine's hair. A quietly stirring experience, which now includes the Labour History archive (free, but appointment required).

St Ann's Church

St Ann's Street, St Ann's Square, M2 7LF (834 0239/www.stanns manchester.com). Metrolink St Peter's Square/City Centre buses/Victoria rail. **Open** 9.45am-4.45pm Mon-Sat; 8.30am-5pm, 6pm-7.30pm Sun. **Admission** free. **Map** p59 D3 ⑫

Built in 1712, this and the Cathedral (p62) have long been the two focal points of surviving old Manchester; indeed, the tower of St Ann's Church is said to mark the geographical centre of the old city. Despite now being swallowed up by the various surrounding temples of commerce, it remains a likeable and visible presence, hosting services and frequent free concert recitals.

St John's Gardens

Lower Byrom Street, M3. Metrolink G-Mex/City Centre buses/Deansgate rail. **Map** p58 B5 ⑬

A nicely laid out patch of green oasis on the site of the demolished St John's church, and a pleasant place to relax after a Castlefield museum visit. A central memorial cross calmly notes that 'around lie the remains of more than 22,000 people'.

Town Hall p65

St Mary's (The Hidden Gem)

Mulberry Street, M2 6LN (834 3547/ www.thehiddengem.papalnet.co.uk). Metrolink St Peter's Square/City Centre buses/Deansgate or Oxford Road rail. **Open** 8am-4pm Mon-Wed, Fri; 8am-6pm Thur; 9.30am-5.15pm Sat; 10.15am. *Exposition* 10am-4pm Mon-Fri; 10.30am-5pm Sat. *Mass* 12.30pm Mon-Fri; noon, 5pm Sat; 10.15am, noon Sun. **Admission** free. **Map** p59 D4 ⑭

The aptly named Hidden Gem – founded in 1794 and claimed to be the oldest post-Reformation catholic church in the country – is approached either from the drably unimaginative Brazenose Street or, more enticingly, via a pair of decorated alleyways leading from John Dalton Street. Outside, an impressively sculpted stone arch haloes the entrance doorway, while inside Royal Academician Norman Adams' beautiful *Stations of the Cross* series of paintings adorns the walls. It's a busy functioning church, so visitors should show discretion if just sightseeing; check for times of services.

Urbis

Town Hall

Albert Square, M60 2LA (234 5000/ www.manchester.gov.uk). Metrolink St Peter's Square/City Centre buses/ Oxford Road rail. **Open** *Albert Square reception* 9am-5pm Mon-Fri. **Admission** free. **Map** p59 D4 ⑮

Alfred Waterhouse's building, completed in 1887, remains a proud symbol of the city. Its imposing halls, host to a range of statuary, city council staff and civic wedding ceremonies are usually, but not always, open to the public – ring in advance to check. Visitors are normally free to visit the ground floor Sculpture Hall (sometimes also with an art exhibition) and, on the first floor, the Great Hall, which features a noted series of 12 Ford Madox Brown murals. Still home to numerous council offices, much of the rest of the building is closed to the public for the usual security reasons, but full guided tours are available by appointment from the Visitor Information Centre (see below).

Urbis

Cathedral Gardens, M4 3BG (605 8200/www.urbis.org.uk). Metrolink Victoria/City Centre buses/Victoria rail. **Open** 10am-6pm Mon-Wed, Sun; 10am-8pm Thur-Sat. **Admission** free. **Map** p59 E2 ⑯

One of the main beneficiaries of the post-bomb rebuilding, this stunning glass structure initially attracted controversy over the extent of its public funding (an alleged £1 million a year council subsidy) before its mission – a museum of the modern city – generated widespread indifference. Abandoning the admission fee has yet to stabilise its reputation. The permanent exhibition – addressing the question 'what is a city?' – is a little over-earnest, and the bars of tinted glass throughout needlessly disrupt any panoramic views. Nevertheless, everything else – from the diagonally rising glass elevator and an engaging series of temporary exhibits – make this a vital part of the city's new landscape.

Victoria Station

Todd Street, Station Approach, M3 1PB. Metrolink Victoria/City Centre buses/Victoria rail. **Map** p59 D1 ⑰

Signs of its former splendour remain – witness the lovely tiled map of the Lancashire and Yorkshire Railway on the entrance walls, the wood-panelled ticket offices, the tea room and the iron and glass canopy along its front – but otherwise this is a distinctly shabby affair, totally overlooked in favour of the Piccadilly Station refit, its roof perpetually cupped by a safety net to catch any collapses. Regional rail services and the Metrolink still run from here, and the Manchester Evening News (MEN) Arena is accessed from the main plaza.

Visitor Information Centre

Lloyd Street, M60 2LA (0871 222 8223/www.manchester.gov.uk). Metrolink St Peter's Square/City Centre buses/Oxford Road rail. **Open** 10am-5.30pm Mon-Sat; 10.30am-4.30pm Sun, bank hols. **Admission** free. **Map** p59 D4 ⑱

A vital stopping-off point for visitors, this centre brims with leaflets and occupies a central location behind the Town Hall (see above). Numerous excellent Blue Badge guided tours are run from here – recommended for the numerous criss-crossings of history which otherwise go unrecorded on the streets.

Eating & drinking

Ape & Apple

28-30 John Dalton Street, M2 6HQ (839 9624). Metrolink St Peter's Square/City Centre buses/Oxford Road rail. **Open** noon-11pm Mon-Sat; noon-9.30pm Sun. **Pub**. **Map** p59 D4 ⑲

A pub of solid Victorian stock, and City Centre bastion for local brewers Holts, who still manage to produce an excellent bitter for around £1.50 a pint. There's a large bar menu, separate dining room upstairs and quaint beer garden out back. Refurbished in mid 2006, the pub is a bit on the bright side, but it shouldn't be long before that rich patina of a true pub returns.

Briton's Protection

memorating the 1819 Peterloo Massacre. See if you can spot the two football managers who feature in the paintings. At lunchtime, punters are mostly business people; later on, Bridgewater Hall concertgoers sneaking in a pre-show quickie. Brews from Jennings and Robinson's are the staples, but the real attractions are the 150-plus whiskies and bourbons.

Corbieres

2 Half Moon Street, M2 7PB (834 3381). Metrolink St Peter's Square/ City Centre buses/Victoria rail. **Open** 11.30am-11pm Mon-Sat; noon-10.30pm Sun. **Bar**. **Map** p59 D3

Corbieres is one of those perplexing places that you go into for one drink and end up leaving five hours later, slightly the worse for wear and wondering where the time went. It is one of those places where time really does stand still, which may be due to its subterranean position. It also claims to have the best jukebox in Manchester, something that the groups of dancing drinkers that regularly fill the place near to closing time will testify to.

Establishment

43-45 Spring Gardens, M2 2BG (839 6300/www.establishment restaurant.com). Metrolink Market Street or Mosley Street/City Centre buses/ Piccadilly rail. **Open** noon-3pm, 6.30-10.30pm Mon-Fri; 6.30pm-10.30pm Sat. **£££**. **Fine dining**. **Map** p59 E4

When this guide went to press, rumours were circulating regarding Establishment's imminent closure or takeover – which is a shame, as the place is currently one of the city's hopes for that elusive Michelin star. Head chef Davey Aspin certainly has the pedigree for a star-studded career: he trained under Marco Pierre White and later became head chef at Paul Heathcote's Longridge restaurant, before moving here in 2005. The reasonable £60 ten-course gourmand menu that we sampled amply demonstrates why Aspin is so highly rated.

Bar 38

Pavillion, Peter Street, M2 5GP (835 3076). Metrolink St Peter's Square/ City Centre buses/Oxford Road rail. **Open** 9am-1am Mon-Thur, Sun; 9am-2am Fri, Sat. **Bar**. **Map** p58 C4

There are no surprises in store at this chain bar, but its good quality dependability can come as a welcome relief to the sometime manic buzz of Manchester's thriving bar scene. If you prefer your bars to be designed more with clean lines, plate glass and laminate flooring than with the student crowd in mind, then this is the place for you.

Briton's Protection

50 Great Bridgewater Street, M1 5LE (236 5895). Metrolink G-Mex/City Centre buses/Deansgate rail. **Open** 11am-11pm Mon-Thur; 11am-midnight Fri; noon-midnight Sat; noon-1.30pm Sun. **Pub**. **Map** p58 C5

Like moths to a flame, drinkers are drawn to the Briton's Protection by the red neon sign over the door. The roomy interior is pub perfection: brass fixtures and fittings, and paintings com-

Evuna

277-279 Deansgate, M3 4EW (819 2752/www.evuna.com). Metrolink G-Mex/City Centre buses/Deansgate rail. **Open** 11am-11pm Mon-Sat. **££. Spanish.** Map p58 C5 ㉔

Spanish restaurant Evuna is a must for oenophiles: it doubles as a wine merchant, selling some cracking Spanish bottles (and cases), and even has its own wine club. We particularly liked Coma Vella, a belting red that went down a treat with the sea bass baked in rock salt. You're encouraged to share. A good place for groups.

French

Midland Hotel, Peter Street, M60 2DS (236 3333/www.qhotels.co.uk). Metrolink St Peter's Square/City Centre buses/Oxford Road rail. **Open** Tue-Sat 7pm-10pm. **£££. French.** Map p59 D5 ㉕

Over the years, the French has quietly got on with being Manchester's premier French restaurant. Indeed, a fair few years ago, it was the recipient of not just Manchester's but the country's first Michelin star; although that honour has since been consigned to the history books, the food still shines. It may not be a buzz restaurant these days, but for authentic French cuisine (try the classic chateaubriand) in richly refined surroundings, there aren't many better.

Gaucho Grill

2a St Mary's Street, M3 2LB (833 4333/www.gaucho-grill.com). Metrolink Market Street/City Centre buses/Victoria rail. **Open** noon-10.30pm Mon-Thur, Sun; noon-11pm Fri, Sat. **£££. South American.** Map p58 C3 ㉖

Gaucho Grill or Grill on the Alley? Let the Steak Wars commence. Argentinian cuisine doesn't often top Must-Try lists but Gaucho suggests it's worth attention. Starters range from salads to an array of cerviches, and the Argentinian beef steaks are served with one of seven sauces and a full choice of side dishes. With a well-chosen wine list that focuses on South America, Gaucho's is a real treat.

Grill On The Alley

5 Ridgefield, M2 6EG (833 3465/ www.blackhouserestaurant.co.uk). Metrolink St Peter's Square/Salford Central rail. **Open** noon-midnight Mon-Sun. **£££. Grill.** Map p59 D4 ㉗

Mancunians don't often get a chance to barbecue, so the Grill is a welcome arrival. With food cooked over live flames to seal in moisture, you can choose from the lobsters that float placidly in their tank or from the display of fresh fish – there is even a chance to sample the notorious beer-fed and massaged Kobe beef. Complete the feast with a split, a delicious fruity milkshake.

Hare & Hounds

46 Shudehill, M4 4AA (832 4737). Metrolink Shudehill/City Centre buses/ Victoria rail. **Open** 11am-11pm Mon-Sat; midday-10.30pm Sun. **Pub.** Map p59 E2 ㉘

This grade II-listed building first opened as licensed premises in 1778; between the wooden panels, tiles and bar service bells, it's obvious that not much has changed here since. Football and boxing memorabilia bring the snug bar a little more in line with the times. Brews from JW Lees, Holt's and Tetley's are well looked after and cheaper than at other places and singalongs sometimes take place around the piano, while the upstairs room has been the scene of many a left-wing debate over the years. And it'd be remiss not to mention the pub's home-produced pickled eggs.

Katsouris Deli

113 Deansgate, M3 2BQ (819 1260). Metrolink St Peter's Square/City Centre buses/Salford Central rail. **Open** 7.30am-5.30pm Mon-Fri; 9am-5.30pm Sat; 10am-5pm Sun. **£. Deli-café.** Map p58 C4 ㉙

Katsouris has descended from Bury Market to bring City Centre punters the sandwiches they deserve. While the salad bar offers healthy options, it's the cakes and roast-meat sandwiches that really stand out. The chicken piri piri sandwich has an entire chicken breast and a world of flavour for £3.

Lounge Ten

Koreana

40a King Street West, Manchester, M3 2WY (832 4330/www.koreana. co.uk). Metrolink St Peter's Square/ City Centre buses/Salford Central or Victoria rail. **Open** noon-2.30pm, 6.30-10.30pm Mon-Thur; noon-2.30pm, 6.30-11pm Fri; 5.30pm-11pm Sat. **££**. **Korean**. Map p58 C3 ③⓪

Operating since 1985, and much-loved by critics and customers alike, Koreana still manages to have the feel of an undiscovered gem. Korean food has spicier flavours than Cantonese cuisine, and traditionally starters, soups and mains are served simultaneously. Koreana have a great special where for £15 per head you can feast on pork, squid and even a Kimchi Hot Pot, consisting of fermented vegetables and chilli peppers.

Le Mont

Urbis, Levels 5&6, Cathedral Gardens, M4 3BG (605 8282/www.urbis.org.uk). Metrolink Victoria/City Centre buses/ Victoria rail. **Open** noon-2pm, 7-10pm Tue-Fri; 7pm-10pm Sat. **£££**. **Fine dining**. Map p59 D2 ③①

When people talk about destination restaurants, it's usually the food that merits the detour. At Le Mont, it's the views that make it a must-visit, but the French cooking of Richard Shaw easily lives up to them. The découverte menu offers ludicrously good value at £20 for three courses, which might include a rich shank of lamb with a light celeriac mash. There's also a Bollinger bar if you're thirsty.

Lounge Ten

10 Tib Lane, M2 4JB (834 1331/ www.lounge10manchester.co.uk). Metrolink St Peter's Square/City Centre buses/Victoria rail. **Open** noon-11pm Tue-Sat. *Supper Club* 11pm-3am Fri. **£££**. **Modern international**. Map p59 D4 ③②

Lounge Ten is rude and lewd, and does obscenely good nosh. This decadent hideaway is the sort of place that could only exist in Manchester. For a debauched evening, try the Friday

Supper Club, which features dishes such as fillet of pork with wild boar sausages, and Sex on Legs (they're dancers).

Luso

63 Bridge Street, M3 3BQ (839 5550/ www.lusorestaurant.co.uk). Metrolink St Peter's Square/City Centre buses/ Salford Central rail. **Open** noon-10.30pm Mon-Sat; noon-10pm Sun. **£££. Portuguese.** Map p58 C3 ③

Arguably Manchester's most universally popular new opening in 2006 was Jane and Carlos Cortes' Luso, which has brought inventive and tasty Portuguese food into the City Centre. Eschewing solely Portuguese staples, Luso's menu boldly ventures in the footsteps of Portuguese travellers. Consequently, vindaloo and tempura dishes feature. Despite this laudable experimentation, favourites like the house-salted salt cod still feature.

Obsidian

Arora International Hotel, 18-24 Princess Street, M1 4LY (238 4348/ www.obsidianmanchester.co.uk). Metrolink St Peter's Square/City Centre buses/Oxford Road rail. **Open** noon-2.30pm, 6-10.30pm Mon-Sat; noon-2.30pm, 6-9.30pm Sun. **£££. Fine dining.** Map p59 D4/E4 ③

This restaurant and bar are located within the chic Arora International hotel (p173), but Obsidian is just as popular with the Manc crowd as it is with expense-accounting visitors to the city. Head chef Adrian Bailey's cooking is adventurous, but never off-puttingly so: aided by ingredients sourced from local suppliers, he lets the flavours of the work. You can't really go wrong with anything on the menu, but the whole Goosnargh duck cooked two ways and served with duck-fat roast potatoes, seasonal vegetables and cherry sauce is ridiculously good. The bar scene is pretty lively.

Old Wellington Inn/ Sinclair's Oyster Bar

4/2 Cathedral Gates, M3 1SW (830 1440/834 0430/0871 2071737). Metrolink Victoria/City Centre

buses/Victoria rail. **Open** 11am-11pm Mon-Sat; noon-10.30pm Sun. **Pub.** Map p59 D2 ③

It's impossible to separate these two icons of the Mancunian spirit, joined as they are at the hip. Having survived all that was thrown at them by the Luftwaffe, they were then threatened by the wrecking ball in the late 1970s before inspired engineering intervened to allow both pubs to be raised several feet and various concrete monstrosities to be built around them. Ironically, it was this concrete that saved the pubs from another bomb, this time of the IRA variety in 1996. In the aftermath, the pubs were dismantled and moved some 300 metres to their current position, an upheaval which has only served to enhance their crooked, wonky appearances. The Wellington is a free house dating back to the early 1500s, while Sinclair's is a couple of hundred years younger. Now a no smoking pub owned by Samuel Smiths, it boasts an excellent downstairs seafood bar, although one lacking in oysters, despite the name. The pubs share a huge outdoor drinking area.

Room

81 King Street, M2 4ST (839 2005/ www.roomrestaurants.com). Metrolink Market Street or Mosley Street/City Centre buses/Piccadilly rail. **Open** *Restaurant* 10am-10pm Mon-Wed; 10am-11pm Thur-Sat. *Bar* 10am-11pm Mon-Wed; 10am-2am Thur-Sat. **££. Retro.** Map p58 D3/E3 ③

Taking its inspiration from the infamous dishes of the 1970s, Room's mission is to put the kitsch back in to the kitchen. That might sound awful but fortunately Room (a mini-chain with branches in Leeds and Liverpool) takes old favourites like prawn and avocado cocktail or chicken Kiev and brings them kicking and screaming into the 21st century, proving that the old(ish) ones are (sometimes) the best ones.

Sam's Chop House

Chapel Walks, M2 1HN (834 3210/ www.samschophouse.co.uk). Metrolink

Sam's Chop House p69

St Peter's Square/City Centre buses/ Victoria rail. **Open** noon-3pm, 5.30-9pm Mon-Thur; noon-3pm, 5.50-10.30pm Fri, Sat; noon-5.50pm Sun. **££**. **British**. Map p59 D3 ③⑦

If you fancy traditional British cooking, then Sam's is the place to go. It might be a beautiful old pub, but you don't go there for the Victorian tiles. Menu highlights include brown onion soup, dumplings, roast beef, corned beef hash and steak and kidney pudding. Don't forget to leave room for dessert: the steamed lemon sponge with custard will make you weak at the knees.

Shlurp

2 Brazenose Street, M2 5BP (839 5199). Metrolink St Peter's Square/ City Centre buses/Deansgate or Oxford Road rail. **Open** 7.30am-3pm Mon-Fri. **£**. **Soup**. Map p59 D4 ③⑧

If you tell your bank manager that you're starting a business and that the unique selling point of said business is soup, then they'll probably tell you that the soup had better be good. Fortunately for Shlurp, their soups are very, very good indeed. The Asian chicken is great for warming you up on a raw, wet Manchester day, and the smoked haddock and corn chowder soup has won an award from the Guild of Fine Food Retailers in 2006. Everything is prepared in-house using fresh ingredients, including the dressings and meats. You can also get early morning bagels and coffee.

Simply Heathcotes

Jacksons Row, off Deansgate, M2 5WD (835 3536/www.heathcotes. co.uk). Metrolink St Peter's Square/ City Centre buses/Deansgate or Oxford Road rail. **Open** noon-2.30pm, 5.30-10pm Mon-Fri; noon-2.30pm, 5.30-11pm Sat; noon-9pm Sun. **££**. **British**. Map p58 C4 ③⑨

Heathcotes might not initially seem cheap, but it does offer some brilliant deals. Two courses and half a bottle of wine for £15 on Mondays is exceptional value, and there's no sense

here of 'feed 'em quick and get 'em out': the polished service remains consistent at all times. If this correspondent was a condemned man, Paul Heathcote's deep-fried Whitby cod in beer batter, hand-cut chips and mushy peas would be on the shortlist for his last meal.

Sinclair's Oyster Bar

2 Cathedral Gates, Manchester M3 1SW (0871 2071737). Metrolink Victoria/City Centre buses/Victoria rail. **Open** 11am-11pm Mon-Sat; noon-10.30pm Sun. **Pub**. Map p59 D2 ④⓪

See p69 Old Wellington Inn.

Stock

4 Norfolk Street, M2 1DW (839 6644/ www.stockrestaurant.co.uk). Metrolink Market Street/City Centre buses/ Victoria rail. **Open** 10am-2.30pm, 5.30-10pm Mon-Sat. **£££**. **Italian**. Map p59 D3 ④①

Stock's name and its imposing atmosphere survive from the building's previous incarnation as Manchester's stock exchange. Hard though it is to match, the Italian menu nonetheless has flavours that rival the venue's stature. The calf's liver and parmesan risotto is wonderful, and there are some excellent Italian wines from which to choose.

Tampopo

16 Albert Square, M2 5PF (819 1966/ www.tampopo.co.uk). Metrolink St Peter's Square/City Centre buses/ Oxford Road rail. **Open** noon-11pm Mon-Sat; noon-10pm Sun. **££**. **Eastern**. Map p59 D4 ④②

Despite its subterranean location, Tampopo has a very light and airy feel and the shared long benches and tables give the restaurant a real buzz when the place is full. Rather than restricting, Tampopo's menu incorporates tastes from Japan, Malaysia, Indonesia and other Eastern destinations to deliver a Most Wanted of the region's cooking. The restaurant is especially recommended for the tasty noodle dishes.

St Ann's Square

Shopping

Exchange Square

This area was entirely rebuilt after the 1996 bomb, and now attracts some of the biggest names in fashion. Stores on New Cathedral Street include Louis Vuitton, Reiss, Massimo Dutti, LK Bennett and Ted Baker and this luxurious parade is book-ended by a vast Zara and an M&S.

Arndale/Market Street

The glittering Arndale Extension opened in 2006, with a huge Next department store, a brand new market area and new or expanded concessions for wildly popular high street brands such as Lush cosmetics, Waterstones and Topshop. The Arndale, part monstrosity of 1970s planning, part rebuilt 21st-century mall, houses almost every significant high street chain in Britain; and if they're not here, they'll be on Market Street.

St Ann's Square

Here, things start getting pricier. St Ann's Square is home to three shopping arcades, the small St Ann's Arcade, the soaring Victorian Barton Arcade and, opposite, the Royal Exchange Arcade which runs past the famous theatre. The square offers a fountain and concrete benches, and often hosts temporary food markets. Shops include Kurt Geiger, French Connection, and Aquascutum.

King Street

The luxury shopping street of Manchester, pedestrianised King Street is home to a *Who's Who* of upmarket household names including Karen Millen, Hobbs, Monsoon, Mulberry, Virgin Bride and Jaeger. At the top end, the street gets even more rarified, with Whistles, Emporio Armani, Joseph, Diesel and DKNY jostling for attention.

Albert Square area

Relatively few must-visit shops crowd the Albert Square area – it's largely business around here. But Bridge Street offers several designer menswear shops, to kit out those who work in its environs.

Arndale

Deansgate

One of the city's main arterial roads, Deansgate runs from Castlefield to the Cathedral. The shopping is relatively sparse at the far ends, but around House of Fraser, there are luxury furniture stores and delis.

Agent Provocateur

Unit GA, Manchester Club, 81 King Street, M2 4ST (833 3735/www.agent provocateur.com). Metrolink St Peter's Square/City Centre buses/Victoria rail. **Open** 10am-6pm Mon-Sat. **Map** p59 D3 ❸

One word: gorgeous. (For men, the one word is 'phwoar'.) But there's nothing sleazy about AP's beautifully constructed lingerie. The shop's interior suits the ethos perfectly, with thigh-deep carpet, glass cases featuring jewelled riding crops and the familiar blush-pink and black colour scheme. The changing room is worth a visit for the candlelit four-poster, birdcages and chandeliers offering a brief glimpse of what your life could be like if you buy those £49 knickers.

Arndale Market

Arndale Centre, 49 High Street, M4 3AH (832 3552/www.arndalemarket.co.uk). Metrolink Market Street/City Centre buses/Victoria rail. **Open** 8am-6pm Mon-Sat; 11am-5pm Sun. **Map** p59 E3 ❹
See box p78.

Aspecto

85-87 Bridge Street, M3 2RE (834 4875/www.aspecto.co.uk). Metrolink St Peter's Square/City Centre buses/ Salford rail. **Open** 9am-6pm Mon-Fri; 11am-5pm Sun. **Map** p58 C3 ❺
Street-style designer clothing for men and women, alongside cool shoes and accessories. Stock includes Duffer, Paul Smith, Maharishi and G Star. The shop is funky and functional and very popular with well-heeled thirtysomethings who still want to cut an urban dash.

C Aston

Unit 8, Royal Exchange Arcade, M2 7EA (832 7895). Metrolink Market Street/ City Centre buses/Victoria rail. **Open** 9am-5.30pm Mon-Sat. **Map** p59 D3 ❻

In-demand designers

Unique Boutique

Manchester is endlessly creative, and fashion design ticks all the right boxes – cool, urban, gorgeous and offering the potential to make serious money. That's why new designers are springing up all over the city, inspired by past giants such as Vivienne Westwood, Wayne Hemingway of Red or Dead and Matthew Williamson, who cut his fashion teeth in the city's nightclubs.

The new generation of designers are equally determined to go global, but they know their own city well enough to understand what sells.

Big hitters such as **Bench** and **Hooch** are stocked in the funkier Northern Quarter boutiques like **Wood** (Oldham Street) and **Westworld** (Church Street), while the quirky, and very successful, street label **Ringspun**, which now owns private members' club the Circle, is stocked by **Intro**, a cutting-edge Deansgate clothes store dedicated to promoting Manchester labels.

Other local successes trade online, avoiding high City Centre rates; www.midasclothing.com has attracted international attention due to its beautifully made range of kilts and skirts for men, while one of the city's best-known labels, **Gorgeous Couture** (www.gorgeouscouture.com), is adored by celebrities, the likes of Girls Aloud.

For glamour with a street edge, **ZuZu Couture** fits the bill. Designed by local girl Fatz Kassim, the studded, shredded and fake-fur trimmed denim club- and day-wear is catnip to fashionistas who long to be noticed, and is currently stocked by **No Angel**, in Afflecks Palace (p94).

After scoring a big hit in the 1990s, urban street style label **Gio Goi** is back. Now worn by the Arctic Monkeys, Hard-Fi and Pete Doherty, the in-demand designer football shirts, hoodies and coats are stocked in **Selfridges** (p79).

Individual labels also thrive in a city that loves to shop, and T-shirt labels **Unknown Pleasures** (Selfridges) and **Cotton Pimp** (Rags to Bitches; p99), funky clubwear experts **Me & Yu** (Afflecks Palace), womenswear designer **Vicky Martin** (the Triangle; p80), and stylish local clothing and accessories brand **Electricity**, at purveyor of women's and men's fashion **Unique Boutique** (the Triangle), all benefit. But most importantly, so do the shoppers.

There are very few good reasons not to give up smoking, but this shop is one of them. It smell immediately transports you to Havana, and the place offers every esoteric kind of cigarette, including a vast range of flavoured tobaccos, pipes, and Habanas in painted boxes. Even if you only smoke once a year, you may be tempted by the glittering Zippo displays, the Swiss army knives, or the giant-size rolling papers. Now whyever would they be of interest?

Co Cu

12 Barton Arcade, M3 2BB (832 8032/www.cocu.co.uk). Metrolink Market Street/City Centre buses/ Victoria rail. **Open** 10.30am-6pm Tue-Sat; appointment only Sun, Mon. **Map** p59 D3 **47**
Resembling an Edwardian boudoir, with its gilt chaise and sweeping silk curtains, Co Cu is devoted to corsetry. And rightly so – their structured pieces in jewel colours will create waists from wet dough, make balloons out of bee-stings, and bestow the fairy gift of confidence on all who wear these be-ribboned, satin masterpieces. There are skirts to match, and a glass-topped counter displaying waspies, basques and other upholstery of an intimate nature.

Early Learning Centre

6 St Ann's Square, M2 7HN (839 1365/www.elc.co.uk). Metrolink St Peter's Square/City Centre buses/ Victoria rail. **Open** 9am-6pm Mon-Wed, Fri, Sat; 9am-7pm Thur; 11am-5pm Sun. **Map** p59 D3 **48**
With the closure of Deansgate's Daisy & Tom in January 2007, mums and dads should turn to its (less chi-chi) sister company the Early Learning Centre to stock up on children's paraphernalia. With hundreds of games and puzzles, outdoor toys (trampolines, playhouses, swings), soft-fabric baby toys, dolls, baby walkers, musical toys, art materials, books and more, it would be hard not to find something here to please the little 'uns – in particular those aged eight and under.

Elite

35 King Street West, M3 2PW (832 3670/www.elitedressagency.co.uk). Metrolink St Peter's Square/City Centre buses/Salford Central or Victoria rail. **Open** 10am-5pm Mon-Sat; 11am-4pm Sun. **Map** p58 C3 **49**
This place should be a secret and now it's not, because the Elite Dress Agency has been clothing Manchester's best turned-out for years. With a rapidly changing stock of barely-worn designer clothes, aficionados can snap up DKNY, Prada and Miu Miu for a fraction of the original price, or seek out more obscure US or European pieces, alongside Jimmy Choos and last season's It-bags. Packed rails and regular sales mean it's almost impossible to leave empty-handed.

Flannels

4 St Ann's Place, M2 7LP (832 5536/www.flannelsgroup.com). Metrolink St Peter's Square/City Centre buses/Victoria rail. **Open** 10am-6pm Mon-Sat; 11am-5pm Sun. **Map** p59 D3 **50**
A Manchester-based independent chain, stocking the cream of each season's fashion crop. Adored by footballers and their wives, the buying tends towards high glamour-Versace, D&G, Gucci and Cavalli – though such tastefully restrained labels as Armani and YSL also feature heavily. This is the flagship store with more formal styles for both men and women – a second branch, for women only, is on King Street, and stocks more casual designer wear such as Juicy Couture. Take your gold card, and an understanding partner.

Fopp

19 Brown Street, M2 1DA (827 1620/www.fopp.co.uk). Metrolink Market Street/City Centre buses/ Victoria rail. **Open** 9am-6pm Mon-Wed, Fri, Sat; 9am-7pm Thur; 11am-5pm Sun. **Map** p59 E3 **51**
We can't all be rarity-obsessed DJs. And that's the brilliance of Fopp: alongside all the new CD releases,

Flannels p75

downstairs there's a huge selection of classic CDs for around £5 to £7. It's horrifyingly easy to rack up a bill of hundreds of pounds, and that's before you've reached the extensive and air-punchingly cheap DVD area. There's a café, too, for a steadying coffee after your tune-binge.

Formes

7 Police Street, M2 7LQ (832 6277/ www.formes.com). Metrolink St Peter's Square/City Centre buses/Victoria rail. **Open** 10am-6pm Mon-Wed, Fri; 10am-7pm Thur; 9.30am-6pm Sat; noon-5pm Sun. **Map** p59 D3 ❷

Clothes often stop being a pleasure during pregnancy, and become a miserable chore, featuring safety pins, elastic panels and your sister's old maternity jeans. Not at Formes. This small but seductive boutique sells tailored and draped collections for the elegantly pregnant, in figure-flattering fabrics such as soft wool, silk and jersey. They're not cheap, but worth it to feel less spacehopper and more yummy tummy.

Harvey Nichols

Exchange Square, M1 1AD (828 8888/www.harveynichols.com). Metrolink Victoria/City Centre buses/Victoria rail. **Open** 10am-7pm Mon-Wed, Fri; 10am-8pm Thur; 9am-7pm Sat; noon-6pm Sun (browsing from 11.30am). **Map** p59 D2 ❸

Harvey Nichols is a beacon of luxury, opened as part of the 2003 Exchange Square development. Its three floors display beauty products, shoes, breathtakingly expensive womenswear – the likes of Marc Jacobs, Stella McCartney and Roberto Cavalli – plus edgy new labels such as Mist and Rock & Republic jeans. There's a floor of choice menswear morsels, and the small jewel of a food department, leading to the restaurant, is a one-stop shop for the rich, and a sublime browsing experience for everyone else. There's also an Aveda spa, a juice bar and an absolutely fabulous handbag department that features the season's most gorgeous armcandy from Luella, Balenciaga and Chloé. The restaurant and brasserie are located on the second floor.

Heal's

*11 New Cathedral Street,M1 1AD
(819 3000/www.heals.co.uk). Metrolink
Victoria/City Centre buses/Victoria
rail.* **Open** 10am-6pm Mon-Fri;
9.30am-6.30pm Sat; 11am-5pm
Sun. **Map** p59 D2 ⑤④

City Centre furniture shops tend
towards either dull and traditional, or
wildly edgy. Heal's, however, understands that your home is an extension
of your personality, and offers a selection of modern classics that look
equally good in a tiny apartment as
in a sprawling Cheshire farmhouse.
The ground floor is devoted to homeware, crockery, quirky cookbooks
and amusing gifts; and while you
couldn't realistically employ the word
'bargain', Heal's relies successfully on
the notion that a thing of beauty is a
joy forever.

Hermès

*31 King Street, M2 6AA (834 5331/
www.hermes.com). Metrolink St Peter's
Square/City Centre buses/Victoria
rail.* **Open** 10am-6pm Mon-Sat.
Map p59 D3 ⑤⑤

Only step inside if you're looking
to offload the irritating amount of
cash you've accumulated. They don't
charge you to breathe the air here, but
they may as well. Sweeping wooden
stairs lead to the salon of scarves,
bags, belts and knick-knackery from
the venerable Parisian design house. It
smells of fine-grain leather, silk and
money – and if you want to bathe in it,
they even do a range of exquisite per-
fumes. Staff are gliding and assured;
customers less so, but it doesn't hurt
to live the WAG dream now and then.

Hotel Chocolat

*Northern Extension, New Cannon
Street, Arndale Centre, M4 3AJ (0870
442 8282/www.hotelchocolat.co.uk).
Metrolink Shudehill or Market Street/
City Centre buses/Victoria rail.* **Open**
9am-8pm Mon-Sat; 11am-5pm Sun.
Map p59 E3 ⑤⑥

Chocolate. In beautiful, minimalist
black packaging, sprinkled with such
enticements as swirls of cream, dried

raspberries and orange peel. It's a long
way from the corner shop's sweetie
counter – and so are the prices. But
worth every calorie and penny for a
very special treat.

House of Fraser

*60 Deansgate, M60 3AU (0870
1607254/www.houseoffraser.com).
Metrolink Market Street or St Peter's
Square/City Centre buses/Victoria
rail.* **Open** 9.30am-7pm Mon-Wed,
Fri; 9am-8pm Sat; 11am-5pm Sun.
Map p58 C3 ⑤⑦

The venerable old auntie of department stores, covering six floors of a
listed art deco building, House of
Fraser (or Kendals, as it was called
until last year, and still is by every
Mancunian) should be praised for moving with the times. Unfailingly stunning window displays signpost six
floors of high fashion, homeware and
cosmetics, a waitress-service café and
a basement annexe crammed with
designer menswear. Have tea and
cakes and check out the fabulous glass
and china department.

Mappin & Webb Ltd

*12-14 St Ann Street, M2 7LF (832
2551/www.mappin-and-webb.co.uk).
Metrolink Market Street or St Peter's
Square/City Centre buses/Victoria
rail.* **Open** 9am-5.30pm Mon-Sat.
Map p59 D3 ⑤⑧

A proper – and proper pricey – jew-
ellers, Mappin & Webb proves that dia-
monds really are a girl's best friend.
And so are watches, earrings, pen-
dants, engagement rings… Glittering
glass cases, smooth staff and a hushed,
plush atmosphere.

Office Sale Shop

*3 St Ann's Place, M2 7LP (834 3804/
www.office.co.uk). Metrolink Market
Street or St Peter's Square/City Centre
buses/Victoria rail.* **Open** 9am-6pm
Mon-Wed, Fri, Sat; 9am-7pm Thur;
11am-5pm Sun. **Map** p59 D3 ⑤⑨

While most bargain shops trade by the
motto 'you get what you pay for', here,
all stock is ex-Office shoe store, and of
generally good quality. The only dif-

Marketing Manchester

Fashion Market

MANCHESTER BY AREA

Everyone likes a bargain, but Manchester's markets are about more than six pairs of socks for a pound. The following venues all offer a compelling alternative to the high street, with unique goods and personal service. Also look out for the less regular markets held in the City Centre throughout the year – in particular, St Ann's Square's sporadic **Fine Food Market** and the Christmas German market.

On the Northern Quarter side of the Arndale lies the permanent **Arndale Market** (p73). Previously a grim repository of cheap tat, it's upped its game and now offers speciality teas, organic breads and arts and crafts. It's worth a look, if only to marvel at the sudden absence of fluorescent lingerie.

At the gateway to the Northern Quarter, the **Fashion Market** (Tib Street, 10am-5pm Sat) allows up-and-coming designers to showcase their collections. Quirky jewellery mingles with customised vintage, one-off leather bags, prints and hand-made silk cushions. And it's always possible you'll be buying from the next Matthew Williamson.

For a traditional and personal vibe, visit the small but bustling **Longsight Market** (Dickenson Road, Longsight, 9am-4.30pm Wed & Fri, 9am-5pm Sat), for cheap and cheery fashions and fabrics, plus meats, veg and exotic spices, while for a slice of bucolic heaven, check out **Manchester Farmers' Market** (Piccadilly Gardens, 10am-6pm 2nd & last Fri & Sat of month). If you want to know the name of the goat that produced the milk for your cheese, this is the place. Smallholders from across the North West sell organic meats, veg, cheese, cakes and wine. You can even find the not-so-native (but organic!) ostrich burgers.

If size is your priority, then **Bury Market** (Murray Road, Bury, Mon-Sat) – the biggest market in the North West, a 20-minute drive from Manchester City Centre – should fit the bill. The most fun happens on Wednesdays, Fridays and Saturdays, when everything from household goods to cheap clothes are rummaged through by tens of thousands of bargain-hunters. For more on the city's markets, visit www.manchester.gov.uk/markets.

ference between this and the main Office store is that stock here has been dramatically marked down due to being end-of-line, last season or marginally scuffed. The place is forever overflowing with canny shoe-lovers of both sexes, loading up on £15 platforms and bargain baseball boots.

Oilily

13a/b Barton Arcade, M3 2BB (839 2832/www.oilily-world.com). Metrolink Market Street or St Peter's Square/City Centre buses/Victoria rail. **Open** 10am-5.30pm Mon-Sat. **Map** p59 D3 **60**
Tucked away in the Victorian splendour of the Barton Arcade, this outpost of the chi-chi children's label is a burst of colour, with bright pink walls and little clothes covered with vibrant gypsy prints, stripes and spots. Cheshire Mums adore it, and the tinies are quite happy to be popped in and out of increasingly adorable outfits in such a jolly shop.

Penhaligon's

St Ann's Square, M2 7TT (835 1155/ www.penhaligons.com). Metrolink Market Street or St Peter's Square rail/City Centre buses/Victoria rail. **Open** 10am-6pm Mon-Sat; 11am-5pm Sun. **Map** p59 D3 **61**
Stepping inside a Victorian parfumerie must have been a similar experience to stepping inside Penhaligon's. Wooden display cabinets house sparkling bottles of the company's own scents, soaps and bath products, based around delightfully old-fashioned ingredients. The pink Love Potion Number 9 is a big seller, and rumour has it that the staff will wrap your gift purchases without the power of sticky tape, using only ribbons and skill.

Ran

8 St Ann's Arcade, M2 7HW (832 9650/www.ranshop.co.uk). Metrolink Market Street or St Peter's Square/ City Centre buses/Victoria rail. **Open** 9.30am-6pm Mon-Sat; 11am-5pm Sun. **Map** p59 D3 **62**
This hard-to-find shoe shop rewards perseverance. Small premises house an eclectic mix of shoes and clothes for men and women, from cutting-edge or rare labels such as Love from Australia, Princess Katrina and Dr Denim. A comfy leather sofa and friendly personal service are further draws.

Richard Crème

64 Bridge Street, M3 3BN (835 2228/www.richardcreme.com). Metrolink St Peter's Square/City Centre buses/Salford Central rail. **Open** times vary; call to make an appointment. **Map** p58 C4 **63**
Richard Crème is said to be the tallest man in Manchester, and used to dress David Beckham. He now provides beautifully cut threads to the city's male great and good from his discreet boutique located just off Albert Square. If you want cheap as chips, go to Primark; if you want an individual, hand-finished suit that will likely last for years, go to Crème and get kitted out properly.

Selfridges

1 Exchange Square, M3 1BD (0870 837 7377/www.selfridges.com). Metrolink Victoria/City Centre buses/ Victoria rail. **Open** 10am-8pm Mon-Fri; 9am-8pm Sat; 10.30am-5pm Sun. **Map** p59 D2 **64**
It would be a crime not to guide the discerning visitor to Selfridges; five floors of loveliness, desirability and luxury. The basement food department is worth a trip in itself, with several counters serving speciality food, plus a Yo! Sushi conveyor belt. For divine wine and top-notch dinner parties, this is the ultimate treat. Upstairs, there are cosmetics, menswear – with a mix of street and classic labels – luxury womenswear and shoes, beside the Champagne bar/restaurant, while the top floor offers younger, funkier (read 'cheaper') high street labels. Not to be missed.

TK Maxx

Basement level, 106-122 Market Street, M1 1WA (236 1885/www. tkmaxx.com). Metrolink Market Street/City Centre buses/Piccadilly

The Triangle

rail. **Open** 9am-8pm Mon-Sat; 11am-5pm Sun. **Map** p59 E3 ⑥⑤

For designer bargains, TK Maxx is unbeatable. Dedicate at least two hours to searching through the endless racks of last-season and surplus stock designer finds. There's menswear, womenswear, underwear, handbags, kidswear and a brilliant homeware section, where the high-quality stock changes regularly and Egyptian cotton sheets are ten a penny (nearly). The shoe department is an essential fashionista spot, with up to 80% off Lulu Guinness and Kurt Geiger. Primark takes up the bottom two floors of this building.

Topshop Shoes

20-22 King Street, M2 6AG (832 5404/www.topshop.com). Metrolink St Peter's Square/City Centre buses/ Victoria rail. **Open** 9am-5pm Mon-Wed, Fri, Sat; 9am-7pm Thur; 11am-5pm Sun. **Map** p59 D3 ⑥⑥

The UK's only dedicated shoe store from the all-conquering Topshop stable. Stock is heavily seasonal and is updated every time Kate Moss clears her throat, but there will almost certainly be bright, shiny shoes in a rainbow of colours, boots – spindly and chunky – and a fashion-forward crowd of women thrusting their credit cards at the checkouts. There's a so-so but affordable vintage section at the back, and lots of mirrors in which to admire potential purchases.

Triangle, Exchange Square

37 Exchange Square, M4 3TR (834 896/www.trianglemanchester.co.uk). Metrolink Shudehill or Market Street/ City Centre buses/Victoria rail. **Open** 10am-6pm Mon-Wed; 10am-7pm Thur-Sat; 11am-5pm Sun. **Map** p59 D2 ⑥⑦

This slick shopping centre sprang from the ashes of the Corn Exchange (another casualty of *that* bomb), and while the old building's unique character has now been obscured by gleaming white walls, chrome and glass stairs, the shops are impeccably chosen. Brands such as Calvin Klein, Karen Millen, Jigsaw (with adjoining café), Mikey jewellery and Body Shop

rub shoulders with funky retailers such as the Japanese homeware store Muji, surf shop O'Neill, Bravissimo lingerie and Joy, the quirky clothing and gift label. On Saturdays, the Triangle resembles a futuristic space station, manned entirely by well-dressed local shoppers.

Vivienne Westwood

47 Spring Gardens, M2 2BG (835 2121/www.hervia.com). Metrolink St Peter's Square/City Centre buses/ Victoria rail. **Open** 10am-6pm Mon-Sat; noon-5pm Sun. **Map** p59 E4 ⑱
Viv is from nearby Glossop, so it's only right that she should have a dedicated boutique here. And it does her justice. Carved mahogany display cases reveal glittering Westwood orb jewellery, the latest collections are hung beside huge gilt mirrors and there's a chaise longue on which to try the latest shoe ranges. The pricey but stunning main collection sells alongside the diffusion line T-shirts – and every self respecting Manc fashionista owns a tartan Westwood bag.

Waterstone's

91 Deansgate, M3 2BW (837 3000/ www.waterstones.com). Metrolink Market Street or St Peter's Square/ City Centre buses/Victoria rail. **Open** 9am-8pm Mon-Fri; 9am-7pm Sat; 11am-5pm Sun. **Map** p59 D3 ⑲
Committed bibliophiles may sigh for the good old days of musty corridors, rickety library steps and personal recommendations; yet Waterstones reigns supreme on high streets up and down the country. Its Deansgate store (another one opened last year in the Arndale extension) is a vast temple to the published word, and has a particularly good arts section. There's a quiet café, helpful staff, and three large floors of shiny, ink-scented stock to get lost in.

White Company

21-23 King Street M2 6AW (839 1586/www.thewhitecompany.com). Metrolink St Peter's Square/City Centre buses/Victoria rail. **Open** 9.30am-5.30pm Mon-Sat; 11am-5pm Sun. **Map** p59 D3 ⑳

MANCHESTER BY AREA

Selfridges p79

Who would have thought that such a simple idea could end up manifesting itself so successfully? The single concept is in the name – everything sold in this shop is white. Towels, sheets, nighties – every type of household linen, in fact – but all made and presented so stylishly, that it's hard to imagine why anyone ever wanted avocado towels to match their bathroom suite. Tasteful pieces of furniture are also on sale.

Nightlife

42nd Street

2 Bootle Street, M2 5GU (831 7108/ www.42ndstreetnightclub.com). Metrolink GMex/City Centre buses/ Deansgate rail. **Open** 10pm-2.30am Mon-Thur; 10pm-3am Fri, Sat. **Map** p58 C4 🕖

An unreconstructed indie club peddling the predictable soundtrack of Manchester tunes past and present, plus assorted Britpop and other guitar-based anthems. Friendly, popular with students and busy most nights of the week.

Ampersand

Longworth Street, off St John's Street, M3 4BQ (832 3038/www. theampersand.co.uk). Metrolink G-Mex/City Centre buses/Deansgate rail. **Open** 10pm-4am Fri; 10.30pm-4am Sat. **Map** p58 C5 🕖

Where most Manchester clubs are in basements, the city's most glamorous nightspot bucks the trend. Ampersand's look is *Goodfellas*-goes-to-Vegas: a large high-ceilinged space that's all chandeliers, sweeping staircases and dramatic potential. The venue comes to life at weekends when DJs for resident club nights Plush and Twisted Elegance play funky house to an appropriately dressed-up crowd.

Circle Club

Barton Arcade, M3 2BJ (839 9767/ www.thecircleclub.com). Metrolink Market Street or St Peter's Square/ City Centre buses/Victoria rail. **Open** noon-6pm Mon; noon-4am Tue-Sat. **Map** p59 D3 🕖

Hidden round the back of St Ann's Square, the Circle is tough to find unless you know where to look: it's a perfect members club location. The door policy is notoriously strict – you won't get in unless you've been invited. But if you make it past the velvet rope, get ready to enjoy a swish bar and a comfy lounge, plus dancing alongside the city's creative elite – and more than the occasional celeb.

Club V

111a Deansgate, M2 6EQ (834 9975/www.venusmanchester.co.uk). Metrolink St Peter's Square/City Centre buses/Salford Central rail. **Open** 11pm-4.30am Fri; 10.30pm-6am Sat. **Map** p58 C3 🕖

Defining this intimate venue is weekly preen-fest Venus (Saturdays), whose promoters pride themselves on providing their dressy, up for it crowd with a top class club experience of Hed Kandi-esque funky, vocal house. This place is hot – literally. Clubbers keep cool with free fans while the terminally frazzled rely on quick-fix hair straighteners in the toilets.

Life Café &
The Late Room

23 Peter Street, M2 5QR (833 3000). Metrolink St Peter's Square/ City Centre buses/Oxford Road rail. **Open** times vary; call for details. **Map** p58 C4 ⑦

Life Café is a café-bar-come-live venue, and its subterranean sister venue the Late Room is a gig/club space. An oasis of credibility among its alcopop-peddling neighbours, they feature up-and-coming acts, established names plus some decent, independently promoted club nights. A place worth stopping by if you're staying in this cheese loving part of town.

Manchester 235

Great Northern, Watson Street, M3 4DT (832 3927/www.manchester 235.com). Metrolink G-Mex/City Centre buses/Deansgate rail. **Open** noon-6am Mon-Sun. **Map** p58 C5 ⑦

The latest venture to inhabit this formerly uninspirational leisure development, Manchester 235 is a luxury, Vegas-influenced restaurant/bar/casino/live music complex. It was the casino that made the headlines on the club's launch; now it's the edgy new music showcased there. A good choice for a slick, smart and sophisticated night out.

MEN Arena

Victoria Station, M3 1AR (0871 226 5000/www.men-arena.com). Metrolink Victoria/City Centre buses/Victoria rail. **Open** times vary. **Map** p59 D1 ⑦

The City Centre's largest concert venue (aka Manchester Arena) is a stopping-off point for those commanding a big crowd: typically big pop acts (à la Aguilera), household name comedians (Eddie Izzard) and (mostly) middle-of-the-road rock bands.

M-two

1 Peter Street, M2 3NQ (839 1112/ www.mtwonightclub.com). Metrolink St Peter's Square/City Centre buses/ Oxford Road rail. **Open** 9.30pm-2.30am Wed; 10pm-2am Thur; 9.30pm-3am Fri, Sat. **Map** p59 D5 ⑦

A favourite with the shirt-and-polished-shoes crowd that prowl Peter Street every weekend, M-two was taken over by the boys behind the influential dance party/club brand Gatecrasher in late 2006. They ushered in a new music policy, with occasional name DJs, and if things go well the club will get a full refurb in 2007. Based on Crasher's (plush) ventures in Sheffield and Leeds, it could be something to get excited about.

Opus

Printworks, Withy Grove, M4 2BS (834 2414/www.opusmanchester. com). Metrolink Shudehill/City Centre buses/Victoria rail. **Open** noon-3am Mon, Wed-Sat; noon-midnight Tue, Sun. **Admission** £4.50-£8; £3-£6 reductions. **Map** p59 E2 ⑦

With a bar, restaurant, comedy, live music and club facilities, this is one of the most well rounded (and liveliest) venues in the mainstream Printworks development. Big name Friday and Saturday night sessions have proved a hit, as have regular club nights, soundtracked to commercial disco, soul and funky house.

One Central Street

1 Central Street, M2 5WR (211 9000/www.onecentralstreet.co.uk). Metrolink St Peter's Square/City Centre buses/Oxford Road rail. **Open** 10pm-3am Thur-Sat, bank hols. **Admission** £4-£6; £4-£5 reductions. **Map** p59 D4 ⑧

A beautifully designed basement club/bar with a big sound system that attracts a mixed crowd of switched-on students and Mancs. Aside from the cocktails, the main draws are fashionably appointed electro disco Romp on Thursdays and Friday's legendary Mancunian electro/tech house session Bugged Out! The great atmosphere rarely disappoints.

Paparazzi

Printworks, Withy Grove, M4 2BS (832 1234/www.theparazzi.co.uk). Metrolink Shudehill/City Centre buses/ Victoria rail. **Open** 9pm-2am Mon, Tue;

One Central Street p83

9pm-2.30am Wed, Thur, Sun; 10pm-3am Fri; 10pm-4am Sat. Map p59 E2 ㉛ Enter the slick and salubrious Paparazzi via a discrete door on its scene-setting red carpet and descend into the split-level club below. Even on student nights this place is super stylish – it's worth making the effort to dress up before heading out, and gives you a better chance of talking your way past the velvet rope into the mezzanine VIP.

Pure

Printworks, Withy Grove, M4 2BS (819 7770/www.puremanchester. com). Metrolink Shudehill/City Centre buses/Victoria rail. **Open** 10pm-3am Mon, Wed; 10pm-6am Fri; 10pm-5am Sat. **Admission** £5-£8; free-£5 reductions. **Map** p59 E2 ㉜ A 2,500-capacity mega club from the people behind London's Heaven, Pure was piloted in the Printworks site in 2006 after its former tenants – the venture Lucid – failed to make it work. They started by stripping out the clutter (a bowling alley, restaurants) and installing a £300,000 Funktion One sound system, with local radio DJs now taking the helm for commercial house sessions at weekends.

South

4a South King Street, M2 6DQ (831 7756/www.south-club.co.uk). Metrolink St Peter's Square/City Centre buses/Salford rail. **Open** 10pm-2.45am Fri; 9.30pm-2.45am Sat. **Map** p58 C3 ㉝ This basic basement club's excellent nights make it well worth risking your new white trainers for. Fridays mean stomping northern soul, Motown and always the best rock 'n' roll at the Rock + Roll Bar. On Saturdays, the Boon Army faithful pile in for indie, dance and disco courtesy of ex-Inspiral (and current Xfm plate spinner) Clint Boon. Get there early – it sells out every week.

Tiger Lounge

5 Cooper Street, M2 2FW (236 6007). Metrolink St Peter's Square/City Centre buses/Oxford Road rail. **Open** noon-

2am Mon-Thur; noon-2.30am Fri; 3pm-3am Sat; 5pm-2am Sun. **Map** p59 D4 ㉞ Renamed after its eponymous Saturday nighter (the place was previously called 'Slice'), this eternally entertaining extravaganza puts on rock 'n' roll, soul, Detroit garage and kitsch covers in swell, although sweaty, leopard-print surroundings. Somewhere to play dress up if you're so inclined – and the quirkier the outfit, the better. Other nights feature live bands and DJs.

Arts & leisure

AMC Great Northern

Great Northern, Deansgate, M3 4EN (0870 755 5657/www.amccinemas. co.uk). Metrolink G-Mex/City Centre buses/Deansgate rail. **Tickets** £5.50; £4.50 before 6pm; £3.50 reductions. **Map** p58 C5 ㉟ Screening standard movie fare in its 16 auditoria, the AMC cinema, which opened in 2001, is set apart by its location – within a Victorian Grade II-listed building that was once a receiving warehouse for deliveries to Central Station (now Manchester Central; p62).

Library Theatre

Central Library, St Peter's Square, M2 5PD (236 7110/www.library theatre.com). Metrolink St Peter's Square/City Centre buses/Oxford Road rail. **Open** Box Office 10.30am-8pm Mon-Fri; noon-8pm Sat. **Map** p59 D4 ㊱ How does one of the city's smallest theatres command so much critical acclaim? Age helps (it's 50-plus years old), as might its unique ethos – it's the only rep theatre in the country funded by a city council, and has performances for the deaf and hard of hearing, as well as programmes in braille and large print. But what sets this theatre apart is the passion with which it puts on its own productions. The blend of drama, modern classics and regional premières keep the plaudits rolling in. The theatre also takes on touring shows from companies with a similar theatrical outlook.

The Royal Exchange

Built in 1729 on the site currently occupied by M&S, Manchester's original Exchange was a grand affair. Over the following century and a half it was demolished, moved, rebuilt, demolished and rebuilt again, before becoming the world's biggest commercial trading floor in the late 19th and early 20th centuries. But as the cotton market faded, so did trading at what was by then known as the Royal Exchange. Business ceased on New Year's Eve of 1968; its last breath is commemorated in cotton prices still posted high on the walls.

The following year, a group of theatrical producers voiced the idea of building a theatre within the existing Victorian shell. Finance was predictably difficult to source, yet seven years and £1.2 million later, the Royal Exchange Theatre was complete, built to designs by architectural firm Levitt Bernstein. The ribbon was cut in September 1976 by Sir Laurence Olivier.

'The aim was to create a theatre of national standing outside London,' explains Founding Artistic Director Braham Murray. 'At that time, audiences outside London either got try-outs for the West End, post-London runs with inferior casts, or rep productions.' It took time, but Murray and colleagues eventually achieved their ambition.

In 1996 came the IRA bomb, detonated a couple of hundred yards away, and which caused severe structural damage to the theatre. While the venue was being rebuilt, loyal audiences watched plays in a makeshift tent. The place reopened in 1998 with a new café and a dedicated studio space given over to new work. The play chosen for the theatre's relaunch was Stanley Houghton's *Hindle Wakes* – the same work that had been running when the explosion went off. A symbol of the theatre's defiance and indefatigability, it was a perfect choice.

Murray has taken to his original task with such enthusiasm that, as the theatre celebrated its 30th birthday in 2006, he was still working within its confines. Here's to another 30 years.

Odeon Manchester & IMAX

Printworks, Withy Grove, City Centre, M4 2BS (0871 224 4007/www. odeon.co.uk). Metrolink Shudehill/ City Centre buses/Victoria rail. **Tickets** £6; £5 Mon-Thur before 5pm; £4 reductions. **Map** p59 E2 ⑥⑦

If size really does matter, the Odeon beats every other City Centre cinema hands down, with 23 screens and an IMAX theatre. Its 'gallery' also gives cinephiles the chance for a more exclusive viewing experience. Here, intimate auditoria, large leather seats and an alcohol licence mean you need to book ahead to bag your spot by the bar.

Opera House

Quay Street, M3 3HP (0870 145 1163/www.manchestertheatres.com). Metrolink St Peter's Square/City Centre buses/Oxford Road rail. **Map** p58 C4 ⑥⑧

Opera House is an ornate 2,000-capacity theatre whose output of West End musicals, comedy, ballet and drama is similar to its sister venue, the Palace Theatre. True to its name, though, this house is also home to regional and national opera.

Portico Library & Gallery

57 Mosley Street, entrance on Charlotte Street, M2 3HY (236 6785/www. theportico.org.uk). Metrolink Mosley Street/City Centre buses/Piccadilly rail. **Admission** free. **Map** p59 E4 ⑥⑨

Tucked unobtrusively away at the side of the Bank pub, and accessed via a buzzer system, the Portico recently celebrated 200 cerebral years of book lending and arts events. Its tightly-packed library, with creaking floorboards, leather-backed chairs and archaic section headings ('polite literature' is one), takes you right back to 19th-century Manchester (but you have to be a member to borrow from the collection). A changing series of art exhibitions take place in the gallery housed beneath a gorgeous Georgian glass dome ceiling, and literary events are held throughout the year.

Royal Exchange

St Ann's Square, M2 7DH (833 9833/ www.royalexchange.co.uk). Metrolink Market Street or St Peter's Square/City Centre buses/Victoria rail. **Open** Box Office 9.30am-7.30pm Mon-Fri; 9.30am-8pm Sat. **Map** p59 D3 ⑨⓪

See box p86.

Sienna Spa Radisson Edwardian

Peter Street, M2 5GP (835 8964/ www.siennaspa.com). Metrolink St Peter's Square/City Centre buses/ Oxford Road rail. **Open** Spa 9am-9pm Mon-Fri, 10am-6pm Sat, Sun. Gym 7am-9pm Mon-Fri, 8am-8pm Sat, Sun. **Admission** Gym £12. Facials from £58. **Map** p58 C5 ⑨①

This five-star day spa in the vaults of the former Free Trade Hall (it famously hosted gigs by Bob Dylan and the Sex Pistols, and was home to the Hallé for many years; it's now the Radisson Edwardian hotel, p177) has a gym, steamroom, sauna and swimming pool (check out the sauna's fibre optic lighting – designed to look like a star-studded night sky). The towels are so thick you could use them as pillows, and the lighting suitably forgiving. Expect top-of-the-range treatments (body wraps, facials, massages, manicures) from exclusive ranges, with prices to match.

Vertical Chill

North Face, 130 Deansgate, M3 2QS (837 6140/www.vertical-chill.com). Metrolink St Peter's Square/City Centre buses/Salford Central rail. **Open** 9.30am-4.30pm Mon-Sat; 11.30am-4.30pm Sun. **Admission** £20-£40. **Map** p58 C3 ⑨②

Step inside outdoor clothing shop the North Face and you may be surprised to see a 23-foot-high sheer wall of ice – known as the Saab Ice Wall – poking up between the fleeces and crampons. The –12°C monolith, operated by Vertical Chill, is perfect for practising climbing and ice-axe moves and, for those Edmund Hillary wannabes, there's an icy overhang to grapple with. Call for details of the various masterclasses.

Craft & Design Centre p95

Northern Quarter

To find Manchester's self-styled creative quarter, just follow the stream of skinny-jean-clad kids heading up Oldham Street. The Northern Quarter's vintage boutiques, galleries and record shops give new meaning to the word 'independent'. It is defiantly chain-free – even the pubs are fiercely singular.

The main action clusters around Oldham Street, but it's worth exploring the side lanes to fully uncover the eclectic shopping experience on offer. The friendly vibe here is exemplified at **Soup Kitchen**, where the close-knit creative community chow down together at communal tables. For more substantial fare, the **Koffee Pot** does good-value breakfasts, or take your pick from the many curry places.

Part of the Northern Quarter's charm comes from its architecture – a slightly ramshackle collection of 18th- and 19th-century warehouses. Some have been beautifully restored (such as the building housing the Buddhist Centre), while others are sadly falling into a state of dilapidation. At the heart of the district is the impressive Neo-Romanesque façade of the former **Smithfield Market**. Now surrounded by rather ugly flats, it fronts onto a small public square. In the same block sits the **Chinese Arts Centre** (its tiny café, serving Chinese tea, is a comfy retreat), while the market's sister building can be found on Oak Street, now converted into the **Craft & Design Centre**. This is a hub of local design and industry; products available include prints, sculptures and leather goods.

Sights & museums

Chinese Arts Centre

Market Buildings, Thomas Street, M4 1EU (832 7271/www.chinese-arts -centre.org). Metrolink Shudehill/City Centre buses/Victoria rail. **Open** 10am-6pm Mon-Sat; 11am-4pm Sun. **Admission** free. **Map** p89 B1 ❶
Established in 1986, this specially designed new building has been open since 2003, and now acts as a national centre for the promotion of Chinese art. A changing programme of exhibitions and events celebrates a variety of international Chinese artists, including an artist-in-residence. There's also an interesting shop and specialist tea room.

Greater Manchester Police Museum

57A Newton Street, M1 1ES (856 3287/www.gmp.police.uk). Metrolink Piccadilly Gardens/ City Centre buses/Piccadilly rail. **Open** 10.30am-3.30pm Tue or by appointment; last admission 3pm. **Admission** free. **Map** p89 C2 ❷
An easily overlooked curiosity tucked into an unfashionable corner of town, this converted former police station – far larger than it looks from the outside, in the appropriate manner of *Dr Who*'s TARDIS police box – contains early *CSI: Miami*-style case histories, the original prison cells, haunting Victorian mugshots and cases of grimly inventive confiscated weaponry, all overseen and explained by retired police officers.

Philips Art Gallery

10a Little Lever Street, M1 1HR (941 4197/www.philipscontemporary art.com). Metrolink Piccadilly Gardens/ City Centre buses/Piccadilly rail. **Open** 11am-7pm Tue-Fri; 11am-6pm Sat. **Admission** free. **Map** p89 C2 ❸
Occupying the higher end of the contemporary art scale, this gallery focuses on internationally accomplished painters – whether those with

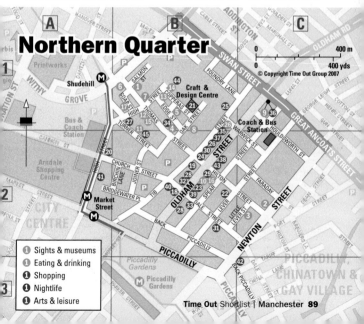

their roots in the city or artists from further afield. Philips also represents Liam Spencer, whose work hangs in Manchester Art Gallery (p62).

Richard Goodall Gallery

59 Thomas Street, M4 1NA (832 3435/www.richardgoodallgallery.com). Metrolink Market Street/City Centre buses/Piccadilly rail. **Open** 11am-6pm Tue-Fri; 11am-5pm Sat. **Admission** free. **Map** p89 B1 ④

On a street tightly packed with skate stores, record shops and quirky boutiques, this commercial gallery's window display pulls in punters with its music and vintage posters and its so-hip-it-hurts illustration, prints and graphic design. A second store round the corner on High Street focuses on rock photography and painting.

Eating & drinking

A Place Called Common

39-41 Edge Street, M4 1HW (832 9245/www.aplacecalledcommon.co.uk). Metrolink Shudehill/City Centre buses/ Victoria rail. **Open** noon-midnight Mon-Wed; noon-1am Thur; noon-2am Fri; 1pm-2am Sat; 2pm-midnight Sun. **Bar. Map** p89 B1 ⑤

A sure-fire bet in the Northern Quarter for consistently friendly staff serving quality drinks in a down-to-earth and lively environment: Common doesn't sacrifice service for boho charm. There's an ever-changing mix of artwork on the walls, DJs spin records most nights of the week, and own-made food is served right until closing time every day. The place also has the latest opening hours in the area. A must for visitors to the city.

Abergeldie Café

40 Shudehill, M4 1EZ (834 5548). Metrolink Shudehill/City Centre buses/ Victoria rail. **Open** 7am-5pm Mon-Sat; 8.30am-3.30pm Sun. **£. Café. Map** p89 B1 ⑥

While the nation's obesity levels are now threatening to sink our little island, some may still find a dirty thrill

This & That p92

in willingly eating fried foods. Greasy spoons like the Abergeldie are now a dying breed, so enjoy the treasure of a traditional full English breakfast (a bargain at £3.90) while you still can.

Bluu

Unit 1, Smithfield Market, Thomas Street, M4 1BD (839 7195/www. bluu.co.uk). Metrolink Shudehill/City Centre buses/Victoria rail. **Open** noon-midnight Mon-Tue, Sun; noon-1am Wed, Thur; noon-2am Fri, Sat. **Bar**. **Map** p89 B1 **7**

This company specialises in *Stepford Wives*-style identikit bars, yet the Manchester branch of Bluu has managed to retain an air of independent dignity that disguises its corporate roots well. This is thanks, in part at least, to its location and to the neighbouring upmarket bars in this alt-cool part of town.

Cord

8 Dorsey Street, M4 1LU (832 9494/ http://mancbars.weshallsee.co.uk). Metrolink Market Street/City Centre buses/Piccadilly rail. **Open** noon-11pm Mon-Thur; noon-1am Fri, Sat; 4pm-10.30pm Sun. **Bar**. **Map** p89 B1 **8**

This aptly-named bar is decked out with cord-covered seating, and the intimate booths give the small but perfectly formed space a homely feel. It can feel terrifyingly cramped at weekends, however, but it's worth braving the crowds for the decent beers and even better DJs who hold court in the basement. In the daytime, stop in for a pickled egg or gourmet pie served with mash and peas.

Crown & Kettle

3 Oldham Street (on corner with Great Ancoats Street), M4 5FE (236 2923). Metrolink Market Street/ City Centre buses/Piccadilly rail. **Open** 11am-11pm Mon-Thur; 11am-midnight Fri, Sat; noon-10.30pm Sun. **Pub**. **Map** p89 C1 **9**

Mothballed for some 20 years, this former haunt of hacks from the nearby Daily Express building has made a

welcome return. Legend has it that the building was originally intended as a law court, hence the intricate ceilings and mullioned windows, although the coloured plaster walls of its refit don't really do the place justice. There's more taste in the range of beers on offer here, which include ales from the local Boggart Hole Clough brewery.

Dry Bar

28-30 Oldham Street, M1 1JN (236 9840). Metrolink Piccadilly Gardens/City Centre buses/Piccadilly rail. **Open** noon-midnight Mon-Wed; noon-2am Thur-Sat; 6pm-midnight Sun. **Bar**. **Map** p89 B2 **10**

A Northern Quarter mainstay long before the area's regeneration kicked in, this former Factory Records-owned DJ bar was one of the first in the country. A must visit for any 'Madchester' or Haçienda (p52) veterans – order a beer at Dry and you'll be perching where countless Mancunian musicians have stood. Stick around into the evening for club nights and live music, when the cavernous interior comes to life. It may be a shadow of its former self, and the former scenesters may have moved on, but the place still holds a certain charm.

Earth Café

16-20 Turner Street, M4 1DZ (834 1996/www.earthcafe.co.uk). Metrolink Shudehill/City Centre buses/Victoria rail. **Open** noon-3pm, 5-7pm Tue-Fri; 10am-5pm Sat. **£**. **Café**. **Map** p89 B2 **11**

This vegan café, in the basement of the Manchester Buddhist Centre (p102), dishes up food that's both fresh and, where possible, organic. The chef's special represents good value for money at £7.65 for rice, a heaped plate of the daily dish (butterbean casserole, for example) and two salads. A range of teas and smoothies is also available.

Hunter's BBQ

94 High Street, M4 1EF (839 5060). Metrolink Market Street/City Centre buses/Piccadilly rail. **Open** 11am-1am daily. **£**. **Barbecue**. **Map** p89 B1 ⑫

The fact that this eccentric restaurant will seemingly barbecue anything they can get their hands on (venison, grouse and quail have all featured on their menu) should be regarded as more than just a mere novelty act. Hunter's curries are all the more interesting for using innovative flavours, and who wouldn't take dark, peppery pheasant over boring old chicken? An odd but enjoyable late-night option.

Market Restaurant

104 High Street, M4 1HQ (834 3743/www.market-restaurant.com). Metrolink Shudehill/City Centre buses/Victoria rail. **Open** noon-2.15pm, 6-9.30pm Wed-Fri; 7-9.30pm Sat. **££**. **Modern British**. **Map** p89 B1 ⑬

The unprepossessing decor may underwhelm, but, as is so often the case in Manchester, the appearance of this place should not be read as an indicator of quality. The Market has racked up a quarter of a century of excellent cooking and has now refined its Modern British style to perfection. The beer list, in particular, comes highly recommended, as do the pudding club events (at £25 for a main and five puds).

Northern Quarter Restaurant & Bar

108 High Street, M4 1HQ (832 7115/ www.tnq.co.uk). Metrolink Shudehill/ City Centre buses/Victoria rail. **Open** noon-10.30pm Tue-Sat; noon-7pm Sun. **£££**. **Modern European**. **Map** p89 B1 ⑭

New head chef Jason Wass has piloted this handsome restaurant away from its former Middle Eastern style, towards a more Modern British/ European proposition. Lovely dishes such as roasted garlic and cherry tomato risotto and oven-roasted wood pigeon have turned the place into a jewel on the Northern Quarter's High Street – an absolute must for any visiting foodies.

Odd

30-32 Thomas Street, M4 1ER (833 0070/www.oddbar.co.uk). Metrolink Shudehill/City Centre buses/Victoria rail. **Open** 11am-midnight daily. **Bar**. **Map** p89 B1 ⑮

A happy haven of eclectic quirkiness, Odd is the antithesis of corporate high street drinking dens, and welcomes a mixed crowd. Even better than the DIY decor, tasty bar snacks (like the to-die-for mini fish and chips), cocktails and continental beers is its background music: kooky jukebox by day, sets from forward-thinking indie advocates by night. Among those giving their expansive music repertoire a regular airing are psychedelic pop-tronica act the Earlies.

Soup Kitchen

31-33 Spear Street, M1 1DF (236 5100/www.soup-kitchen.co.uk). Metrolink Market Street/City Centre buses/Piccadilly rail. **Open** 9am-4pm Mon-Fri. **£**. **Café**. **Map** p89 B2 ⑯

From the team behind supreme boozer the Bay Horse comes this communal canteen. After collecting your food from the counter you transport your grub to one of the long benches and tables and say hello to fellow diners. Select large bowls of freshly-made soup (which change daily) and hunks of fresh bread for less than a fiver, or go for the daily hot special. A good, cheap and tasty lunch option.

This & That

3 Soap Street, M4 1EX (832 4971). Metrolink Shudehill/City Centre buses/Victoria rail. **Open** 11.30am-5pm Mon-Fri; 11.30am-4pm Sat, Sun. **£**. **Curry**. **Map** p89 B1 ⑰

There's an enjoyable sense of the old school canteen about this curry café, with its plastic chairs and steaming bain-marie (across which you place your order). Asking for 'rice and three' gets you a hearty plate of boiled rice with three different curries mingling joyously together on top. The varieties vary daily, but you can expect a good choice of meat (chicken and lamb) and vegetable (from daal to cabbage) varieties,

Afflecks Palace p94

and for less than a fiver you'll get a heap of spicy wholesome food, fresh naan bread and a jug of mango lassi. The one drawback is the hard-to-find location – the place is tucked away in the sort of alley that you might see featured on *Crimewatch* reconstructions. But think of the food that awaits, and be brave.

Shopping

The best place in the city to find independent boutiques, quirky one-off shops and cutting-edge styles, the Northern Quarter attracts hip shoppers, students and fashionistas who aren't afraid to wander between dodgy curry houses, garment warehouses and the odd remaining tramp, as they rack up their purchases.

Afflecks Palace

52 Church Street, M4 1PW (834 2039/ www.afflecks-palace.co.uk). Metrolink Market Street/City Centre buses/ Piccadilly rail. **Open** 10.30am-6pm Mon-Fri; 10am-6pm Sat. **Map** p89 B2 ⑱
At weekends, this four-floor alternative shopping institution crawls with disaffected teens – for a leisurely browse, go midweek. You'll find new designers, clubwear, vintage, fancy dress, records, homeware, cute and kitsch gifts, posters and a vast range of black T-shirts. The building used to be Affleck & Brown's – Manchester's premier department store – and with careful purchasing, you can still emerge with gorgeous items at suitably teenage prices.

Beatin' Rhythm

42 Tib Street, M4 1LA (834 7783/ www.beatinrhythm.com). Metrolink Market Street/City Centre buses/ Piccadilly rail. **Open** 10am-5.30pm Mon-Sat; 11am-4pm Sun. **Map** p89 B2 ⑲
This place lives up to the wildly overused phrase 'a real gem'. It stocks 1960s soul, doo-wop, northern soul, blues, country, girl bands and rock 'n' roll on vinyl and CD, and carries the biggest rare 45s section in the UK. If you crave obscure vinyl from Barbara Lynn or Dobie Gray, you'll think God has answered your prayers. And if you don't, simply enjoy entering a place where the Pussycat Dolls would be laughed out of town.

Christopher Wray Lighting

38 High Street, M4 1QB (832 5221/ www.christopherwray.com). Metrolink Market Street/City Centre buses/ Piccadilly rail. **Open** 9.30am-6pm Mon-Sat. **Map** p89 A2 ⑳

If you seldom find yourself overcome with passionate yearning at the sight of a stunning Rococo chandelier or sweeping velvet sofa, then you'll enjoy a pleasant browse at Christopher Wray. Everyone else will be carried out weeping with longing for the frankly gorgeous lighting effects, lamps and exquisite furniture, because you might need to remortgage to get the chandelier of your dreams. Then again, it'll probably add several thousand pounds to the value of your house.

Craft & Design Centre

17 Oak Street, M4 5JD (832 4274/ www.craftanddesign.com). Metrolink Market Street/City Centre buses/ Piccadilly rail. **Open** 10am-5.30pm Mon-Sat; *Dec only* times vary Sun. **Map** p89 B1 ㉑

This long-established creative hub continues to draw the best local talent. Each floor is lined with small shops and studios, and many traders design on site and sell their work fresh from the drawing board, sewing machine or workbench. Products include one-off bags, intricate jewellery, large-scale photographic prints, paintings, sculpture and leather wares. There's also a pleasant café, and changing exhibitions throughout the year. And if you're after something really special, most of the artisans will work to commission.

Fred Aldous

37 Lever Street, M1 1LW (236 4224/ www.fredaldous.co.uk). Metrolink Piccadilly Gardens/City Centre/ Piccadilly rail. **Open** 8.15am-5.15pm Mon-Sat. **Map** p89 B2 ㉒

'Supplying the creative mind since 1861' states the sign. It doesn't sell opium, but Fred Aldous does offer a huge basement packed with everything the social sketcher, dedicated designer and committed craftsperson could ever want. Aisles groan with pens, paints, glue, paper, glitter and all the little bits and pieces you need to make jewellery, cards and felt things to sell at the church fête. Staff are immensely helpful, and it's easy to

Magma p96

MANCHESTER BY AREA

believe you're a successful artist simply by sniffing the creative air.

Magma

24 Oldham Street, M1 1JN (236 8777/ www.magmabooks.com). Metrolink Piccadilly Gardens/City Centre buses/ Piccadilly rail. **Open** 10am-6.30pm Mon-Sat; 11am-5pm Sun.
Map p89 B2 ㉓

Though this is a small chain, Magma has the feel of an independent bookshop, with obscure, fascinating and glossy photographic and art books. Some of the coffee table books are the price of a, er, coffee table but for a £10 gift, the 'Cool Shops' series from Taschen is ideal. You can easily spend hours here, leafing through the volumes. There's also a selection of funny, quirky postcard books and adult cartoons for those who find proper 'Art' too tiresome.

Northern Flower

58 Tib Street, M4 1LG (832 7731/ www.northernflower.com). Metrolink Market Street/City Centre buses/ Piccadilly rail. **Open** 9am-6pm Mon-Sat. **Map** p89 B2 ㉗

A flower shop with personal service and knowledgeable staff is something of a rarity in a world where the choice is often limited to wilted garage chrysanths and supermarket spider plants. At Northern Flower, you can believe that the blooms have just been picked by an elf skipping through a dew-drenched field. Find rare pot plants to liven up a dull office, get staff to make up a customised romantic bouquet or just pluck a few bold blooms to cheer yourself up on the way home.

NÚA Lifestyle

49 Tib Street, M4 1LS (839 5580/ www.nualifestyle.com). Metrolink Market Street/City Centre buses/ Piccadilly rail. **Open** 11am-6pm Mon-Sat; noon-5pm Sun. **Map** p89 B1 ㉕

Most sex shops in the Northern quarter are blacked-out and seedy as a hamster's food-bowl, thereby repelling nervous browsers. NÚA, however, is light, bright, arranged like a particularly exquisite ornament-shop and features the very best in sex toys, lingerie and those bits of scary bedroom paraphernalia you always thought were only for Angelina Jolie. And if you're still unsure, the female owners are always happy to talk you through the, er, ins and outs of their range.

Oi Polloi

70 Tib Street, M4 1LG (831 7870/ www.oipolloi.com). Metrolink Market Street/City Centre buses/Piccadilly rail. **Open** 10am-6pm Mon-Sat.
Map p89 B2 ㉖

Oi Polloi seems to have the menswear market nailed, offering a selection of upmarket casualwear labels such as Penguin, Belstaff and Fred Perry. The owner's resident bulldog adds a rakish air to the proceedings.

Oklahoma

74-76 High Street, M4 1ES (834 1136). Metrolink Market Street/City Centre buses/Piccadilly rail. **Open** 8am-7pm Mon-Sat; 11am-5pm Sun.
Map p89 B1 ㉗

If a giant *piñata* were to explode in Manchester, the results might resemble Oklahoma. Defying categorisation, this airy, wooden-floored shop-cum-café stocks the best selection of retro and quirky cards in town alongside bizarre and amusing cheap gifts, imported and designer homeware and a healthy dose of kitsch. If you're after Virgin Mary charm bracelets, or magic trees, you're in the right place. If you'd rather buy a subtitled Korean DVD and eat vegetarian chilli washed down with a banana smoothie, you're also catered for. Anyone who dares to leave this place disappointed is a joyless soul indeed.

Oxfam

8-10 Oldham Street, M1 1JQ (228 3797/www.oxfam.org.uk). Metrolink Piccadilly Gardens/City Centre buses/ Piccadilly rail. **Open** 10am-6pm Mon-Sat; noon-5pm Sun. **Map** p89 B2 ㉘

Mint Lounge

The city's club of the moment.

Back in early 2005, the Mint Lounge (p100) was a burlesque bar – the only venue of its type in the city. But some two years on, the showgirls have more or less vanished from the basement space. Having taken the decision to shake off its feather boa, Mint now hosts an array of house, hip hop, reggae, mix 'n' mash and live music events, making it one of the city's most exciting venues.

Despite the owners' intentions to avoid all the club venue clichés, it's hard to avoid the feeling that the transition was inevitable. In a city lacking quality spaces for dancing, there was pressure from the start for Mint to evolve. 'We'd been interested in Mint since it opened,' confesses Huw Morgan of local promoters the Electriks, whose fantastic Saturday-nighter Nish Nash Nosh was the first to move in. 'It's got the perfect basement feel, but – more importantly – it's not your typical damp and dirty basement. It has a real warmth.'

Also quick to capitalise on Mint's change in direction were the organisers of New York-style deep house, disco and soul-based soirée Development, which, like Nish Nash Nosh, proved perfectly suited to the space. Development's guests have so far included Ben Watt, Danny Krivit, Hippie Torales and Phil Asher – yet the nights aren't just about big-name visitors. 'The guests have been strong, but hopefully people also come because they know they'll get two rooms of quality, varied music every month', stresses co-promoter Tom Lynch.

Perhaps the most notable arrival over the past few months has been Fat City hip hop session Friends & Family, which has landed a regular residency at Mint.

So was Mint's journey purely serendipitous or a calculated plan? 'Mint's evolution was half planned, half not,' says Miss M, one third of the venue's management. 'But we wanted to create a club that's defined by good music, good vibes and a great social, rather than by which DJs are on. And I think we've achieved that.'

Matt & Phred's Jazz Club p100

This huge Oxfam is not a bargain-hunter's paradise – its city centre location is reflected in the prices. But it does specialise in collectibles, and has a vinyl section that's well worth a peek, plus several shelves of rare books. Give it a miss for clothes, though, and go to Oxfam Originals across the road (Unit 8, Smithfield Building, 839 3160), which sells the fashionista's pick of the charity bundles, including cool bags and shoes from the '60s to the '90s.

Pop

34-36 Oldham Street, M1 1JN (236 5797/www.pop-boutique.com). Metrolink Piccadilly Gardens/City Centre buses/Piccadilly rail. **Open** 10am-6pm Mon-Sat; 11am-5pm Sun. **Map** p89 B2 ❷

Pop is a student institution, selling original and recreated '60s and '70s styles upstairs, including jeans, cute tops and cotton dresses, and featuring retro records and a '50s-style café, with chrome chairs and a vegetarian-friendly menu, downstairs. For a quick, painless trip back in time, it's well worth a visit – though if you're a retro purist, it may seem a bit sanitised.

Rags to Bitches

60 Tib Street, M4 1LG (835 9265/ www.rags-to-bitches.co.uk). Metrolink Market Street/City Centre buses/Piccadilly. **Open** 11.30am-6pm Mon, Tue, Thur, Fri, Sat; noon-6pm Wed. **Map** p89 B2 ❸

This upmarket vintage boutique is decorated like a Victorian jewellery box, and offers one-offs, designer and customised pieces from the '40s to the '80s. It also stocks a fabulous selection of costume jewellery, handbags and shoes. The downstairs area houses further hand-picked stock including vintage menswear, bridal and homeware. The owner gives tarot readings on Fridays and, on Saturdays, free fairy cakes are served. Regular events, such as clothes swap parties and Dansette disco nights, are also held in the '30s-speakeasy-style basement.

Rockers

20A Dale Street, M1 1EZ (236 5607/ www.rockersengland.co.uk). Metrolink Piccadilly Gardens/City Centre buses/Piccadilly rail. **Open** *Café* 8.30am-6pm Mon-Sat. *Shop* 10am-6pm Mon-Sat. **Map** p89 B2 ❸

Some specialist shops can be unnerving – this one, however, is notably down-to-earth, and has something for everyone who's ever eyed up a Harley. Having recently moved to new premises, the shop now has a small café, alongside racks of cool T-shirts, bags, jewellery, iron-on patches and spectacular '50s-style dresses. Staff live the dream with quiffs, chains and hefty turn-ups, but they welcome all comers, even if you're a lightweight who just fancies a skull-decorated lighter.

Thunder Egg

22 Oldham Street, M1 1JN (235 0606/www.thunderegg.co.uk). Metrolink Market Street/City Centre buses/Piccadilly rail. **Open** 10.30am-6pm Mon-Fri; 10am-6pm Sat; noon-5pm Sun. **Map** p89 B2 ❸

This funky little gift shop looks like the inside of a Japanese teenager's bedroom. It's packed with Hello Kitty ephemera, design-your-own T-shirt kits, funny cards, cute bags and Paul Frank pinboards. It might be a little too visually exhausting for the over-30s, but for a desirable and affordable gift for your funky mate, it's a great bet.

Travelling Man

4 Dale Street, M1 1JW (237 1877/ www.travellingman.com). Metrolink Piccadilly Gardens/City Centre buses/Piccadilly rail. **Open** 9.30am-6pm Mon-Sat; 10.30am-4pm Sun. late opening 7-10pm Thur. **Map** p89 B2 ❸

Are you male? Like the odd action adventure? Love computer games? Then you'll be drawn to this shop like a moth to a light bulb. US and Japanese comics are displayed on ceiling-high racks, there are obscure board games featuring pneumatic vixens, computer quests, figurines from the crazed imaginations of reclusive animators and rare publications for the dedicated collector. They even have weekly animation workshops (Thursday nights). Your girlfriend may end up dumping you due to your newly developed geekiness – but you will hardly notice.

Vox Pop Music

53-55 Thomas Street, M4 1NA (832 3233/www.voxpopmusic.com). Metrolink Shudehill/City Centre buses/ Victoria Rail. **Open** 8.30am-7pm Mon-Fri; 10am-6pm Sat; 11am-5pm Sun. **Map** p89 B1 ③④

This relatively recent addition to the parade of Manchester record shops is large, easy to navigate and has the added attraction of a miniature branch of local deli Love Saves the Day (p131), selling coffee and snacks at the front. A small CD section and several time-sapping aisles of rare and desirable vinyl mean that whole days can pass and marriages crumble as DJs and aficionados truffle for audio gold – and generally find it.

Nightlife

Centro

74 Tib Street, M4 1LG (832 1325/ www.centro-bar.co.uk). Metrolink Market Street/City Centre buses/ Piccadilly rail. **Open** noon-11pm Mon-Wed; noon-1am Thur-Sat; noon-12.30pm Sun. **Map** p89 B2 ③⑤

A wide range of continental beers and highly munchable, reasonably priced bar food make up just a small part of this bar's kaleidoscopic appeal. Split over two floors, the Northern Quarter stalwart makes for a relaxed retreat during the day and an unpretentious but hip hangout at night. Cool DJs playing Thursday to Saturday make weekends go with an extra swing.

Frog & Bucket

102 Oldham Street, M4 1LJ (236 9805/www.frogandbucket.com). Metrolink Piccadilly Gardens/City Centre buses/Piccadilly rail. **Open**

7.30pm-2am Mon, Thur-Sat; 7.30pm-midnight Sun. **Map** p89 C1 ③⑥

The Frog has given an early boost to comedians like Dave Gorman, Peter Kay and the inimitable Johnny Vegas over the years – a list the venue hopes to add to through its 'Beat the Frog' amateur stand up session held every Monday. Weekends at this welcoming old-school style comedy club see more established names in charge of entertainment, after which a cheerfully cheesy disco ensues.

Matt & Phred's Jazz Club

64 Tib Street, M4 1LW (831 7002/ www.mattandphreds.com). Metrolink Market Street/City Centre buses/ Piccadilly rail. **Open** 5pm-2am Mon-Sat. **Map** p89 B2 ③⑦

A much-loved Oldham Street staple and Manchester's only live jazz music club, Matt & Phred's also provides legendarily good pizza (try the Dave Walsh Special, £6.95) and cocktails. The cosy interior is the perfect setting for the live background music, provided by local and international musicians.

Mint Lounge

46-50 Oldham Street, M4 1LE (228 1495/www.mintlounge.com). Metrolink Piccadilly Gardens/City Centre buses/Piccadilly rail. **Open** 8pm-2am Thur; 10pm-4am Fri, Sat; 7pm-1am Sun. **Map** p89 B2 ③⑧ See box p97.

Night & Day Cafe

26 Oldham Street, M1 1JN (236 4597/www.nightnday.org). Metrolink Piccadilly Gardens/City Centre buses/ Piccadilly rail. **Open** 10am-2am Mon-Sat. **Map** p89 B2 ③⑨

Dingy but full of character, Night & Day is perfectly situated among Oldham Street's record shops: first do some crate-digging, then head on over for a relaxed beer and catch tomorrow's big act or cult faves hanging out, having fun and – if you're lucky – playing intimate sets. Relaxed café-bar by day, world-class rock 'n' roll bar by night: no self-respecting music fan can claim a 'proper' trip to Manchester without a visit here.

Art attack

Manchester's new art space.

Take one former sewing machine shop and a Manchester artist famous for his mosaics. Add a liberal dose of quirky furniture. Season with one-off gigs, exhibitions and musical friends. And there you have it: **Bamber's Art Space** (p102), one of the city's most eclectic cultural experiences.

Bamber's is the brainchild of artist Mark Kennedy and furniture designers Lorna Lucas and Danny Healey, who took over the vacant sewing shop in 2006. It's slap bang in the centre of the Northern Quarter, and is the perfect location for Kennedy to show off his work (he's also spent a decade constructing the tiled artworks that adorn Afflecks Palace, just round the corner; p94). And Bamber's huge windows make it the ideal shop window for Lucas and Healey's mix of new, salvaged and mid 20th-century furniture.

But Bamber's is not simply a vanity project. It puts on events, performances and art shows. The Fall's frontman Mark E Smith is a patron – the band sometimes rehearse in the basement and Bamber's hosts occasional exhibitions of their artwork. Papier-mâché-headed comedian Frank Sidebottom has shown paintings here, while the organisers of Viva La Muralists (p39) chose Bamber's to debut a new street art festival in 2006. Bamber's also has a 'performance window' – a glass-sided room fronting on to the street that's a favourite for fashion photographers.

What makes Bamber's interesting is its unpredictability – you can never be sure what you might find. Entirely self-funded, Kennedy and friends are free to do what they like and are always open to new ideas. When the Koffee Pot café next door was due to close, for example, Bamber's decided to rescue it, transforming it with a mosaic sign, lashings of street art and a new menu. So if you don't find what you're looking for at Bamber's, you can always pop next door for a consolatory bacon buttie.

North

*35 Tib Street, M1 5NJ (839 1989/
www.clubnorth.co.uk). Metrolink
Market Street/City centre buses/
Piccadilly rail.* **Open** 10pm-4am Fri-
Sat; 10pm-5am last Sat of mth.
Map p89 B2 **40**

This underground dance club features
a bustling roster of independently promoted nights for hardcore clubbers,
where two rooms, a big sound system
and a friendly atmosphere come as
standard. Saturdays are for funky
vocal and electro house, while Fridays
fluctuate between drum 'n' bass, hard
house and hard trance.

OHM

*28-34 High Street, M4 1QB (834
1392). Metrolink Market Street/City
Centre buses/ Piccadilly rail.* **Open**
11pm-4am Fri, Sat. **Map** p89 A2 **41**

Take a wrong turn during a Market
Street shopping spree and you could
end up at Club OHM – a recently
revamped venue with a massive
sound system that's squeezed in
between High Street shops. Once
inside, you'll wish you'd dressed for
the occasion: at flagship weekly residency 2Risque, in particular, the outfits are taken as seriously as the funky
vocal house music.

Roadhouse

*8 Newton Street, M1 2AN (237 9789/
www.theroadhouselive.co.uk). Metrolink
Piccadilly Gardens/City Centre buses/
Piccadilly rail.* **Open** times vary daily.
Map p89 B3/C3 **42**

Walking down the flight of steps into
the Roadhouse is akin to kicking open
the doors of a blast furnace: downstairs, you're always guaranteed the
hottest new talent in town. This ace
Piccadilly basement dive is the stopping-off point for a cutting edge selection of bands as well as home to
respected club nights like '60s-inspired
indie disco Revolver (Mondays) and
block partying hip hop session C'mon
Feet (days vary).

Arts & leisure

Bamber's Art Space/ Koffee Pot

*Hilton Street, M1 1JJ (07970 101
699/www.bambersartspace.co.uk).
Metrolink Market Street/City centre
buses/Piccadilly rail.* **Open** *Bamber's*
10am-5pm Mon-Sat. *Koffee Pot* 7am-
4pm daily. **Admission** free.
Map p89 B2 **43**
See box p101.

Inner Sanctuary Spa

*112 High Street, M4 1HQ (819 2465/
www.innersanctuarysspa.com). Metrolink
Market Street/City Centre buses/
Piccadilly rail.* **Open** 10am-8pm Mon-
Fri; 9.30am-7pm Sat; 11am-4pm Sun.
Admission *Day spa pass* £25.
Map p89 B1 **44**

Since it shifted from its Oldham Street
loft, Inner Sanctuary's treatment menu
has expanded quicker than a
Christmas day waistline. It offers
everything from a 'detox box' to
colonic irrigation, and from therapeu-
tic soaks to a hydro pool with eight different massage settings. Excellent
sports massages for aches and sprains,
plus hypnotherapy, life coaching and
the more usual facials, manicures and
pedicures are also available.

Manchester Buddhist Centre

*16-20 Turner Street, M4 1DZ (834
9232/www.manchesterbuddhistcentre.
org.uk). Metrolink Shudehill/City Centre
buses/Victoria rail.* **Open** 10am-7pm
Mon-Fri; 10am-5pm Sat. *Library* by
arrangement. **Admission** free.
Map p89 B2 **45**

One of the most beautifully-refur-
bished warehouses in the Northern
Quarter (think narrow wooden staircases and exposed brickwork) houses two shrine halls (the Vajra Hall is
open throughout the day for drop-in
meditation), a library and a bookshop.
The Bodywise centre offers everything from yoga to Qi Gong, while the
award-winning vegetarian Earth Café
(p91) means both body and mind
leave satisfied.

Piccadilly Gardens p104

Piccadilly, Chinatown & the Gay Village

Strolling down **Canal Street** can sometimes feel a little like walking onto the set of *Queer as Folk*, the late-1990s TV show that propelled it into the national consciousness. Bars, clubs and restaurants cluster around the canal, and sitting out on this traffic-free street to watch life's parade pass by is a treat. **Tribeca**, **Taurus** and **Mantos** are good places to start the night, while the large choice of clubs means you won't stop until sunrise. Canal Street is also the focal point of **Manchester Pride** – ten days of parades, picnics, sport, comedy and partying. The **Pride Parade** won't fail to raise a smile and, sometimes, a lump in the throat.

Close by sits the civic centrepiece of **Piccadilly Gardens**, remodelled in 2002. Tadao Ando's concrete 'bunker' at its foot provides a barrier to the fuming buses at the interchange beyond, making for a more pleasant open-air experience. A fountain attracts kids – daring each other to race through – and bars and cafes have marginally improved the ugly office block that sits to the east.

A few minutes' walk away, a towering, multi-tiered **Chinese Imperial Arch** marks the start of **Chinatown**. Built in 1987 as a gift from the Chinese people, the arch was the first of its kind in Europe. Chinatown is lively all year round, but **Chinese New Year** is celebrated with particular vigour. Fireworks, food and an enormous dancing dragon top off the festivities, while institutions like **Yang Sing** serve top-class Chinese food, dish after dish, without fail.

Sights & museums

Alan Turing Memorial
Sackville Park, Sackville Street.
Map p105 B2 ❶
Turing, a hero of the World War II Bletchley Park codebreakers, came to Manchester and helped found one of the world's first computers (a copy of which can be seen in the Museum of Science & Industry, p127). His story ended tragically – he committed suicide in 1954, two years after his arrest for a then-illegal homosexual relationship. This statue, unveiled in 2001, sits at the heart of the city's gay village.

Imperial Chinese Archway
Faulkner Street, M1. Metrolink Street Peter's Square/City Centre buses/Oxford Road rail. **Map** p105 B2 ❷
Manchester is home to one of Europe's largest Chinese communities, and this

Barry Dodds at Retro Bar p112

striking piece of architecture commemorating the fact – a gift to the city from the people of China – sits in the middle of a rather shabby square, surrounded on all sides by bustling human and vehicular traffic.

International 3
8 Fairfield Street, M1 3GF (237 3336/ www.international3.com). **Open** Call for information. **Admission** free.
Map p105 C3 ❸
A small, independent artist-run space, this whimsically eccentric gallery consists of a single room with a changing programme of work. The specialism is conceptual art.

Piccadilly Gardens
Metrolink Piccadilly Gardens/ City Centre buses/Piccadilly rail.
Map p105 B1 ❹
Donated for public use over two centuries ago, the land that is now Piccadilly Gardens first housed an infirmary, demolished in 1909; today's Labour council have operated a loose interpretation of the initial intentions by selling off the Portland Street corner for office and shop development (now belatedly coming to life and shaking off its bad reputation) in order to finance the 2002 overhaul of the rest of the gardens. The area now contains new seating, a popular walkthrough fountain, a thoughtful metal tree sculpture commemorating the World War II civilian dead, and a much reviled concrete wall courtesy of Japanese architect Tadao Ando.

Eating & drinking

Barburrito
1 Piccadilly Gardens, M1 1RG (228 6479/www.barburrito.co.uk). Metrolink Piccadilly Gardens/City Centre buses/ Piccadilly rail. **Open** 11am-9pm Mon-Sat; noon-6pm Sun. **£**. **Mexican**.
Map p105 B1 ❺
It seems amazing that Barburrito, 'the UK's first burrito bar', opened so recently (in 2006). The compile-your-own burrito format has caught on so quickly that the only downside is the queue the

place can generate. We're reliably informed that the menu goes beyond the slow-braised pork flavoured with bay leaves and orange (£3.10/£4.50), but we haven't got past it yet.

Brasserie on Portland

Princess on Portland, 101 Portland Street, M1 6DF (236 5122/www. princessonportland.co.uk). Metrolink St Peter's Square/City City Centre bus/ Oxford Road rail. **Open** noon-2.30pm, 6.30-10pm daily. **£££**. **International Cuisine**. Map p105 A2 ⑥

The Brasserie on Portland is the restaurant at the distinguished Princess on Portland hotel (p177), now part of the Best Western chain. The arrival of head chef Ashley Clarke has greatly improved the standard of the cooking – the à la carte menu now displays Italian, French and even Eastern influences, all handled with consummate care.

Circus Tavern

86 Portland Street, M1 4GX (236 5818). Metrolink St Peter's Square/City Centre buses/Oxford Road rail. **Open** 11am-11pm daily. **Pub**. Map p105 A2 ⑦

Another listed boozer that dates back to the 1790s, when the place is said to have been the hangout of choice for performers from the city's then permanent circus. One of Tetley's heritage pubs, it's popular with football fans – despite its diminutive size – and there's a good smattering of United and City paraphernalia on the walls. There's no food and no music, but bags of atmosphere.

EastZEast

Ibis Hotel, Princess Street, M1 7DG (244 5353/www.eastzeast.com). Metrolink St Peter's Square/City Centre bus/Oxford Road rail. **Open** 5pm-midnight Mon-Thur, Sun; 5pm-1am Fri-Sat. **££**. **Indian**. Map p105 B3 ⑧

Although you might be tempted by the curry mile's bright lights, be warned: it's rare to find good food among the gaudiness. The Punjabi specialist EastZEast is, however, an altogether classier proposition. The family behind

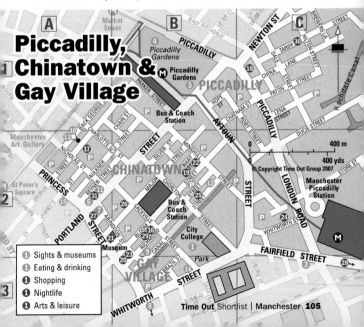

Piccadilly's Station Approach

Technically this is just one venue but it has two separate sections – with Chinese food downstairs and Thai food upstairs – that operate almost as two different restaurants, complete with separate opening hours. Both sections share a chic, modern look but the Thai section probably offers the better food, with deep-fried fish in sweet tamarind sauce the house speciality.

Red Chilli

70-72 Portland Street, M1 4GU (236 2888/www.redchillirestaurant. co.uk). Metrolink St Peter's Square/ City Centre buses/Oxford Road rail. **Open** noon-11pm Mon-Thur, Sun; noon-midnight Fri, Sat. **££**.
Cantonese. Map p105 A2 ⑪

Most Chinese restaurants focus on Cantonese dishes, but Red Chilli differentiates itself from the norm by offering cooking from Sichuan and Beijing. As a result, the menu may seem unfamiliar, listing dishes such as the curious offal-based 'husband and wife lung slices' and an excellent deep-fried sea bass. The presentation makes a real impact and the flavours are equally impressive.

Taurus

1 Canal Street, M1 3HE (236 4593/ www.taurus-bar.co.uk). Metrolink Piccadilly Gardens/City Centre buses/ Piccadilly rail. **Open** noon-11pm Mon-Thur; noon-1am Fri, Sat; noon-10.30pm Sun. **Bar**. Map p105 B2 ⑫

Owned and run by Canal Street stalwarts Mike 'Polly' Pollard and Iain Scott, Taurus owes its success to the twin tenets of excellent service and a sense of mischievousness. The decor is homely rather than super stylish, but who cares when the food, cocktails and company are this good? A night out here is always bags of fun.

Teppanyaki

Connaught Building, 58-60 George Street, M1 4HF (228 2219/ www.teppanyaki-manchester.co.uk). Metrolink St Peter's Square/City Centre buses/Oxford Road rail. **Open** noon-2pm, 5.30-11pm Mon-Fri; 6-11pm Sat. **££££**. **Japanese**. Map p105 A2 ⑬

this hotel-restaurant previously worked in Bradford for over 50 years, and all of this experience shows in the superb service and delicious karahi dishes.

Manto

46 Canal Street, M1 3WD (236 2667/ www.mantobar.com). Metrolink Piccadilly Gardens/City Centre buses/ rail. **Open** 11am-2am Mon-Thur; 11am-3am Fri; 11am-4am Sat; noon-2am Sun. **Bar**. Map p105 B2 ⑨

Along with Dry Bar (p91), Manto provided the catalyst for Manchester's now burgeoning bar scene, proudly showcasing the creativity and vibrancy of the gay scene behind a glass frontage for the first time. Now more institution than rebellious innovator, it's nevertheless still a big draw.

Pacific

Connaught Building, 58-60 George Street, M1 4HF (228 6668/www. pacificrestaurant.co.uk). Metrolink St Peter's Square/City Centre buses/ Oxford Road rail. **Open** Thai noon-3pm (buffet), 6pm-midnight Mon-Sat; noon-4pm (buffet), 4-10pm Sun. *Chinese* noon-midnight daily. **£££**. **Thai/Chinese**. Map p105 A2 ⑩

Chinatown

positive+

advice, information, courses, groups, financial help, counselling
and other support for people with HIV in the North West

call us on **0161 274 4499** or visit our website **www.ght.org.uk**

george house trust
still life with HIV

registered charity 700364

Teppanyaki is the Japanese style of cooking that originated among Samurai warriors cooking on the battlefield, using the inside of their metal armour as a sizzling hot pan. Here, awesome chefs prepare the ingredients in the kitchen and then cook them in front of your eyes, so that you can see the skill and fresh ingredients that go into your dish. With excellent sushi and sashimi as a further draw, it's worth splashing out at Teppanyaki.

Tribeca

50 Sackville Street, M1 3WF (236 8300/www.tribeca-bar.co.uk). Metrolink Piccadilly Gardens/City Centre buses/ Piccadilly rail. **Open** noon-1am Mon-Thur, Sun; noon-2.30am Fri, Sat. **Bar**. **Map** p105 B3 ⑭

Tribeca's laid-back take on bar culture made it an instant hit when it opened in 1999; eight years on, it's still as popular as ever, pulling an eclectic bag of customers – whether gay, straight or bi, the bar, situated on the edge of the gay village, has something for everyone. Friendly rather than achingly fashionable, it can be counted on for reasonably priced cocktails and space to chat. Downstairs, take time out to recline on supper club-style beds in between stints on the small dancefloor.

Yang Sing

34 Princess Street, M1 4JY (236 2200/ www.yang-sing.com). Metrolink St Peter's Square/City Centre buses/ Oxford Road rail. **Open** noon-11pm Mon-Thur; noon-midnight Fri, Sat; noon-10.30pm Sun. **£££**. **Chinese**. **Map** p105 A2 ⑮

This fantastically glamorous Chinese restaurant has had a tumultuous 30-year history, with a fire and a reality TV show being just two of the events it has been associated with. Through everything, it's kept a consistency in the kitchen that would shame many other restaurants. Don't bother with the menu: simply explain to your waiter what you like and don't like, agree a price per head, and then your banquet will be devised for you.

Gay karaoke

Canal Street isn't quiet at the best of times. However, the trend for karaoke nights in and around the Gay Village means that even early in the week, there's always music (of sorts) in the air. You'll find amazingly supportive crowds at the various karaoke nights, just waiting to join in on the chorus. And, best of all, you won't have to pay for your three minutes of fame: most events are free, and some even offer prizes for the best crooner.

Tuesday is a big night for karaoke in the Village, and few places are able to better the New Union on Princess Street (9pm-2am). It's hosted by fabulous showgirl Petra Fied, who has been kind enough to break into her family allowance and offers a prize of £50 for the top singer of the night. If you manage to grab the moolah, you can spend it the following Tuesday at Coyotes on Chorlton Street (9pm-1am), which offers more of the same. And if neither of those take your fancy, there's always Tribeca (p109) on Sackville Street (9pm-1am), where you can sing for your supper from one of their famous beds.

On Thursdays at the New Union (9pm-2am), there's more karaoke (and another £50 prize) with DJ Carl. And from October, the Hollywood Studio & Lounge (p112) on Bloom Street (8pm-late) will provide you with the opportunity to give your vocal cords a public workout.

MANCHESTER BY AREA

Essential p112

Shopping

Shopping opportunities in and around Piccadilly are largely limited to functional stores such as Superdrug, M&S and Somerfield. The area doesn't offer many browsing opportunities, but there are a few specialist stores worth seeking out.

Clone Zone

36-38 Sackville Street, M1 3WA (236 1398/www.clonezone.co.uk). Metrolink Piccadilly Gardens/City Centre buses/Piccadilly rail. **Open** 11am-10pm Mon-Thur; 11am-11pm Fri, Sat; noon-7pm Sun. **Map** p105 B2 ⑯
A Gay Village institution, Clone Zone stocks a wide range of gay and lesbian magazines and publications, obscure, arty and erotic magazines, and, most famously, rubber and fetish gear and toys that are much admired by clubbers, bedroom poseurs and experimental lovers alike.

Woo Sang Chinese Supermarket

19-21 George Street, M1 4HE (236 4353/www.woosang.co.uk). Metrolink St Peter's Square/City Centre buses/ Oxford Road rail. **Open** 10.30am-7pm Mon-Fri, Sun; 10.30am-7.30pm Sat. **Map** p105 A2 ⑰
Air-dried meats, exotic vegetables, incense sticks, Hello Kitty bubblegum – a visit to the Woo Sang is nearly as good as a quick whisk around Hong Kong. Fabulous packaging, fascinating ingredients you won't find at Tesco, and the odd but rewarding experience of being immersed in a completely different culture for fifteen minutes are all draws at this supermarket. If you can't afford the cost of a long-haul flight to China, this option is second best.

Nightlife

Bierkeller

77 Piccadilly, M1 2BU (236 1807/ www.bierkeller.co.uk). Metrolink Piccadilly Gardens/City Centre buses/ Piccadilly rail. **Open** times vary; call for information. *Club nights* 10pm-2am Wed; 9pm-2am Fri; 8pm-1am Sat. **Map** p105 C1 ⑱
This would-be run-of-the-mill pub draws the crowds with the band-breaking, barnstorming antics of Blow Out. These gig nights (held on selected Fridays) have secured the Bierkeller a central place in the city's indie elite. Those in the know also grace the dancefloor at fashionable and fun electroclash club-night Tramp!, every Wednesday.

Charlie's Karaoke Bar

1 Harter Street, M1 6HY (237 9898). Metrolink St Peter's Square/City Centre buses/Piccadilly rail. **Open** 8pm-2am Mon-Thur; 10pm-4am Fri, Sat. **Map** p105 B2 ⑲
Tatty but charming, Charlie's mutates from karaoke hangout into club proper at weekends. Saturday night belongs to the Heart of Soul crew that play soul, funk and hip hop to an up-for-it crowd. Friday's club nights rotate throughout the month; most notable is the decadent cabaret soiree the Whim Wham Club. If you've spent the day shopping for vintage garb in the Northern Quarter's quirky boutiques, this is the place to show it off.

Club Alter Ego

105-107 Princess Street, M1 6DD (237 1749/www.clubalterego.co.uk). Metrolink St Peter's Square/City Centre buses/Oxford Road rail. **Open** 11pm-3.30am Tue; 11pm-4am Fri, Sat. **Map** p105 B3 ⑳
If the bland Gay Village soundscape of homogenised house turns your shimmy into a shudder then take refuge at Club Alter Ego, home of evergreen innovative indie shindig Poptastic. Its two weekly sessions are the venue's main draw, with a new Friday nighter boasting DJs like Norman Jay and Allister Whitehead and bringing a more dance-focused crowd into the mix.

Cruz 101

101 Princess Street, M1 6DD (950 0101/www.cruz101.com). Metrolink St Peter's Square/City Centre buses/ Oxford Road rail.. **Open** 11pm-5am

Mon, Thur, Sun; 11pm-3.30am Tue; 11pm-6am Fri, Sat. **Map** p105 A2 ㉑
Really two clubs in one, with a large main room and smaller lower level, Cruz is Manchester's oldest gay club – but the (mostly) bright young things on its dancefloors each week keep its appeal fresh. Though it started as a gay disco (think Chic and Donna Summer), Cruz's music policy has since evolved, and now features a more varied mix of funky house, pop, trance and R&B.

Essential

8 Minshull Street, M1 3EF (236 0077/www.essentialmanchester.com). Metrolink Piccadilly Gardens/City Centre buses/Piccadilly rail. **Open** 11pm-4am Thur, Sun; 11pm-5am Fri; 11pm-7am Sat. **Map** p105 B2 ㉒
Run by Take That's former manager and de facto king of camp Nigel Martyn Smith, Manchester's first gay superclub took Canal Street by storm when it burst onto the scene about a decade ago. Visits by gay deities like Kylie Minogue kept the buzz going, and on a scene defined by the new and fresh, the longevity of the biggest gay club outside the capital now seems assured.

Hollywood Studio & Lounge

100 Bloom Street, M1 3LY (228 1666/www.hollywoodshowbar.co.uk). Metrolink Piccadilly Gardens/City Centre buses/Piccadilly rail. **Open** 9am-2am Mon-Thur; 9am-3am Fri; 9pm-8am Sat; 9pm-2am Sun. **Map** p105 B2 ㉓
As camp as Christmas, this show-bar offers a raucous mix of drag acts, karaoke, singalongs and unreconstructed Canal Street frolicking. The new management seem to be adding fresh excitement to the familiar charms, if their recently launched Tuesday night porn parties – where customers are invited to douse themselves in oil and wrestle – are anything to go by. The spot sometimes has an air of being more of a tourist destination than a venue proper, yet it still manages to retain its place at the heart of the Village scene.

Legends

4-6 Whitworth Street, M1 3QW (236 5400/www.legendsmanchester.com). Metrolink Piccadilly/City Centre buses/Piccadilly rail. **Open** *Legends* 10.30pm-late Fri; 10pm-4am Sat. *Outpost* noon-11pm Mon-Thur; noon-2am Fri, Sat; 1pm-11pm Sun. **Map** p105 C2 ㉔
A brilliantly disorientating labyrinthine set-up on the site of seminal 1960s nightspot the Twisted Wheel. Legends plays host to the original antidote to gay Canal Street clubbing, Homo Electric. Run by the people behind Electric Chair, this awesome, cutting-edge club-night famously welcomes enthusiastic 'homos, hetros, lesbos and don't knows' into its sweaty, occasional embrace.

Queer

4 Canal Street, M1 3HE (228 1360/ www.queer-manchester.com). Metrolink Piccadilly Gardens/City Centre buses/Piccadilly rail. **Open** 11am-2am Mon-Sat; noon-12.30am Sun. *Club night* 5am-midday Sun. **Map** p105 B2 ㉕
A glamorous bar that's a favoured spot in which to warm-up before moving on to Essential (see above). Queer serves food to a chilled soundtrack during the day, with resident DJs and full-on club vibe at night.

Retro Bar

78 Sackville Street, M1 3NJ (274 4892/www.retrobarmanchester.com). Metrolink Piccadilly Gardens/City Centre buses/Piccadilly rail. **Open** *Pub* 9am-3am daily; *Club* 8pm/9pm-3am daily. **Map** p105 B2 ㉖
A mere stone's throw from the Canal Street strip but a million miles away in terms of outlook, Retro is – as its name suggests – a defiantly run-down yet charming little venue. The place hosts a variety of off-the-wall underground indie nights, typically run by young, up-and-coming promoters.

Satan's Hollow

101 Princess Street, M1 6DD (236 0666/www.satanshollow.net). Metrolink St Peter's Square/City Centre buses/ Oxford Road rail. **Open** times vary daily. *Club nights* 7pm-11pm. *Gigs* 10pm-3am. **Map** p105 A2 ㉗

Gothic decor, wilfully eclectic club nights (rock/pop/bhangra) and regular gigs define this theatrical set up. But despite its devilish architecture, fearsome lighting and at times oddly styled bar staff, this is one goth that never takes itself too seriously. The entrance is on Silver Street.

Star & Garter

18-20 Fairfield Street, M1 2QF (273 6726/www.starandgarter.co.uk). Metrolink Piccadilly/City Centre buses/ Piccadilly rail. **Open** *Club nights* 9pm-3am selected Fri, Sat. **Map** p105 C3 ㉙
This Piccadilly bolthole has been vying for the title of most indie venue in Manchester, with disco monthlies dedicated to the Smiths and Belle and Sebastian, plus regular up-and-coming and unsigned gigs. Gladioli and hearing aids are optional.

Vanilla

39-41 Richmond Street, M1 3WB (228 2727/www.vanillagirls.co.uk). Metrolink Piccadilly Gardens/City Centre buses/ Piccadilly rail. **Open** 5pm-midnight Tue, Wed; 5pm-1am Thur; 4pm-4am Fri; 3pm-4am Sat; 3pm-12am Sun. **Map** p105 B2 ㉙

Vanilla is the only bar on Canal Street with a female focus, and one of the most famous in the country. DJ nights through the week offer everything from pop to indie rock and funky house. In possession of a Y chromosome? Then take a female chaperone or you won't get in.

Arts & leisure

Basement

18 Tariff Street, Piccadilly, M1 2FN (237 9996/www.basementcomplex. co.uk). Metrolink Piccadilly Gardens/ City Centre buses/Piccadilly rail. **Open** 24 hrs. **Map** p105 C1 ㉚
A gay owned and run sauna that has a round-the-clock licence.

Colin Jellicoe Gallery

82 Portland Street, M1 4QX (236 2716/ www.colinjellicoe.co.uk). Metrolink St Peter's Square/City Centre buses/ Oxford Road rail. **Open** noon-5pm Tue-Fri; 1pm-5pm Sat. **Admission** free. **Map** p105 A2 ㉛
A 40-odd-year-old commercial art gallery that's still run by proprietor Colin Jellicoe. As well as showcasing Jellicoe's own work, the gallery also puts on group exhibitions.

Metrolink tram

Cornerhouse p124

Oxford Road & Around

Infamous for its thundering traffic, Oxford Road nevertheless packs in so many galleries, museums and theatres that locals have christened it Manchester's 'cultural corridor'. It's also home to two universities (the University of Manchester and Manchester Metropolitan), whose 69,000 or so students inevitably lend a unique flavour.

At the northern end sits **Cornerhouse**, the city's arthouse film and contemporary art complex, while at the other, at the start of the **Curry Mile**, sits the Victorian red-brick **Whitworth Art Gallery** and historic Whitworth Park. With a solid gathering of artworks and an important collection of textiles and wallpapers, the Whitworth squeezes in an award-winning café serving locally-sourced sustenance.

In between Cornerhouse and the Whitworth are theatres, **Manchester Museum**, the **University of Manchester**'s collegiate campus (a quadrangle of Gothic buildings designed by Alfred Waterhouse; check the atmospheric Whitworth Hall and Christie Bistro inside), and two Danish-inspired **Kro** bars. Halfway up the road, **Grosvenor Park** occupies the site of a former church. In summer, this grassy retreat is reassuringly dotted with sun-loving students.

Rumours of large-scale redevelopment may yet solve Oxford Road's traffic problems; before then, don't let the honking and spluttering jams put you off exploring this area of the city.

Sights & museums

CUBE Gallery

113-115 Portland Street, M1 6DW (237 5525/www.cube.org.uk). Metrolink St Peter's Square/City Centre buses/ Oxford Road rail. **Open** noon-5.30pm Mon-Fri; noon-5pm Sat. **Admission** free. **Map** p116 B1 ①

Focusing on architecture, the gallery at the Centre for the Urban Built Environment has a changing programme of exhibits ranging from the dry to the inspired, and has been particularly relevant in offering a European and global context during the city's recent rebuilding boom. One for the expert and layman alike.

Manchester Museum

University of Manchester, Oxford Road, M13 9PL (275 2634/www. museum.man.ac.uk). Metrolink St Peter's Square/Bus 11, 16, 41, 42, 47, 147, 190, 191/Oxford Road rail. **Open** 11am-4pm Mon, Sun, bank hols; 10am-5pm Tue-Sat. **Admission** free. **Map** p117 D5 ❷

Formerly a rather dusty example of a museum in the old-school mould, this building (designed in 1890 by Alfred Waterhouse, the architect of London's Natural History Museum) received a refit and general sprucing up in 2003, allowing some much needed daylight to reach its murky corners – although its corridor layout would still confound a tomb raider. Persevere, though, for highlights that include a notable collection of Egyptian mummies and artefacts and a striking skeleton of a Tyrannosaurus (named Stan), posed in full hunting mode.

Refuge Assurance Building

Oxford Street, City Centre, M60 7HA. Metrolink St Peter's Square/City Centre buses/Oxford Road rail. **Map** p116 B2 ❸

Designed by Alfred Waterhouse for the Refuge Assurance Company, this late 19th-century Grade-II listed building is a landmark in Manchester, with its distinctive red brickwork and 217ft clock tower. It was converted to a hotel in the mid 1990s and, after a £7million refurbishment in 2005, now houses the Palace Hotel (p177).

University of Manchester

Oxford Road, M13 9PL (306 6000/ www.manchester.ac.uk). Metrolink St Peter's Square/Bus 16, 41, 42, 47, 190, 191/Oxford Road rail. **Map** p117 C5 ❹ (Visitors Centre)

Newly merged with the city centre campus of UMIST, this sprawling complex is one of the country's largest educational establishments. Amid the beautiful collection of redbrick, theatre venues (Martin Harris Centre, the John Thaw studio theatre) and history abound – the golden generation of British alternative comedy (Ben Elton, Rik Mayall, Ade Edmondson) met and studied here, while Ernest Rutherford's research led to the splitting of the atom and 'the Baby', one of the world's first computers, was built here in 1948.

Whitworth Art Gallery

Oxford Road, M15 6ER (275 7450/ www.whitworth.man.ac.uk). Metrolink St Peter's Square/Bus 15, 16, 41, 42, 43-45a, 47, 48, 50, 87, 111, 141-145, 157/Oxford Road rail. **Open** 10am-5pm Mon-Sat; 2-5pm Sun. **Admission** free. **Map** p117 D4 ❺

With the Manchester Art Gallery generally grabbing most of the limelight, the University-owned Whitworth is a quieter, more spacious place, with holdings divided between fine art and industrial design and crafts. Opening with Jacob Epstein's dramatic Genesis sculpture, the gallery specialises in wallpapers, textiles, prints and watercolours. It has a light-flooded sculpture gallery and a regular schedule of temporary exhibitions and talks.

Eating & drinking

Abdul's

133-135 Oxford Road, M1 7DY (273 7339/www.abduls.net). Metrolink St Peter's Square/Bus 15, 16, 41, 42, 43-45a, 47, 48, 50, 87, 111, 141-145, 157/Oxford Road rail. **Open** 11am-3am daily. **£. Kebabs**. **Map** p116 C3 ❻

When people leave Manchester, Abdul's often appears on the list of things they'll miss. This is no nostalgia-driven regret – the food here is in a different galaxy to the standard greasy post-pub kebab. Think spicy-tikka chunks of flame-grilled chicken served in fresh naan bread with salad and sauces. Manchester loves Abdul's, and with good reason.

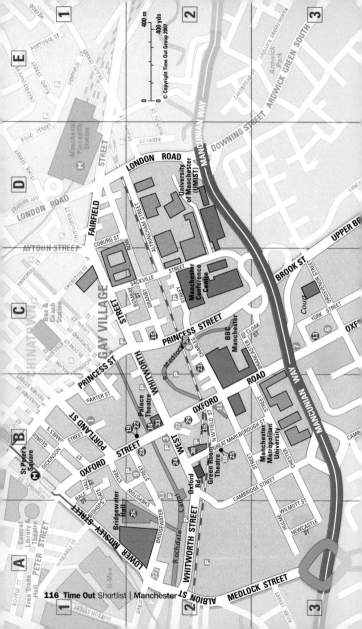

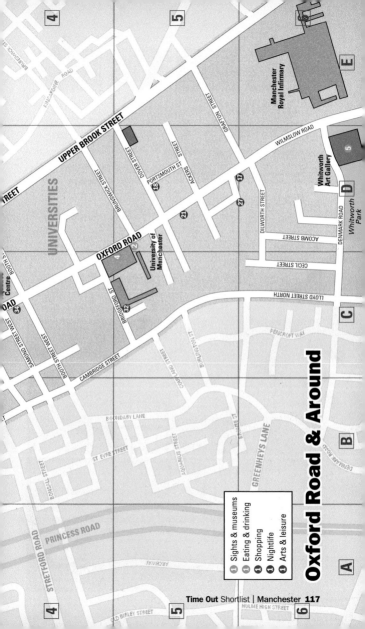

Oxford Road & Around

- Sights & museums
- Eating & drinking
- Shopping
- Nightlife
- Arts & leisure

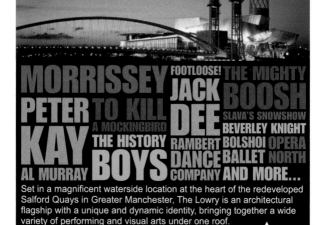

Kro 2

*Oxford House, Oxford Road, M1 7ED
(236 1048/www.kro.uk). Metrolink St
Peter's Square/Bus 15, 16, 41, 42,
43-45a, 47, 48, 50, 87, 111, 141-145,
157/Oxford Road rail.* **Open** 8.30am-
midnight Mon-Thur; 8.30am-2am Fri;
10.30am-2am Sat; 10.30am-midnight
Sun. **Bar**. **Map** p116 C3 ❼

The largest of the ever-expanding
homegrown chain of Kro bars, Kro 2
pays the strongest homage to Danish
minimalism, and is all the more loved
for it. The abundance of glass gives it
an inside-out feel, and offers some of
the best people-watching opportunities
in the city. It also has one of
Manchester's largest and best beer gardens, and the presence (and effective-
ness) of the plentiful outdoor heaters
make it a viable choice even on a crisp
November afternoon.

Lass O'Gowrie

*36 Charles Street, M1 7DB (273
6932/www.thelass.co.uk). Metrolink St
Peter's Square/City Centre buses/
Oxford Road rail.* **Open** noon-7.30pm
daily. **£**. **Gastropub**. **Map** p116 C2 ❽

The Lass is a Manchester institution;
since being taken over in 2005, its stated aim has been to create the perfect
village inn. The simple food ably
assists that aim with brilliant own-
make pies and artisan-made sausages.
There are nine ales on tap, including
three guest beers, which sometimes
make an appearance on the food menu,
too, for example in the steak and Black
Sheep ale pie.

Peveril of the Peak

*127 Great Bridgewater Street, M1
5JQ (236 6364). Metrolink G-Mex/
City Centre buses/Deansgate rail.* **Open**
11.30am-3pm, 5-11pm Mon-Fri; 11am-
2pm, 7-11pm Sat; 11am-2pm, 7-10.30pm
Sun. **Pub**. **Map** p116 B2 ❾

This Grade II-listed building, named
after a famous stagecoach renowned
for the speed at which it made its trips
from Derbyshire, is arguably the most
distinctive pub in the city. You can
see all sorts of people inside the green-
tiled exterior, at all times, but it gets
particularly packed on Fridays and

Saturdays, and United fans are in
abundance on match days. The pub is
also said to have its very own ghost.
The brews vary too, but favourites
include Boddingtons, Marston's
Pedigree, Timothy Taylor Landlord
and Bombardier. There's a pool table
in the cramped back room, and darts
and table-football in the front. Look out
for the occasional folk nights.

Pure Space

*11 New Wakefield Street, M1 5NP
(236 4899/www.purespacecafebar.
co.uk). Metrolink St Peter's Square/
City Centre buses/Oxford Road rail.*
Open noon-midnight daily. **Bar**.
Map p116 B2 ❿

With a roof terrace that offers protection from the elements during
Manchester's rainy season – so, essen-
tially, all year round, apart from a week
or so in July or August – Pure Space is
a hidden gem. Stylish without being
pretentious, the bar is one of those
trusted choices that unites a range of
different tastes.

Revolution

*90-94 Oxford Street, M1 5WH (236
7470/www.revolution-bars.co.uk).
Metrolink St Peter's Square/City
Centre buses/Oxford Road rail.*
Open 11.30am-2am Mon-Thur;
11.30am-4am Fri, Sat; 11.30am-2am
Sun. **Vodka bar**. **Map** p116 B2 ⓫

Part of a national chain, this depend-
able choice for a quiet pint in the daytime and more raucous proceedings in
the evening has recently undergone an
impressive interior overhaul. Like
many of the best bars in Manchester, it
has something for everyone and you'll
find a mixed bunch of visitors no matter when you pop in.

Temple of Convenience

*100 Great Bridgewater Street, M1
5JW (278 1610). Metrolink St Peter's
Square/City Centre buses/Oxford Road
rail.* **Open** noon-midnight Mon-Thur;
noon-1am Fri, Sat; noon-11pm Sun.
Pub. **Map** p116 B2 ⓬

This place spent a former incarnation
as a public lavatory (Temple of
Convenience, geddit?), and is now

Manchester v Cancer

How to top the first Manchester v Cancer? A benefit gig for Christie Hospital , it featured no less than 14 major league Mancunian acts who played classics and covers and collaborated on new material to send the rapt crowd into paroxysms of joy.

MvC was jointly conceived by ex-Smiths bassist Andy Rourke and his manager Nova Rehman after Rehman's sister was diagnosed with cancer in 2005. A trawl through their combined contacts revealed universal good will and, crucially, availability. And so, in January 2006, 14,000 people converged on the MEN Arena (p83) to witness New Order (pictured above) play an entire set of Joy Division tracks, see Elbow's Guy Garvey and Doves combine for an atmospheric rendition of 'There Goes The Fear' and watch Andy Rourke and Johnny Marr take to the stage together for the first time in 20 years – fuelling rumours of a Smiths reunion that just won't go away.

The gig's unforgettable finale was a full-cast rendition of Happy Mondays hit 'Wrote for Luck', with Shaun Ryder and Bez taking charge. According to Rourke, three minutes after leaving the stage, they knew that this wasn't going to be a one-off event. Sure enough, in March 2007 Rourke and his team returned to the arena with new headliners and a fresh line-up of talent (not exclusively Mancunian this time), raising yet more money for Christie. Two new events were also organised for 2007: Comedy v Cancer (3 May) and Acoustic v Cancer (4 May) at the Carling Apollo, giving different sets of artists and their respective audiences a chance to get in on the act. Even more exciting for completist music fans was not a gig but an auction – in which a Fender guitar signed by the entire MvC cast, along with signed and framed Mick Rock photos of the artists, will be up for grabs. For the chance to rub shoulders with original MvC artists, bag yourself a piece of music history and raise money for charity at the same time, check out www. manchestervcancer.co.uk.

another of the city's more cramped boozers. The pub lays claim to one of the finest jukeboxes in town, and is certainly the place to go if you like your beer strong, continental and bottled.

Shopping

Known as the Student Corridor, Oxford Road is functional, full of bars and cafés and lacking in one-offs and individual shops. It's essential to take a trip out of the city centre to Rusholme, otherwise known as the 'curry mile', where the endless (though variable) eateries are punctuated by Asian stores selling exotic groceries, saris, books and music and gold jewellery.

Johnny Roadhouse

123 Oxford Road, M1 7DU (273 1111/www.johnnyroadhouse.co.uk). Metrolink St Peter's Square/Bus 14, 16, 41-45a, 47, 48, 50, 87, 111, 140, 142, 143, 147, 157, 197, 250, 291/Oxford Road rail. **Open** 9.30am-5.30pm Mon-Sat. **Map** p116 C3 ⓭

Trading from the same premises for over 50 years, Johnny Roadhouse is a rite of passage for every Manc musician and wannabe. Still overseen by 86-year-old Johnny himself, the much-loved superstore offers three floors of brass, string and percussion instruments and effects and was recently featured in an Oasis video (for 'Masterplan'). There should be a *Wayne's World*-style 'No Stairway to Heaven' sign in the guitar department, where customers sample the stock.

Venus

95 Oxford Street, St James' Building, M1 6ET (228 7000/www.venusflora. co.uk). Metrolink St Peter's Square/ City Centre buses/Oxford Road rail. **Open** 8am-6pm Mon-Fri; 9am-5pm Sat. **Map** p116 B2 ⓮

One of the first designer flower shops in the city, Venus continues its modern floral revolution. There are no feeble carnations here, just lush, verdant bursts of tropical colour, spiky, graphic shapes and imaginative arrangements.

Nightlife

5th Avenue

121 Princess Street, M1 7AF (236 2754/www.5thavenuemanchester.com). Metrolink St Peter's Square/City Centre buses/Oxford Road rail. **Open** 10pm-2am Mon, Thur; 10pm-3am Fri, Sat. **Admission** £3-£4; £2 reductions. **Map** p116 C2 ⓯

This popular, student-friendly club features the usual cheap drinks and indie tunes most nights of the week.

Attic

50 New Wakefield Street, M1 5NP (236 6071/www.thirstyscholar.co.uk). Metrolink St Peter's Square/City Centre buses/Oxford Road rail. **Open** 10pm-2/3am Thur-Sat; 8pm-midnight Mon-Wed, Sun.* **Map** p116 B2 ⓰

Climb the rickety spiral staircase to reach this small club, located under a railway arch. The place is home to some of the city's best underground club-nights. Find cutting-edge techno, electro, house, drum 'n' bass and more from the local and international DJ talent. On big nights and special events, promoters take over both floors (once the pub downstairs closes).

Big Hands

296 Oxford Road, M13 9NS (272 7779). Metrolink St Peter's Square/Bus 14, 16, 41-45a, 47, 48, 50, 87, 111, 140, 142, 143, 147, 157, 197, 250, 291/Oxford Road rail. **Open** 10am-3am Mon-Thur; 10am-4am Fri; noon-4am Sat; 6pm-2am Sun. **Map** pp117A5/A6 ⓱

The musical smarts of Big Hands' defiantly independent crowd – compounded by regular after-gig visits from touring musicians – have made this bar an essential indie hangout for those in the know. Stop off here for a pre-Academy pint, and warm your ears up on an eclectic variety of tunes – the music policy ranges from reggae to northern soul.

Jabez Clegg

2 Portsmouth Street, M13 9GB (272 8612/www.jabezclegg.co.uk). Metrolink Oxford Road/Bus 15, 16, 41-44, 46-48, 50, 53, 111, 113, 130, 140-143, 145, 157, 158, 191, 197/Piccadilly rail.

Open 11am-11pm Mon-Wed; 11am-midnight Thur; 10pm-3am Fri, Sat; noon-11pm Sun. Map p117 D5 ⑱

In the mood for a booze-fuelled singalong to Chesney Hawkes in the middle of a crowded dancefloor? The unre-constructed student cheesefest the Bop will give you the Saturday night out you desire in a shame-free setting. Indie and dance anthems (Fridays) and live music (Thursdays) are slightly less cringe-worthy reasons to board the Magic Bus down busy Oxford Road.

Jilly's Rockworld

65 Oxford Street, M1 6FQ (236 9971/www.jillys.co.uk). Metrolink St Peter's Square/City Centre buses/Oxford Road rail. **Open** 9pm-2am Mon-Thur; 9pm-7am Fri; 9pm-3am Sat. **Map** p116 B2 ⑲

One of the longest-running rock clubs in the country, Jilly's is testament to the eternal appeal of playing it fast and loud. The place hosts four weekly club nights, at which joyful headbanging is positively encouraged, and claims to be 'Manchester's number one rock club' – which sounds about right.

Joshua Brooks

106 Princess Street, M1 6NG (237 7336/www.joshuabrooks.co.uk. Metrolink St Peter's Square/City Centre buses/Oxford Road rail). **Open** 10pm-2am Mon-Sat; 8pm-12.30am Sun. **Map** p116 C2 ⑳

This lo-fi student hangout manages to keep everyone happy, with match screenings for sports fans, a lively atmosphere early evening for drinkers, and a basement space after dark for clubbers. Independently promoted events rotate through a monthly schedule, with something good happening on most nights.

Manchester Academy 1/2/3 & Club Academy

Manchester University Students Union, Oxford Road, City Centre, M13 9PR (275 2930/www.manchesteracademy.net). Metrolink St Peter's Square/Bus 14, 16, 41-45a, 47, 48, 50, 87, 111, 140, 142, 143, 147, 157, 197, 250, 291/Oxford Road rail. **Map** p117 D5 ㉑

Three different sized spaces in the heart of the university campus accommodate a range of acts across all genres, from unsigned to established acts. The Academy now also includes Club Academy, home to Manchester's longest-running club night Tangled (trance/breaks) and a range of other student-orientated promotions.

Music Box

65 Oxford Street, M1 6QF (236 9971/www.themusicbox.info). Metrolink St Peter's Square/City Centre buses/Oxford Road rail. **Open** 9/10pm-3/4am Fri, Sat. *Weekly Gigs* 7.30pm-11pm. **Map** p116 B2 ㉒

A landmark 800-capacity sweaty basement club that Manchester's most celebrated leftfield eclectic dance sessions call home: Mr Scruff's Keep it Unreal and the Unabombers' Electric Chair being the most famed nights. Serious clubbers of all stripes should find something to their liking here, with drum 'n' bass, hip hop and house sessions on monthly rotation. Live music events take place during the week.

Po Na Na Souk Bar

42 Charles Street, M1 7DB (272 6044/www.ponana.co.uk). Metrolink St Peter's Square/City Centre buses/Oxford Road rail. **Open** 10pm-3am Mon, Thur-Sat; 10pm-2am Tue, Wed. **Map** p116 C2 ㉓

Local DJ/promoter Luke Unabomber's infamous midas touch has brought added sparkle to an already accomplished line up at Po Na Na. His Thursday night disco/punk/funk party, Tikkerty Boo, has further bolstered a well-executed weekly roster spanning breaks, Brazilian and boogaloo. Occasional big name guests (Jazzy Jeff, The Cuban Brothers) complete the package at this friendly, warren-like club.

Ritz

100 Whitworth Street West, M1 5NQ (236 4355/www.ritznightclub.co.uk). Metrolink St Peter's Square/City Centre buses/Oxford Road rail. **Open** 9.30pm-3am Mon,Wed; 10pm-3am Fri, Sat. **Admission** £3-£6; £2-£5 reductions. **Map** p116 B2 ㉔

Refuge Assurance Building p115

MANCHESTER BY AREA

This ex-ballroom's sprung dancefloor has been graced by generations of Mancunians. The Ritz's nondescript, cheesy weekends are best avoided altogether; try, instead, the student sessions (Monday and Wednesday). Even better (and worth keeping an ear out for) are the occasional gigs from acts like Arctic Monkeys, Chemical Brothers or Elbow that temporarily realise the club's true potential.

Sub Space

New Wakefield Street, M1 5NP (236 4899/www.purespacecafebar.co.uk). Metrolink St Peter's Square/City Centre buses/Oxford Road rail. **Open** 10.30pm-3am Mon, Wed-Sat. **Map** p116 B2 ㉕
A late night counterpart to the Pure Space bar (p116), basement venue Sub Space runs busy club sessions most nights. Specialising in soul and funk, the nightclub is popular with a mixed, but always friendly, crowd.

Arts & leisure

Bridgewater Hall

Lower Mosley Street, M2 3WS (907 9000/www.bridgewater-hall. co.uk). Metrolink G-Mex/City Centre buses/Deansgate rail. **Map** p116 A2 ㉖
With impressive musical accoutrements such as a 5,500-pipe organ, and a menu of 300-plus events every year, there's no better place to tune into classical, jazz, pop and world music. The decade-old £42-million concert hall is also the performing home of the Hallé and the BBC Philharmonic orchestras.

Contact Theatre

Devas Street, off Oxford Road, M15 6JA (274 0600/www.contact-theatre. org). Bus 16, 41, 42, 47, 48, 50, 111, 157/Oxford Road rail. **Map** p117 C5 **27**

With its castles-in-the-air façade, funky bar with weekend DJs, regular street art shows and free WiFi, Contact has the advantage when it comes to attracting a younger crowd to its dance, theatre, music, DJ, art and spoken word events.

Cornerhouse

70 Oxford Street, M1 5NH (200 1500/ www.cornerhouse.org). Metrolink St Peter's Square/City Centre buses/ Oxford Road rail. **Map** p117 D5/D6 **28**

With three galleries, arthouse cinemas, two specialist bookshops and two rather chi-chi café-bars, Cornerhouse is the original champion of independent visual arts and film in the city. Its three floors of odd-shaped gallery space sometimes break up the changing temporary exhibitions (there's no permanent collection) a little awkwardly. Weekend nights feature DJs, while the film programme, with regular festivals, talks and indie selections, is arguably the best in town.

Dancehouse

10 Oxford Road, M1 5QA (237 9753/ www.thedancehouse.co.uk). Metrolink St Peter's Square/City Centre buses/ Oxford Road rail. **Map** p116 B2 **29**

Although best known for its comedy nights, this art deco former cinema puts on dance, drama and music gigs, and is the home of the Northern Ballet School.

Greenroom

54-56 Whitworth Street West, M1 5WW (615 0500/www.greenroomarts.org). Metrolink G-Mex, City Centre buses/ Oxford Road rail. **Map** p116 B2 **30**

This unusual venue champions experimental theatre (including some great kids' stuff), live art, dance and spoken word events and expects the audience to muck in, too. You've been warned…

Manchester Aquatics Centre

2 Booth Street East, M13 9SS (275 9450). Bus 16, 41, 42/Oxford Road rail. **Open** 6.30am-10pm Mon-Fri; 7am-6pm Sat; 7am-10pm Sun. **Admission** *Swimming pools* £2.80; £1.70 reductions. **Map** p117 C3/C4 **31**

Built for the 2002 Commonwealth Games, and the city centre's only public swimming pool, the Aquatics Centre houses two 50-metre pools (with diving facilities), as well as fitness studios.

Martin Harris Centre for Music & Drama

University of Manchester, Bridgeford Street, M13 9PL (275 8951/www. manchester.ac.uk). Bus 16, 41, 42/ Oxford Road rail. **Map** p117 C5 **32**

The Martin Harris Centre quietly hosts some of the city's best music, theatre and literary events. Its concert hall is home to the the Quatuor Daniels string quartet (which often gives free lunchtime concerts), while the John Thaw Studio Theatre puts on critically acclaimed theatre and film and holds a reading series that has in the past featured such literary luminaries as Will Self, John Banville and Sarah Waters.

Palace Theatre

Oxford Street, M1 6FT (0870 145 1163/www.manchestertheatres.com). Metrolink St Peter's Square/City Centre buses/Oxford Road rail. **Map** p116 B2 **33**

Massive musicals, big-name comedians and the celeb-stuffed Christmas pantos regularly play to a packed house. The theatre also puts on dance, from highbrow English National Ballet productions to the more popular *Riverdance*.

Royal Northern College of Music (RNCM)

Oxford Road, M13 9PL (907 5555/ www.rncm.ac.uk). Metrolink St Peter's Square/Bus 15, 16, 41, 43-45a, 47, 48, 50, 87, 111, 141-145, 157/Oxford Road rail. **Map** p117 C4 **34**

One of the UK's leading conservatoires, RNCM balances a fierce reputation for teaching against an international reputation for top-notch performance. If mention of student musicians conjures up images of amateurs, think again. Only the very gifted study here. It also pulls in international players for festivals such as the international cello festival and the annual festival of brass.

Castlefield & Deansgate Locks

With its railway arches, cleaned-up canals and seemingly endless supply of tiered locks and cobblestones, Castlefield remains one of the city's loveliest outdoor spots. Even the addition of the 47-storey **Beetham Tower** doesn't detract from the 150-odd-year-old industrial architecture. Though it can be quiet on weekdays, Castlefield offers something that the rest of the city often overlooks: peace and tranquillity.

Overlooked by a vast Victorian viaduct (if you come to Manchester from Liverpool by train, you'll look down from it onto Castlefield), the main draws are the sprawling **Museum of Science and Industry**, the outdoor arena (it was here residents burst into a spontaneous rendition of Monty Python's *Always Look on the Bright Side of Life* at the news of Manchester's second failed Olympic bid) or sitting outside **Dukes 92** tucking into man-size slabs of cheese and bread.

Closer to town, **Deansgate Locks** hosts a series of bars frequented by the 'in crowd', and the excellent **Comedy Store**, each one tucked inside a railway arch and facing onto the canal. Across the road and nestling beside the redbrick entrance to Deansgate Station is one of the city's best delis and purveyors of locally-sourced food, **Love Saves the Day** – great for stocking up on picnic treats.

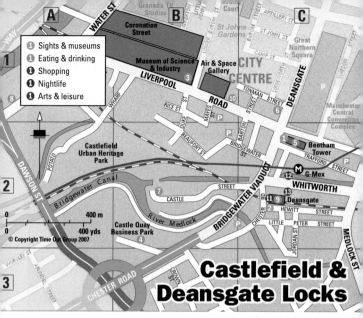

Sights & museums

Beetham Tower

301-303 Deansgate, M3 4LQ.
Metrolink G-Mex/City Centre
buses/Deansgate rail. **Map** p127 C2 ❶
Beetham Tower is one of the newest
and certainly most prominent additions
to 21st-century Manchester. Its
current fame rests chiefly on its height
– 47 storeys and 561 feet (171 metres)
high, by far the tallest building in the
city and reputedly the tallest in the UK
outside of London – although these are
statistics that are unlikely to last for
long. Taller projects are already under
construction by the side of Piccadilly
station. Split between residential apartments (the Olympian penthouse is
occupied by the building's architect,
Ian Simpson), offices and the Hilton
hotel (p174), there's little except the
pricey Sky Bar available for the casual tourist – but standing at its base and
gawping to the heavens may be
enough. See also box p129.

Castlefield Gallery

2 Hewitt Street, Knott Mill, M15 4GB
(832 8034/www.castlefieldgallery.co.uk).
Metrolink G-Mex/City Centre buses/
Deansgate rail. **Admission** free. **Map** p127 C2 ❷
An artist-run gallery specialising in the
more conceptual end of the creative
scale, and which frequently showcases
emerging practitioners and new media.
This twin-level building reopened in its
current (and somewhat well-hidden)
location in 2002.

Museum of Science & Industry in Manchester

Liverpool Road, M3 4FP (832 2244/
www.msim.org.uk). Metrolink G-Mex/
City Centre buses/Deansgate rail.
Open 10am-5pm daily. **Admission**
free. **Map** p127 B1 ❸
A family-friendly playground of vintage technology set amid the converted
remains of Liverpool Road's 1830s railway station. Highlights include a walkthrough replica of the Victorian sewer

Scaling new heights

Make no bones about it: the £150-million **Beetham Tower** (p127), on Deansgate, truly divided Mancunian opinion when it was completed in 2006. Many have now been swayed by the skyscraper, and are proud that the city is currently home to the UK's tallest building outside London; others still consider the tower to be a monolithic blot on the landscape. One thing's for sure: with 47 floors and a height of 561 feet (171 metres), you certainly can't miss it.

Half Hilton hotel (p174), half residential apartments, the tower stands on a site that was the underpinnings of a railway viaduct that crossed Deansgate and connected with Central Station (now the junction of Great Bridgewater Street and Liverpool Road). The viaduct was demolished in the mid 1960s by an explosives demolition contractor called Simpson, assisted by his boy Ian; the lad from Heywood grew up to become the renowned architect of Manchester-based Ian Simpson Architects. The firm designed the tower for Liverpool-based developers the Beetham Organisation, which has also commissioned several other eponymous towers (some of which have now been completed, while others are still in the pipeline) in Liverpool, Birmingham, Brighton and the capital. London's tower, planned for the South Bank, will be the tallest, with a planned height of 590 feet (180 metres).

With its glass and steel envelope, vertical louvres and polished concrete podium, the Beetham Tower does feel more than a touch last-century, and will not be everybody's favourite building. Yet even those who dislike the tower might concede that it turns something of a corner for Manchester. The city has no waterfront and little topography, and needs to rewrite itself from time to time. The Town Hall (p65) did it in the 1870s; Sunlight House did it in the 1930s; CIS did it in the 1960s; and now it could well be the turn of the Beetham Tower. All those strained necks and squinting eyes are looking at something. In some intuitive way, the lad from Heywood and his team have made a quintessentially Manchester building. And even if you don't like the tower itself, you're sure to be impressed by the fabulous views afforded from the Hilton's Cloud 23 bar (p130).

Cloud 23

The new Hilton bar affords fabulous views of the city.

Manchester's newest tall building, the Beetham Tower (p127, and box p129) is home to one of its most talked-about new bars, the Hilton's Cloud 23, billed as Manchester's first 'sky bar' (it's located on – as you may have guessed – the 23rd floor). Designed by the Gorgeous Group, which has previously worked wonders on ventures such as London's award-winning Hakkasan, the bar itself has the feel of the world's coolest airport lounge. With floor-to-ceiling windows laying bare every section of Manchester, all guests can do is stare out of the windows and take in the incredible views. If you'd rather look down, there are two portholes cut out of the floor where you gaze on the city below. Not for vertigo sufferers.

The drinks menu has a full selection of wines and beers but a special view demands a drink to match. Gorgeous Group has plundered Mancunian history to bring you a range of Manc-themed cocktails. Rather than featuring anything with stout in it, Ena's Sparkles finally grants Mrs Sharples some glamour and commemorates the *Coronation Street* star with a fruit juice and champagne drink. The Stone Roses also get the cocktail treatment with Sally Cinnamon, a brandy and cider concoction flavoured with tarragon and, naturally enough, cinnamon.

With most cocktails coming in around the £8 mark, make sure you make the most of the view. To avoid disappointment you should probably also try and book a booth in advance (0161 870 1788), or go the whole hog and book an entire room. It's possible that you'll still find a few Mancs who don't like the tower as a whole, but it would be amazing if you found someone who didn't enjoy a drink or two at Cloud 23.

system (more interesting than it sounds), a huge Power Hall of thrusting, steaming turbines like something from the feverish dreams of Brunel, and the equally impressive Air and Space Hall featuring a pantheon of airborne greats including a colossal Shackleton bomber.

Eating & drinking

Choice Bar & Restaurant

Castle Quay, M15 4NT (833 3400/ www.choicebarandrestaurant.co.uk). Metrolink G-Mex/City Centre buses/ Deansgate rail. **Open** noon-11pm daily. **£££. Modern British. Map** p127 B2 ❹

Choice has already won several awards since launching in 2001, and its menu should suit those with a taste for refined British flavours and an eye for outstanding presentation. Scallops on a Cheshire-cheese scone with saffron sauce makes for a surpisingly successful combination of flavours. The team also has a flair for finding good local suppliers.

Cloud 23

Hilton, 303 Deansgate, M3 4LQ (870 1600/www.hilton.co.uk). Metrolink G-Mex/City Centre buses/Deansgate rail. **Open** 5pm-2am Mon-Thur; 5pm-3am Fri; 2.30pm-3am Sat; noon-midnight Sun. **Bar. Map** p127 C2 ❺

See box p130.

Dimitri's

Campfield Arcade, Tonman Street M3 4FN (839 3319/www.dimitris.co.uk). **Open** 11am-midnight daily. **££. Greek. Map** p127 C1 ❻

No prizes for guessing that there's a Greek lineage lurking at this lively restaurant. The menu is alive with tasty meze dishes, great for soaking up the ouzo. If you can tolerate crimes against language, order the Kalamata Plata – a feast of nibbles to share. A great place for group outings. Service can be a bit slack.

Dukes 92

18-25 Castle Street M3 4LZ (839 8646/ www.dukes92.com). **Open** 11.30am-11pm Mon-Thur; 11.30am-1am Fri, Sat; noon-10.30pm Sun. **Pub. Map** p127 B2 ❼

Dimitri's

MANCHESTER BY AREA

One of the first bars to open in these parts, Dukes 92 is still as popular as ever, and the canalside patio is one of the best outdoor spots from which to enjoy a summer pint and a chunky gourmet sandwhich or cheese and pâté plate; choose from over 30 types of cheese from Britain and around Europe.

Harry Ramsden's

1 Water Street, M3 4JU (832 9144/ www.harryramsdens.co.uk). Metrolink G-Mex/City Centre buses/Deansgate rail. **Open** 11.30am-9.30pm Mon-Thur; 11.30am-10pm Fri, Sat. **££. Fish & chips.** Map p127 C2 **8**

Although Ramsden's is more expensive than your average chippy, it does have a sit-down restaurant, which obviates the need to drive at high-speed to get your chips home still-warm. The place may be relocating in spring 2007.

The Knott

374 Deansgate, M3 4LY (839 9229). Metrolink G-Mex/City Centre buses/ Deansgate rail. **Open** noon-12.30am Mon-Wed, Fri-Sun; noon-1am Thur. **Bar.** Map p127 C2 **9**

The transformation from unloved bar to much-cherished real ale haven has been as swift as it has been amazing. Another Marble Brewery offering, the Knott has been squeezed in underneath railway arches, and shakes violently when a loco rumbles overhead (slightly unnerving the first time it happens). An excellent food menu complements the range of organic and bottled beers.

The Ox

71 Liverpool Road, M3 4NQ (839 7740/www.theox.co.uk). Metrolink G-Mex/City Centre buses/Deansgate rail. **Open** noon-3pm, 5.30-9.30pm Mon-Sat; 12.30pm-7pm Sun. **££. Gastropub.** Map p127 B1 **10**

An award-winning gastropub with a largely British menu garnished with Asian twists. Suitably dark, there's a mishmash of furniture dotted around and a raft of well-kept real ales. For those who can't face the journey home – or afford the Hilton, opposite – there are nine guest rooms upstairs (see p178).

Shopping

Love Saves the Day

345 Deansgate, M3 4LG (834 2266/ www.lovesavestheday.com). Metrolink G-Mex/City Centre buses/Deansgate rail. **Open** 8am-7pm Mon, Tue; 8am-8pm Wed, Fri; 8am-9pm Thur; 10am-6pm Sat; 10am-4pm Sun. Map p127 C2 **11**

Foodie hearts were broken when the Oldham Street LSTD closed – but lifted when the Deansgate outpost re-opened. Reminiscent of an Italian neighbourhood deli, it emits a delicious smell of fresh coffee that attracts customers from all over Castlefield; passers-by are often seized by sudden cravings for fresh pasta, own-made bread or a sit-down with soup at the window tables.

Nightlife

Comedy Store

Deansgate Locks, M1 5LH (08705 932 932/www.thecomedystore.co.uk). Metrolink G-Mex/City Centre buses/ Deansgate rail. **Open** Regular shows from 8pm. Map p127 C2 **12**

The northern outpost of the long-running London laugh-bastion, this venue is at the heart of Manchester's current comedy renaissance, with big names from the stand-up circuit regularly dropping by to play its theatre-style auditorium. Launched in 2000, and propping up one end of the bustling Deansgate Locks cluster, it's a good option for drinks, dinner and a (non-smoking) show.

Emporia

2B Whitworth Street West, M1 5WZ (236 8833/www.emporia .co.uk). Metrolink G-Mex/City Centre buses/ Deansgate rail. **Open** 10pm-4am Thur-Sat. Map p127 C2 **13**

A stylish dance venue run by club promoters-turned-operators, Emporia is the latest in a succession of ventures to call this space home, and seems to have finally ushered in a degree of stability. As it's situated a stagger away from the bars of Deansgate Locks, promoters can enforce the club's strict dress code with confidence. Inside, find VIP wannabes getting down to funky house sounds.

Imperial War Museum North p137

Salford & the Salford Quays

Salford

Let's get one thing straight: Salford isn't in Manchester. There's nothing that will rile locals more than mistaking the two – on both sides of the divide. Salford and Manchester are two separate cities that just happen to share a border (and, arguably, a city centre).

Salfordians are proud of their industrial heritage and tight-knit communities, and the Smiths' *The Queen is Dead* album cover (shot in front of **Salford Lads Club**) put Salford on the musical map. The **King's Arms** is testament to Salford's eclectic independence. A regular theatre and gig venue, it's one of the hosts of the Sounds of the Other City mini music festival.

As well as a number of superb watering holes, there is now fine dining here, courtesy of the Lowry Hotel's **River Restaurant**. Eyck Zimmer's British and Modern European menu are a real draw.

Sights & museums

Ordsall Hall

Ordsall Lane, Salford, M5 3AN (872 0251/www.salford.gov.uk). Metrolink Exchange Quay/Bus 71, 73, 84, 92. **Open** 10am-4pm Mon-Fri; 1-4pm Sun. **Admission** free. **Map** p134 A3 ❶
Ordsall is now an unlikely setting for this splendid Grade-I listed house, which comprises elements of medieval, Tudor, Stuart and Victorian construction. The patchwork of functions persists to this day, with a pottery the latest addition. Only the Great Hall, the 'star chamber' bedroom and the kitchen are accessible to the general public – although an ambitious restoration project will hopefully open up more of the building in years to come. The regular family open days really bring the building to life.

Salford Lads Club

Coronation Street, Salford, M5 3RX (872 3767/www.salfordladsclub.org.uk). Bus 33/Deansgate rail. **Open** by appointment. **Admission** free. **Map** p134 A2 ➋

Featured on the cover of the Smiths' *The Queen Is Dead* album (p51), this registered charity, established in 1903, still fulfils its original function as a sports club and community centre, although it's now open to both boys and girls. The spot is a mecca for all Smiths devotees, and the surrounding streets host regular pilgrimages of often rather worried-looking foreign fans. Inside, the club has a specific room devoted to the band, where you'll find all sorts of memorabilia, as well as a collection of images that fans have sent in of themselves in the classic cover pose. There's also a colourful collection of notes covering the walls, with words and lyrics from visitors. If you'd like to visit the room, email info@salfordladsclub.org.uk to arrange a time.

Salford Museum & Art Gallery

Peel Park, The Crescent, Salford, M5 4WU (778 0800/www.salford.gov.uk). Bus 7, 8, 12, 26, 31, 32, 36, 37, 67, 68, 100/Salford Crescent rail. **Open** 10am-4.45pm Mon-Fri; 10am-5pm Sat, Sun. **Admission** free. **Map** p134 A2 ➌

Inevitably overshadowed by its more prestigious neighbours both up and down the road (its Lowry collection has been transferred to the Lowry; p138), this gallery nevertheless has a good selection of Victorian art, including Dollman's striking *Famine* painting and an exquisite Burne-Jones drawing of a woman's head. The recreated Victorian Street, Lark Hill Place, is crammed with vivid period sights and sounds.

Eating & drinking

Crescent

18-20 The Crescent, Salford, M5 4PF (736 5600). Bus 7, 8, 12, 26, 31, 32, 36, 37, 67, 68, 100/Salford Crescent

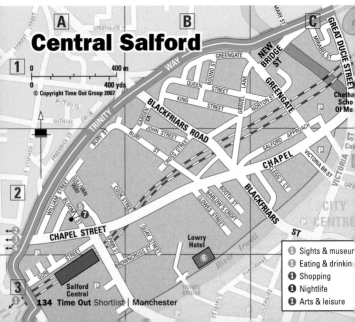

Central Salford

0   400 m
0   400 yds
© Copyright Time Out Group 2007

➊ Sights & museur
➊ Eating & drinkin
➊ Shopping
➊ Nightlife
➊ Arts & leisure

rail. **Open** 11am-midnight Mon-Thur; 11am-1am Fri, Sat; noon-midnight Sun. **Pub**. **Map** p134 A2 ❹

Don't be put off by the grey exterior and basic furniture: it's the beer that counts at the Crescent, one of Greater Manchester's older pubs, dating back to the mid 19th century. You'll fight for a seat with CAMRA types and eggheads from the nearby University of Salford (who really should be doing other things); all crowd in for cask ales, with up to ten available at any one time. Beers from the Roosters Brewing Company are particularly good, as is the Black Pig mild from Salford's very own Bazens' Brewery. Regular quiz nights, a great jukebox (at least if Led Zeppelin is your idea of great music) and frequent beer festivals are additional highlights.

King's Arms

11 Bloom Street, Salford, M3 6AN (832 3605/www.studiosalford.com). Bus 3, 7, 8, 10, 12, 25-27, 31, 32, 36, 37, 67, 68, 71, 93, 98, 100, 137, 138/Salford Central rail. **Open** noon-11pm Mon-Thur; noon-midnight Fri, Sat; noon-6pm Sun. **Pub**. **Map** p134 A2 ❺

This is a real gem, an alcopop-free zone sitting pretty in the no-man's-land between Manchester and Salford (it's an easy stroll from the city centre). Beers include offerings from Bazens and Flintshire beer-meisters Facers, with Timothy Taylor a staple. A newly launched menu promises hearty grub sourced from local suppliers, while the fantastic vaulted room upstairs (home to Studio Salford, below) hosts regular band nights and plays. All told, it's hard to fault this pub – even the jukebox has won awards.

River Restaurant

Lowry Hotel, 50 Dearmans Place, Salford, M3 5LH (827 4041/www.the lowryhotel.com). Bus 1, 2, 7, 8, 10, 12, 25-27, 31, 32, 36, 37, 67, 68, 70, 71, 93, 98, 100, 137, 138, X34/Salford rail. **Open** noon-2.30pm, 6-10.30pm Mon-Sat; 12.30pm-4pm, 7-10.30pm Sun. **£££**. **Modern European**. **Map** p134 B2/B3 ❻

Eyck Zimmer is a technically peerless chef, having honed his craft in London at the Dorchester, Claridge's and the Ritz. He's come to Manchester because he predicts big things for the city's food future. His à la carte menu at the River Restaurant is pleasingly varied, featuring the likes of slow-cooked fois gras or roasted scallops for starters and pumkin risotto, grilled whole Dover sole or Cheshire beef fillet for mains. There's also a Modern British Pie menu (a different pie features nightly, Monday to Friday), plus accomplished and hugely comforting desserts such as sherry trifle or rice pudding. Set daily menus cost a very reasonable £20 for two courses or £25 for three. The views over the Irwell may be uninspiring, but the cooking is triumphant.

Arts & leisure

Studio Salford

11 Bloom Street, Salford, M3 6AN (834 3896/www.studiosalford.com). Bus 3, 7, 8, 10, 12, 25-27, 31, 32, 36, 37, 67, 68, 71, 93, 98, 100, 137, 138/Salford Central rail. **Open** *Shows* 8pm Tue-Sat. **Admission** £6.50; £4 reductions. **Map** p134 A2 ❼

Studio Salford concentrate on new theatre performances – and its consistent quality has seen the Studio snatching awards and nominations from under the noses of bigger rivals. The real ale setting (the King's Arms, above) is another award-winner and is known for secret gigs, and film and club nights. In the rafters of this old boozer resides an eleven artist-strong art studio.

Salford Quays

Salford has taken longer to redevelop than Manchester, though clever regeneration schemes such as Urban Splash's 'upside down' houses in Langworthy are definitely a sign that change is a-coming. And for all its down-at-heel terracing, Salford has something Manchester doesn't: a spectacular waterfront.

A 15-minute tram hop west of the city centre, the **Lowry** arts centre sits by the Manchester Ship Canal, surrounded by made-for-footballer apartments and a designer outlet shopping mall. Plans are in place to build a waterside 'media village' by 2010, which will become the home of the BBC's planned northern outpost. In the meantime, a bridge connects the Lowry to the **Imperial War Museum North**. Strictly speaking, the museum isn't in Salford: it's in the borough of Trafford. We just thought we'd better set the record straight before you start asking for directions.

Sights & museums

Imperial War Museum North

The Quays, Trafford Wharf, M17 1TZ (836 4000/http://north.iwm. org.uk). Metrolink Harbour City/ Bus 205. **Open** *Mar-Oct* 10am-6pm daily; *Nov-Feb* 10am-5pm daily. **Admission** free. **Map** p137 A2 **⑧**

Closely competing with Urbis (p65) for the title of most striking new building from the past decade, the brain-boggling design of the Imperial War Museum was based on renowned architect Daniel Libeskind's concept of a shattered globe (representing the world divided by conflict). Inside, the floors and doors gently slope and disorientate. More a museum of peace than a museum of war, the place works hard – and mainly succeeds – at being an entertaining and educative multimedia-led venue. Its permanent displays – which include artillery, audio-visual shows and hands-on, interactive exhibits such as The Trench – are supplemented by temporary exhibitions, like the photographic exhibition to mark the 25th anniversary of the Falklands War (31 Mar-22 July 2007). The tower has an impressive view, but should be avoided by the vertiginous.

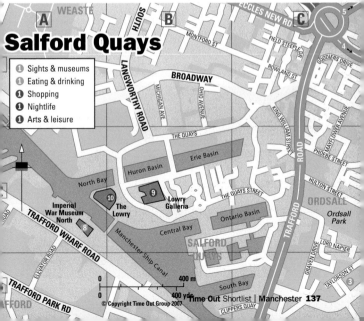

Shopping

Lowry Outlet Mall

The Quays, Salford, M50 3AH (848 1850/www.lowrydesigneroutlet.com). Metrolink City/Bus 69. **Open** 10am-6pm Mon-Wed, Fri; 10am-8pm Thur; 10am-7pm Sat; 11am-5pm Sun. **Map** p137 B2 **❾**

This sprawling indoor factory outlet offers clothes, books, gifts and homeware at discounts of between 25 and 75 per cent. What you'll get depends largely on how happy you are to devote hours to rummaging. The selection of shops are generally classy, and include Karen Millen, Flannels, Whistles and Mikey Jewellery, which almost always has something glittery and worth snapping up for peanuts. If you want to make a day of it, the mall also houses cinemas and a range of eateries.

Arts & leisure

The Lowry

Pier 8, Salford Quays, M50 3AZ (0870 787 5780/www.thelowry.com). Metrolink Harbour City/Bus 69, 290, 291. **Open** *Galleries* 11am-5pm Mon-Fri, Sun; 10am-5pm Sat; call or see website for shows and events. **Admission** *Galleries* free; call or see website for show and events. **Map** p137 B2 **❿**

A long way from the grimly functional mill buildings so often captured by its eponymous subject and raison d'etre, the Lowry marked a tipping point for the previously isolated Salford Quays development area when it opened in spring 2000. The landmark waterside building houses an extensive collection of LS Lowry's art, as well as an excellent changing programme of painting, sculpture and photography, often based around the local area.

Lowry is only half of the story, however, as the centre brings together an amazing variety of visual and performing arts projects all under one roof. As well as the contemporary arts shows in its galleries, the steel-clad wonder has also hosted more award-winning theatre productions than any other regional venue. Its two theatres and additional performing arts space receive blockbuster musicals, dance, opera, comedy, ballet, children's shows, jazz, folk and popular music acts and West End productions. There are restaurants, cafés and bars situated in the south side of the building – offering breathtaking views with your cappuccino – while its close proximity to Imperial War Museum North (p137) make a trip to Salford Quays doubly worthwhile.

The Lowry

City of Manchester Stadium p146

North Manchester

Sometimes overlooked in favour of some of South Manchester's more affluent suburbs, the north races ahead of its southern sister when it comes to international sporting facilities. Two miles from the centre, **Sportcity** is a sprawling complex that houses the National Squash Centre, a 6,000-seat athletics arena, the Regional Tennis Centre and **Manchester Velodrome**.

Sportcity is part of the legacy of the 2002 Commonwealth Games, an event that single-handedly reversed economic decline in north-east Manchester. The city tackled the huge event with typical gusto, pulling off a 'best ever' Games and in the process creating some of the best sporting facilities in the country.

No tour of Sportcity would be complete without Manchester City's ground – the **City of Manchester Stadium**. The stadium is a match for United's 'theatre of dreams' and arguably draws a more loyal and local crowd. It's due to host the UEFA cup final in 2008.

Close by is the **B of the Bang**, Thomas Heatherwick's monumental sculpture that resembles a firework caught mid-explosion. It's not without its detractors, but the *B of the Bang* is a dramatic statement of the renewed fortunes of north-east Manchester, commissioned in response to the success of the Games.

Further north, **Heaton Park** continues the sporting theme. As well as 600 acres of parkland, an 18th-century house and a farm centre, Heaton Park has four championship-standard bowling greens built for, you guessed it, the Commonwealth Games.

B of the Bang

Sights & museums

B of the Bang

Alan Turing Way, Sportcity (www.bof thebang.com). Bus 11, 28, 309, 310, 368, 369, 371/Piccadilly rail.
Commissioned to commemorate the 2002 Commonwealth games, the *B of the Bang* is the tallest piece of sculpture in England, at over 183 feet (56 metres) – making it more than twice the height of the *Angel of the North*. It was designed by Thomas Heatherwick and named after Linford Christie's quote on when to set off in a sprint (not just at the bang of the pistol, but at the 'b' of the bang). Constructed from rust-proof 'weathering steel', the sculpture's 180 spikes radiate outwards from a central core, resembling a dramatic frozen firework explosion. It is visible for miles when illuminated at night. With blackly humorous ill-timing, some of its spike tips loosened and fell soon after its unveiling (by Christie) in 2005, and its immediate surrounds have since been fenced off for safety reasons.

Heaton Hall

Heaton Park, Prestwich, M25 2SW (773 1231/www.manchestergalleries. org/our-other-venues/heaton-hall). Metrolink Heaton Park/Bus 56, 59, 64, 64a, 89, 137, 138, 150, 151,167, 484, 495. **Open** Apr-Oct 11am-5.30pm Wed-Sun, bank hols. **Admission** free.
An elegant Grade I-listed neo-classical country house designed by James Wyatt in the late 18th century and expanded by Lewis Wyatt in the 1820s. It was home to the Earls of Wilton until purchased by the council in 1902. In 1906, a section of the hall became a branch of Manchester City Galleries, used to house its growing collection of paintings and decorative objects. The organisation restored the houses in the 1980s and '90s. Only half of the house (13 rooms) is currently open to the public – a fire-damaged wing remained gutted at the time of writing, but the ground floor still hosts interesting temporary exhibitions.

Heaton Park

Off Middleton Road, Prestwich, M25 2SW (773 1231/www.heatonpark. org.uk). Metrolink Heaton Park/Bus 56, 59, 64, 64a, 89, 137, 138, 150, 151, 167, 484, 495. **Open** 8am.
Closing hours vary. **Admission** free.
Nestled in the foothills of the Pennines, Heaton Park is one of Europe's largest municipal parks, at over 600 acres; it contains eight English Heritage listed buildings, a boating lake, an 18th-century hall, four championship-standard bowling greens (built for the Commonwealth Games), a golf course, a herd of highland cattle and a farm. The park is host to numerous concerts throughout the year, and a summer outdoor theatre.

Heaton Park Tram Museum

Heaton Park, Prestwich, M25 2SW (740 1919/www.mtms.org.uk). Metrolink Heaton Park/Bus 56, 59, 64, 64a, 89, 137, 138, 150, 151, 167, 484, 495. **Open** Easter-Oct noon-5pm Sun, bank holidays. **Admission** free.
Tram fares £1; 50p reductions.
Run by volunteers, this small but lovely museum is housed in an old tram shelter, from which restored vehicles run from Easter to October. The original system fell into disuse in the 1930s, and the park's tramlines were only released from beneath a layer of tarmac in the late '70s. The building includes transport memorabilia, demonstration models, a shop and a maintenance pit where the trams can be seen undergoing restoration.

Manchester Jewish Museum

190 Cheetham Hill Road, Cheetham, M8 8LW (834 9879/www.manchester jewishmuseum.com). Metrolink Victoria/ Bus 59, 89, 135, 167/Victoria rail. **Open** 10.30am-4pm Mon-Thur; 10.30am-5pm Sun. Closed Jewish hols. **Admission** £3.95; £2.95 reductions; £9.50 family ticket (2 adults & up to 4 children).
Just beyond the outskirts of the City Centre lies the Jewish museum, in an old synagogue founded in 1874. Downstairs is a fully restored former place of wor-

ship. Upstairs, the former ladies gallery houses a permanent display cataloguing the history of the still prominent local Jewish community. Helpful guides explain the ritual and history, and there are monthly heritage trails.

Manchester Museum of Transport

Boyle Street, Cheetham, M8 8UW (205 2122/www.gmts.co.uk). Metrolink Victoria/Bus 53, 54, 59, 88, 89, 135, 151, 167/Victoria rail. **Open** *Mar-Oct* 10am-5pm Wed, Sat, Sun, public hols. *Nov-Feb* 10am-4pm Wed, Sat, Sun, public hols. **Admission** £4; free-£2 reductions.

Two huge halls house over a century's worth of lovingly restored public transport history; the continually expanding collection is one of the largest of its kind. The timeline starts with a 19th-century horse-drawn carriage and concludes with a Metrolink tram. Not just for anoraks.

Strangeways

1 Southall Street, Manchester, M60 9AH (817 5600). Metrolink Victoria/Bus 134, 135/Victoria rail.

The intriguingly named Strangeways – officially HM Prison Manchester since the 1990s – owes its fame to the

Smiths' 1987 album *Strangeways, Here We Come* and to the 1990 riot that led to extensive rebuilding. It was designed by Manchester Town Hall architect Alfred Waterhouse in the 1860s; only the most disastrous of tourist excursions will end up within its walls, but its panopticon 234-foot (71-metre) tower makes it one of the city centre periphery's more distinctive landmarks.

Eating & drinking

Lamb Hotel

33 Regent Street, Eccles, M30 0BP (789 3882). Metrolink Eccles/Bus 10, 33, 63, 67, 68, 70/Eccles rail. **Open** 11.30am-11pm Mon-Thur; 11.30am-11.30pm Fri, Sat; noon-11pm Sun. **Pub**.

As good as it gets when it comes to original pub decor. Built in 1906, this is a pretty much unspoilt Grade II-listed Holts pub, with a superb wood-panelled billiards room, complete with full size table. Other features include exquisite glazed tiles, a clutch of high ceilinged rooms and a huge mahogany bar, enclosed with thick acid-etched glass. Some of the regulars can be a bit intimidating; it's best to visit during the day.

MANCHESTER BY AREA

Marble Arch Inn p144

Marble Arch Inn

73 Rochdale Road, Manchester, M4 4HY (832 5914). Metrolink Victoria/ Bus 17, 17a, 24, 51, 56, 64, 65, 74-78, 80-83, 89, 112, 113, 118, 123, 124, 131, 163, 180-184/Victoria rail. **Open** 11.30am-11.30pm Mon-Wed, Sun; 11.30am-midnight Thur-Sat. **Pub**. Victorian tiling and a sloping floor give this place a classic feel. The brewery at the back makes it a magnet for real ale aficionados, who share the space with postmen from the nearby sorting office. Guest beers from Marston's, Bazens' and Greene King supplement the brewery's own. Traditional pub food is available, and there's a decent jukebox.

Olive Lounge & Bistro

254 Moston Lane, Moston, M40 9WF (203 4967/www.purpleolive.co.uk). Bus 51, 52, 88, 149/Moston rail. **Open** 10am-3pm, 5-10pm Tue-Sat; 11am-4pm Sun. **£££. Classic**. The downright superb Olive Lounge should encourage more restaurateurs to look towards the north of Manchester as a potential location. A focus on local ingredients, and sumptuous à la carte dishes like Bury black pudding and mushroom wontons, shredded duck hotpot, and polenta cake with roasted vegetables keep customers coming back for more. The popular Sunday roasts are a very reasonable £8.95.

Slattery

197 Bury New Road, Whitefield, M45 6GE (767 7761/www.slattery.co.uk). Metrolink Whitefield/Bus 90, 95, 98, 135, 484/Whitefield rail. **Open** *Dining room* 9am-4pm Mon-Fri; 9am-3.30pm Sat. *Shop* 9am-5.30pm Mon-Fri; 9am-5pm Sat. **££. Tea room**. Remember the orgasm scene in *When Harry Met Sally…*? Such behaviour should be expected here by customers sampling Slattery's beautiful Swiss hot chocolate (£3.15). The Slattery family have been baking since 1967, and crafting chocolates since 1991. They now run a dining room that serves breakfasts and lunches, as well as the range of chocolate-based goodies.

The School of Excellence teaches the arts of chocolate making. With a third generation of Slatterys now helping to run the business, the restaurant has become a classic venue.

Nightlife

Sankeys

Beehive Mill, Radium Street, Ancoats, M4 6JG. (950 4201/www.sankeys.info). Metrolink Market Street/Bus 75-78, 80, 82, 83, 89, 180-182, 184, 216-218, 231-237/Piccadilly rail. **Open** 11pm-3am Tue-Thur; 11pm-5am Fri, Sat; 7pm-1am Sun. **Admission** varies. See box p147.

Arts & leisure

Manchester Climbing Centre

Bennett Street, West Gorton, M12 5ND (230 7006/www.manchesterclimbing centre.com). Bus 205,206/Ardwick rail. **Open** *Climbing wall* 10am-10pm Mon-Fri; 10am-6pm Sat, Sun. *Café* noon-9.30pm Mon-Fri; 10am-5.30pm Sat, Sun. **Admission** *Before 4pm* £5 members; £7 non-members; £5-£7.50 reductions. *After 4pm* £6.50 members; £8 non-members; £6-£7.50 reductions. Practice your belaying and leading in this Grade-II listed church, which now houses one of the largest climbing walls in Europe. Hang around under the huge stained-glass windows on the 75 tied routes and two bouldering walls. Get to grips with the mezzanine-level Rocks Café (good cakes, Wi-Fi access and a great viewing gallery from which to watch the surrounding action), or brush up on your rope skills with specialist courses. All levels are catered for here, from complete beginners (including children) to experienced climbers.

Manchester Velodrome

Stuart Street, Philips Park, M11 4DQ (Velodrome 223 2244/Revolution 0700 594 2579/www.manchestervelodrome. com). Metrolink Piccadilly/Bus 217, 219, 53/Piccadilly rail. **Open** *Taster sessions* 5pm-6pm Mon; noon-1pm Tue, Thur, Fri, Sun; 1pm-2pm Wed;

Heaton Park p141

5pm-6pm Thur, Sun; 6pm-7pm Sat. **Admission** From £8; £6 reductions.
As the home of the British Cycling Team, the Velodrome's track is one of the best in the world, but the place still welcomes all levels of ability. If riding a fixed-gear bike appeals, hour-long taster sessions provide full kit and advice on riding the steep banking (and how to stop a bike without brakes). 'Revolution' events held during the winter season pull in crowds of 3000-plus with a 'night at the races' combo of sprinting and endurance races, music, food and booze. The Velodrome will close for resurfacing in April and May 2007.

Manchester City Football Club/City of Manchester Stadium

Sportcity, M11 3FF (0870 062 1894/ www.mcfc.co.uk). Bus 216, 217, 230, X36, X37/Manchester Piccadilly rail. **Open** *Tours* 9.45am-4.15pm Mon-Sat; 11am-2.45pm Sun. **Admission** *Tours* £8.75; £4.75 reductions.
The 48,000 capacity City of Manchester Stadium has housed the city's less glamorous but more endearing second football club, Manchester City, since 2003.

On site you'll find a club shop, a restaurant, a museum, athletics track and squash courts. Stadium tours are available; call to book. The stadium successfully hosted the 2002 Commonwealth Games (it was originally designed as part of the failed bid for the 2000 Olympics) before being converted into a football stadium. On top of Manchester City home games, the stadium will be the venue for the UEFA Cup Final in 2008. Big-name rock concerts take place here over the summer.

Octagon Theatre

Howell Croft South, Bolton, BL1 1SB (01204 529407/www.octagonbolton. co.uk). Bus 8, 12, 36, 37, 68/Bolton rail. **Open** times vary. **Admission** £10.95-£15.95 Mon-Fri; £12.50-£17.50 Sat; £8-£12.75 reductions. *Matinees* £9.50; £7.50 reductions.
This multi-award winning theatre takes its name from its octagonal auditorium. This isn't the result of architectural whimsy: clever design means directors can choose from theatre-in-the-round, traditional end-on or 'thrust', depending on the production, and audiences are guaranteed excellent sightlines.

Manchester Velodrome p144

Open all hours

The club that's raising the stakes for after-hours venues.

Even at its quietest moments, the Mancunian clubbing scene has never been less than loud. Since September 2006, though, the volume has been cranked up to 11, as a new – or at least, rematerialised – heavyweight addition to the scene, Sankeys, arrived in the city. Situated in a landmark building, and featuring serious line-ups, it now commands a substantial slice of the action.

Following a radical refit that mirrored the rapid regeneration of its formerly industrial surroundings, Mancunian clubbing institution **Sankeys** (formerly Sankeys Soap) is open for business once again. The Beehive Mill-based club was closed from May to September 2006, during which time its owner, David Vincent, was busy rewriting the script. A third room was added, the sound and light was bolstered, the music policy reinvented and the grimy interior radically overhauled to reveal a new club space primed for futuristic fun.

'We're aiming to be the most forward-thinking venue north of Fabric [in London],' says Vincent. '85 per cent of the DJs we've got booked have never played Manchester before, and that's always good for the scene. It helps music move forward and evolve.'

Sankeys relaunched on 22 September 2006 and is open five nights a week with stalwart minimal house, breaks, electro and techno-based Tribal Sessions, including the mixed/gay electro event Bitch at weekends. The place also hosts a mix of student and live music nights, including Thursday's Club NME sessions, to round out the calendar.

The recent refurbishment may have given Sankeys a more slick and mainstream image, but the place continues to push the musical envelope.

Hulme Arch Bridge

South Manchester & Stockport

South Manchester

Manchester's wealthier communities are most populous in its southern reaches, whose suburban boutiques, eateries and gardens make the short trip out of the centre worth the effort. Though non-southern Mancunians tend to roll their eyes at mention of the organic-buying media types who populate **Didsbury** and **Chorlton** (rumour has it that one newsagent in Chorlton sells more *Guardian* newspapers than anywhere else in the UK), there is much to recommend these suburbs.

While the City Centre isn't particularly rich in open space, the southern suburbs have enough of the green stuff to make up for it.

From **Fletcher Moss** in Didsbury to **Tatton Park** (p150) further out, there's enough parkland to get you pink-cheeked after overindulging in the city's more urban pursuits.

Heading south along Oxford Road takes you towards Rusholme's **Curry Mile,** a riotous strip of neon lights, booming Banghra, swishing saris and curry houses so tightly packed that it'd be rude not to stop off and sample a bhuna or balti (the curries aren't always great, but the experience is). The traffic here can be horrendous during early evening.

Fallowfield is primarily a student stomping ground with little to recommend it; instead, head over to Gorton in the south-east to visit **Gorton Monastery,**

or down to **Withington**, **West Didsbury** and **Didsbury Village**. West Didsbury's **Burton Road** has become an eating destination for urbanites, with pubs such as the **Metropolitan** dishing up reliable, hearty fare. Across the road, **Greens** regularly serves up staggering veggie dishes capable of sating even the most hardened of carnivores. Further west, though there's little else in leafy **Urmston**, is **Isinglass**, a superb restaurant serving up English dishes and showcasing local produce.

Further south, along Princess Parkway, the dramatic **Hulme Arch Bridge** straddles the carriageway, a symbol of the area's recent regeneration. Once a concrete jungle of dank flats and gloomy walkways, Hulme was rebuilt in the 1990s with smart red-brick townhouses and green spaces that replaced the 1960s high-rises.

Comfy boozers abound in the south, and it's easy to lose a Sunday afternoon switching between the papers and downing pints of locally-brewed or organic beer. Chorlton's **Marble Beer House** is a good

bet, and you can head here feeling virtuous after stocking up on treats at nearby vegan superstore **Unicorn**.

Those seeking retail therapy will be delighted by the quirky boutiques and independent record stores that clutter the streets in West Didsbury and Chorlton. Burton Road is again the place to head for in the former, while Chorlton's equivalent is **Beech Road**. Here, boutiques and boozers vie for space between delis and restaurants. While they're undoubtedly great for weekend downtime, locals have been grumbling about just how much tapas and focaccia a community really needs, especially as post offices and more practical shops have been forced to pull down their shutters.

As with the north, this slice of Greater Manchester is awash with sports venues. **Old Trafford** is home to **Manchester United**'s 'theatre of dreams', as well as to **Lancashire County Cricket Club**'s ground. Both provide a jumping-off point for the **Imperial War Museum North** and, on the other side of the Ship Canal, Salford's **Lowry** arts centre (p138).

MANCHESTER BY AREA

Tatton Park p150

Fletcher Moss Gardens

Wilmslow Road, Didsbury, M20 2SW (434 1877/www.manchester.gov.uk). Bus 42, 42a, 196 /East Didsbury rail. **Open** 8am-dusk (times vary). **Admission** free.

Donated to the public by the eponymous Alderman Moss in 1914, these lovely gardens – nestled in the suburbs across 21 acres – are notable for their rare and unusual plant species that bloom throughout the year. A nature trail winds through woods before opening out onto the Mersey river, but the real draw is the tiered rock and heather garden overlooking tennis courts. A tiny teahouse opens sporadically (afternoons only) for tea and ice-cream.

Gallery of Costume

Platt Hall, Rusholme, M14 5LL (224 5217/www.manchestergalleries.org). Bus 41-44, 46-48, 54, 140-143, 145, 157, 158. **Open** 10am-4.45pm Mon-Fri (ring bell on arrival); 10am-4.45pm last Sat of mth. **Admission** free.

Housed in an 18th-century textile merchant's home, this collection is the largest of its type in Britain (but with only a fraction of the 20,000-plus items on display). High fashion from the 17th century to the present is represented, and the contrasting selections of working people's attire and clothes from the neighbouring South Asian community are also interesting.

Gaskell House

84 Plymouth Grove, Ardwick, M13 9LW (225 1922/01663 744 233). Bus 50, 113, 130, 147, 191, 197/ Ardwick rail. **Open** *Mar-Dec* noon-4pm 1st Sun of mth or by appointment; *Sept* Heritage Days; call for information. **Admission** free (donations welcome).

Neglected for years, the home of Elizabeth Gaskell is now finally undergoing a renovation. The author – one of Manchester's most esteemed novelists and social commentators – lived with her family in this Regency-style villa between 1850 and 1865, hosting visits from Charlotte Bronte, Dickens, Thackeray and John Ruskin. Access may be limited during the renovation period – phone to check before visiting.

Gorton Monastery

Endcott Close, Gorton, M18 8BR (223 3211/www.gortonmonastery.co.uk). Bus 205, 206/Ashburys rail. **Open** 9am-4.30pm Mon-Fri; tours by appointment. **Admission** suggested donation £5.

Designed by Edward Pugin and built between 1863 and 1867, this spectacular piece of ecclesiastical architecture, officially called the Monastery of St Francis, served as a focus for the local community for over a century. Falling attendances (and declining numbers of monks) meant it was abandoned by the Franciscan order in 1989, and thereafter stripped of most of its contents by successive property developers, vandals and art thieves. A decade later the building was on the World Monuments Fund list of the globe's 100 most endangered sites. Much of the pilfered statuary has since been recovered at auction, however, and the still-impressive shell of the building is currently undergoing a renovation, and is due to reopen in May 2007.

Pankhurst Centre

60-62 Nelson Street, Chorlton on Medlock, M13 9WP (273 5673/ www.thepankhurstcentre.org.uk). Bus 15, 16, 41-44, 46-48, 50, 111, 113, 140-143/Manchester Piccadilly rail. **Open** 10am-4pm Mon-Thur. **Admission** free.

Saved from demolition in 1979, this Georgian house is where the remarkable Emmeline Pankhurst brought up her daughters Sylvia, Christabel and Adela, all active suffragettes. She founded the militant Women's Social and Political Union here in 1903. Today the Pankhurst Centre functions on two levels: as a women-only space for workshops and training, and as a bookshop and exhibition room (men admitted) recreating Pankhurst's parlour.

Tatton Park

Knutsford, Cheshire (01625 534400/ www.tattonpark.org.uk). Bus 26, 27,

MANCHESTER BY AREA

Gorton Monastery

Manchester's Michelin star

For a city used to having stars around every corner (see if you can trawl the bars along Deansgate at the weekend and *not* bump into a celeb), there's one type of star that's proved very elusive indeed in Manchester. In fact, you'd need to go back to the Midland Hotel's French restaurant circa 1975 if you wanted to eat in a city centre restaurant which held the coveted Michelin star. Subsequent years have seen the stars disappear from the city altogether.

For Michelin-starred dining on your visit to Manchester you'll need to take the tram or bus to Altrincham and find your way to 21 The Downs, where for the last 11 years professional Geordie Paul Kitching (pictured) and Katie O'Brien have run **Juniper** (p157). In their 34-cover space, the Juniper team have created and refined an almost uniquely inventive form of cuisine.

'I keep waiting to get bored at work, but it just doesn't seem to happen', Kitching says, and given the sort of experimentation that goes on in his kitchen, it's not surprising that his interest has held firm. The varied menus include themes around a single ingredient, such as olives, or cheese, which magically inveigle their way into every course served on that particular night. Other evenings might revolve around a concept or phrase, such as 'It's all white on the night' – a celebration of just one end of the edible colour spectrum. Although the food may be outlandish, the prices are the opposite; most bills come to around £30 per person.

It appears that Manchester's best hope of getting another Michelin star lies with Kitching opening another restaurant. However, the owners remain cautious about expansion plans. Rumours that Urbis (p65) almost became home to Juniper II indicate that if the place were to expand it would need to find a building as inventive and exciting as the food. 'It's either that, or we do a Juniper brasserie', Kitching muses – an interesting proposition indeed.

289/Knutsford rail. **Open** *Mansion* Mar-Oct 1pm-5pm (last entry 4pm) Tue-Sun. Closed winter except half-term and Christmas. *Gardens* Mar-Sept 10am-6pm Tue-Sun (last entry 5pm). Oct-Feb 11am-4pm (last entry 3pm) Tue-Sun. Guided tour of Japanese Garden 1.20pm, 2.20pm Wed, Sat. *Farm* Mar-Sept noon-5pm (last entry 4pm) Tue-Sun. Oct-Feb 11am-4pm (last entry 3pm) Sat, Sun. *Old Hall* Mar-Sept (guided tour only) noon-5pm Sat, Sun. Closed winter except autumn half-term. *Park* Mar-Sept 10am-7pm (last entry 6pm) daily. Oct-Feb 11am-4pm (last entry 4pm). **Admission** £3.50; £2 reductions; £9 family ticket (2 adults and up to 3 children); £4.20 park entry.

Get lost in the Cheshire countryside in this 1,000-acre park with free-roaming deer, lakes and a farm. A walled garden boasts fruit trees, tomato and fig houses; sample some fresh produce and own-baked cakes in the on-site restaurant and shop. The 200-year-old Mansion features unchanged state rooms, but the real attractions are outside – the gardens include a 1850s fernery and beech maze, and Japanese landscaping.

Victoria Baths

Hathersage Road, Chorlton-on-Medlock, M13 OFE (224 2020/www.victoria baths.org.uk). Bus 191, 197/Ardwick rail. **Open** email info@victoriabaths.org.uk for details. **Admission** £1; free reductions.

The winner of the BBC's *Restoration* programme in 2003, Victoria Baths is finally approaching a functional state after funding issues delayed development. The Turkish baths will reopen, as will at least one of the pools. Ongoing restoration will limit visitor access, so call for up-to-date details. See box p160.

Wythenshawe Hall

Wythenshawe Park, Northenden, M23 0AB (998 5083/www.manchester galleries.org). Bus 41. **Open** *June-Sept* 11am-5pm Sat. **Admission** free.

Isinglass p154

MANCHESTER BY AREA

Built in 1540, many of the hall's original Tudor timbers survived traumas inflicted when it held out as a Royalist stronghold in a three-month siege during the English Civil War (hence the Oliver Cromwell statue opposite). Much of the building is occupied by council departments, but key rooms with period memorabilia (such as the superb dining room) are open to the public. The hall stands in 250-acre Wythenshawe Park.

Eating & drinking

Asian Fusion
489-491 Barlow Moor Road, Chorlton, M21 8ER (881 7200). Bus 22, 23, 23a, 46, 47, 84, 85, 270, 297. **Open** 5pm-11.30pm Mon-Thur, Sun; 5pm-midnight Fri, Sat. **££. Asian**.
It's interesting to watch the chefs, led by Salim Ahmed, at work in this open-plan restaurant. The team prides itself on giving everyone a first-class welcome, which is perhaps why the restaurant is always filled with families, couples and groups. Balti bangla – sizzling chunks of chicken topped with red onions – is a popular, medium-strength dish.

Beech
72 Beech Road, Chorlton, M21 9EG (881 1180). Bus 46, 276. **Open** 11am-11pm Mon-Thur, Sun; 11am-midnight Fri, Sat. **Pub**.
This pocket-sized local, hidden away off the main drag near leafy Chorlton Green, is known for its superb choice of real ales. Football match screenings are a regular fixture in the back bar, while there's a snug feel in the front room, where flock wallpaper dominates. Seats are at a premium most nights; if you can't find a perch here, the Trevor Arms opposite is also worth a visit. The Beech also has a large beer garden.

Café Jem&I
1C School Lane, Didsbury, M20 6RD (445 3996). Bus 23A, 42, 142, 157, 158, 171, 196, 370/East Didsbury rail. **Open** 5.30pm-10pm Mon; noon-2.30pm, 5.30-10pm Tue-Fri; noon-2.30pm, 6-10pm Sat, Sun. **££. Modern British**.

This popular Didsbury restaurant, run by the gifted Jem Sullivan (previously of the Lime Tree, p157), has been awarded the Michelin Bib Gourmand – a prize that identifies establishments that represent good value for money. Expect dishes such as pumpkin, asparagus and petit pois risotto for a tenner.

Greens
43 Lapwing Lane, Didsbury, M20 2NT (434 4259/www.greensrestaurant.net). Bus 46, 47, 111, 169, 178, 179/East Didsbury rail. **Open** 5.30-10.30pm Mon, Sat; noon-2pm, 5.30-10.30pm Tue-Fri; 12.30-3.30pm Sun. **££. Vegetarian**.
After a visit to Greens, it's more or less compulsory for carnivores to say 'I loved it, and I'm not even vegetarian'. The inclusive menu (two courses for £12.95, Tue-Fri and Sun lunch) is fab, but if you're out on a Saturday night, we recommend the Cheshire goat's cheese and pine nut salad with rocket, spinach and watercress, followed by potato hash and artichokes, sun-blush tomatoes, kalamata olives and dill. Oh, and save a little room for the white chocolate cheesecake with dark chocolate sauce.

Isinglass
46 Flixton Road, Urmston, M41 5AB (749 8400/www.isinglassrestaurant.co.uk). Bus 22, 23, 23a, 46, 47, 84, 85, 270, 297/Urmston rail. **Open** 6pm-9.30pm Tue-Thur, Sun; 6pm-10pm Fri, Sat. **££. Modern British**.
Suburban Urmston is the unlikely home of Isinglass, one of Manchester's most impressive restaurants. The name refers to a gelatin-like substance made from fish bladders that's used to clarify beer and wine – but don't let that put you off. Opened by Julie Bagnoli and magnificent Manchester chef Lisa Walker, the idiosyncratic establishment takes the oft-empty promise of only using local ingredients – and shows what can be achieved when experts hold themselves to it. Salad leaves from Chat Moss, rich Dunham Massey ice-cream, meat from Knutsford… the menu doubles up as a local geography guide. Most impressive of all, the evident quality comes at very affordable prices.

Sifters p161

Not what you would expect from a Museum and Tour, but everything you would expect from UNITED.

The Museum and Tour Centre is open all year round. For more information or to book a tour please call: **0870 442 1994** or email: **tours@manutd.co.uk**

Juniper

*21 The Downs, Altrincham, WA14 2QD
(929 4008/www.juniper-restaurant.
co.uk). Metrolink Altrincham/Bus 41,
263, 264.* **Open** *7pm-9.30pm Tue-Thur;
noon-2pm; 7-9.30pm Fri, Sat.* **£££**.
Modern French.
See box p152.

Jai Kathmandu

*45 Palatine Road, Northenden,
Manchester, M22 4FY (946 0501).*
Open noon-2.30pm, 6-11.30pm Mon-
Thur; noon-2.30pm, 6pm-midnight Fri,
Sat; 6pm-11pm Sun. **££. Nepalese**.
Although this restaurant (unconnected
to West Didsbury's Great Kathmandu)
may not appear to be much from the
outside, inside, the Nepalese-centred
cooking is a cut above most curry house
fare. Spicy kidney kebabs and a rich
bhuna gosht stand out on the menu.

Lime Tree

*8 Lapwing Lane, West Didsbury,
Manchester, M20 2WS (445 1217/
www.thelimetreerestaurant.co.uk).
Bus 46, 47, 111, 169, 178, 179/East
Didsbury rail.* **Open** noon-2.30pm, 5.45-
10.15pm Tue-Fri, Sun; 5.45-10.15pm
Mon, Sat. **£££. Modern French**.
Patrick Hannity's refined operation has
loyal customers who can border on the
fanatical in their evangelising, but their
fervour is well placed. The place wears
its French influences lightly, so dishes
of calves liver are served with (a delicious) bubble and squeak.

Marble Beer House

*57 Manchester Road, Chorlton, M21
9PW (881 9206). Bus 84, 86, 270.*
Open noon-11pm Mon-Wed; noon-
midnight Thur-Sun. **Pub**.
Small and intimate, this pub has a nice
line in reclaimed furniture and an ever-
changing choice of guest beers. There's
a well-stocked chiller, with some mighty
strong Belgian bottles. Snacks come by
the bowl courtesy of Chorlton's famous
organic grocers Unicorn, across the road.

Metropolitan

*2 Lapwing Lane, West Didsbury,
Manchester, M20 2WS (374 9559/
www.the-metropolitan.co.uk). Bus 46,
47, 111, 169, 178, 179/East Didsbury
rail.* **Open** 11.30am-11.30pm Mon-
Wed; 11.30am-midnight Thur-Sat;
noon-11.30pm Sun. **£££. Pub**.
This sprawling, loveable pub is a prime
venue in which to enjoy a traditional
roast dinner – but booking is advisable.
With its assortment of large tables and
ramshackle bookshelves, the Met is a
great venue for a lost Sunday. Evening
dishes tend towards high quality pub
fare (Thai green curry, chicken supreme).

Palmiro

*197 Upper Chorlton Road, Whalley
Range, Manchester, M16 0BH (860
7330/www.palmiro.net). Bus 84, 86,
270.* **Open** 6-10.30pm Mon-Sat; noon-
10.30pm Sun. **£££. Modern Italian**.
This trattoria-style Italian is well worth
the trip out to Whalley Range. The food
takes its cue from the family-owned
restaurants of Italy, featuring brilliant
flavours. Special ingredients are imported by owner Stefano Bagnoli's Venetian
father, and there's a superb wine list.
One of the greats of the city's suburbs.

Petra Restaurant

*267 Upper Brook Street, Victoria Park,
Manchester M13 0HR (274 4441/
www.petra2eat.co.uk).* **Open** 11.30am-
2.30pm; 5-11pm Mon-Fri; 5pm-11pm
Sat, Sun. **££. Middle Eastern**.
As an unlicensed restaurant off a busy
main road, this place needs to big-up its
charms to bring in customers. Petra's
strength is its tasty take on Middle
Eastern cuisine: from the delightful
Babaghanouj – an aubergine and garlic
dip sweetened with pomegranate – to
the range of delicately spiced kebabs.

Red Lion

*532 Wilmslow Road, Withington,
M20 4BT (434 2441/www.redlion
withington.com). Bus 50, 113, 130, 147/
Burnage rail.* **Open** 11am-11pm Mon-
Wed; 11am-11.30pm Thur; 11am-12.30am
Fri, Sat; noon-11.30pm Sun. **Pub**.
A cavernous pub with a white-washed
200-year-old façade, where the prevail-
ing beer of choice is Matson's. Outside
is an oddly-shaped bowling green (part
of it was lopped off to extend the beer

garden). It's one of the city's most popular boozers, especially during the summer, with additional highlights being the long-running Monday night quiz and a tremendous chippy (Andy's) opposite, to satisfy those post-pub munchies.

Royal Oak

729 Wilmslow Road, Didsbury, M20 6WF (434 4788). Bus 23, 42, 42a, 142, 157, 158, 171, 196, 370. **Open** 11am-11pm Mon-Wed; 11am-11.30pm Thur; 11am-1am Fri; 11am-12.30am Sat; noon-11.30pm Sun. **Pub**.

Among the glitz and neon of the numerous chains that have taken over south Manchester's most affluent suburb, this place is a haven for traditionalists. The pub is full of lovely little spaces in which couples can share a Marston's and one of the pub's famed cheese and pâté lunches. It's also one of the only remaining places where you can quaff a pint of dark mild too. Drama buffs will love the theatrical posters and memorabilia.

That Café

1031 Stockport Road, Levenshulme, M19 2TB (432 4672/www.thatcafe. co.uk). Bus 191, 192/Levenshulme rail. **Open** 6-10.30pm Tue-Sat; noon-2.30pm Sun. **££. Modern European**.

Kingbee Records

The name undersells this south Manchester venture (this isn't eggs, chips and beans territory), but who needs savvy branding when the food's as good as this? The menu changes weekly, and generally features assured dishes such as venison carpaccio and locally reared pork chops with crackling. Drawing inspirations and flavours from around the world, the standard of cooking is generally superb.

Trof

2A Landcross Road, Fallowfield, M14 6NA (224 0467/www.trof.co.uk). Bus 41, 42, 43, 48, 142. **Open** 9am-midnight daily. **£. Café-bar**.

This café is a stone's throw from Fallowfield's many boozers, so most of the customers will be students eating off a hangover with a hearty breakfast, or, more likely, a hefty Trof burger. The chocolate milkshakes are a joy.

Shopping

Hub

190 Burton Road, West Didsbury, M20 1LH (448 9438). Bus 46, 47, 111, 169, 171, 172, 178, 179, 196/East Didsbury rail. **Open** 10.30am-6pm Mon-Sat; noon-5pm Sun.

This cute and compact boutique is much-loved in south Manchester for its well-chosen collections from lesser-known and upcoming designers, plus owner Louise's popular Beth Graham range. Pretty accessories and a soothing, no-pressure environment for trying clothes on make it a favourite among fashion-forward girls who can't face the City Centre bustle.

Kingbee Records

519 Wilbraham Road, Chorlton, M21 0UF (860 4762/www.kingbeerecords. co.uk). **Open** 10am-5.30pm Mon-Sat.

Record shops are ten a penny in Manchester – but some still achieve legendary status. Despite sitting on an anonymous suburban drag, Kingbee is the worst-kept secret in town. DJs, obsessives and musicians (both famous and aspiring) make regular visits to stock their collections

Mountain excitement

The Trafford Centre goes Alpine with a new snow centre.

Anyone familiar with the UK's swelling ranks of indoor ski slopes will know that skiing in them can be a far from atmospheric experience – more akin to sliding around a refrigerated aircraft hanger than cruising through mountains. It's a problem that planners are determined to address at Manchester's forthcoming Chill Factor (www.chillfactore.com), the country's first self-styled indoor mountain village, where the harmonious Alpine character of the centre's various elements is key. Most of the UK's indoor ski centres are owned by property developers; 'by contrast,' says the project's MD David Sterland, 'we're an indoor ski company developing our own building, so everything is themed around the slope itself: there's an Alpine crêperie, a North American ski bar and a Savoyard-style restaurant.'

It's an ambitious plan: when Chill Factor opens next to the Trafford Centre in October 2007, it will have cost £31 million and will house the country's longest indoor slope, at 180 metres. There'll also be an abundance of mobile ramps and rails for designated freestyle nights, plus a range of amenities for less confident visitors – from a 60-metre beginner slope, toboggan run and supervised snow-play crèche to a programme of ski and snowboard lessons overseen by Andrew Lockerbie, chairman of the British Association of Snowsports Instructors.

The cost of maintaining such an installation means that hour-by-hour skiing will be priced higher than even the priciest of Alpine paradises at roughly £20 per 90 minute session. But, of course, it also saves you the price of a flight, as well as the environmental impact. And though snow-making is never going to be green, Chill Factor is at least trying to be responsible, using environmentally sound building materials and refrigerant, plus renewable energy sources.

No bombing, no petting

Victoria Baths (p153), that fragile old dame of splashing and swimming, celebrated her 100th birthday in 2006 with the news that restoration work is at last going ahead. Although one of Manchester's most sumptuous Grade II-listed Victorian remnants, the Baths closed in 1993, and for ten years thereafter its future looked uncertain.

Thanks to local campaigners, the Baths claimed the attention of *Restoration*, the BBC TV show about buildings on the verge of collapse. Charming its way into first place, the Baths won the hearts of the voting public, plus £3.5 million (£500,000 from the BBC, the rest from the Heritage Lottery Fund).

The funds are being used to restore just one part of this aquatic complex – the Turkish Baths. More important for the baths' long-term future is the TV show's impact: it jump-started a campaign to raise the further £20 million needed to fully restore the rest of the building.

As we went to press, the council was selecting a development partner, with the aim of opening at least one pool for swimming.

Now is the time to enjoy this watery wonder. A multi-coloured brick exterior gives way to floor-to-ceiling tiled rooms. Original signs still hang. A 1950s aeratone (a giant metal jacuzzi) squats in one room, while peeling paintwork can't detract from the grandeur of the stained glass windows. The echoes of a grand past resonate across now-empty pools.

Visitors are still allowed inside, to sneak a peak at renovations and to get to the three untouched pools. Although the building lacks the mod cons you'd expect of a museum, volunteer staff pull out all the stops to give a warm welcome. The free guided tours, gift shop and refreshments are just the icing on this wonderful architectural cake – visit while restoration is still taking place in order to sample Victoria Baths' faded splendour.

with rare, deleted and obscure 45s, and albums from the annals of ska, soul, rock and psychobilly.

Longsight Market

Dickenson Road, Longsight, M13 0WG (225 9859). Bus 53, 54, 168, 170, 173, 191, 192, 196, 197/Levenshulme rail. **Open** 9am-4pm Tue; 9am-4.30pm Wed, Fri; 9am-5pm Sat.
See box p78.

McQueen

54 Beech Road, Chorlton, M21 9EG (881 4718). Bus 16, 46, 47, 85, 168, 276. **Open** 10.30am-6pm Mon-Sat; noon-5pm Sun.
Not to be confused with the notorious fashion designer, McQueen is a small, independent boutique with hand-picked stock featuring up-and-coming labels, established designers and quirky one-offs for women. Men also benefit from the individual buying policy. Shoes and bags add to the offerings, while the shop's style is warm, welcoming and delightfully British.

Mortens

6 Warburton Street, Didsbury, M20 6WA (445 7629). Bus 23, 42, 142, 157, 158, 171, 196, 370/East Didsbury rail. **Open** 9.30am-5.30pm Mon, Tue, Thur-Sat; 9.30am-5pm Wed.
For lovers of rabbit-warren, what-will-you-find-next bookshops, Mortens is unbeatable. It's as rickety and eclectic as Waterstones is corporate and on-message, and none the worse for it. A series of rooms lead you through biography, fiction, arts, children, history and travel, and the low-rise building itself is tucked away down a little cobbled lane.

Pixie

6 Albert Hill Street, Didsbury, M20 6RF (445 5230/www.pixiechildrens wear.com). Bus 23, 42, 142, 157, 158, 171, 196, 370/East Didsbury rail. **Open** 10am-5.30pm Mon-Sat.
This place could probably only work in Didsbury – the flashy, moneyed part of Manchester – and offers maximum appeal to mums who don't believe in cheap and cheerful when it comes to dressing their children. It sells clothes,

shoes and gifts for under-8s, and a small but perfectly formed maternity range; the cutest collections come from Timberland, Quiksilver and Ali Bali.

Sifters

177 Fog Lane, Burnage, M20 6FJ (445 8697). Bus 44, 50, 130, 145, 169, 170, 179, 196/Burnage rail. **Open** 9.30am-5.30pm Mon, Tue, Thur-Sat; 9.30am-1pm Wed.
Enjoying the timeless publicity of a mention in an Oasis song (Mr Sifter in 'Shakermaker') this small second-hand record shop emits a high-pitched whistling noise that only obsessive collectors, generally young men in student jackets, can hear. Not that 'normal' people won't find anything great – Sifters has everything from Loretta Lynn to Les Negresses Vertes – it's just that they'll need sharp elbows to snatch up that rare Nirvana import.

Trafford Centre

M60 junctions 9, 10, Manchester, M17 8AA (746 7777/www.traffordcentre. co.uk). Metrolink Stretford/Bus 23, 23a, 250. **Open** 10am-10pm Mon-Fri; 10am-8pm Sat; noon-6pm Sun.
This huge, shiny mall – home to over 250 shops – caters for every whim and is, therefore, generally pulsing at the seams with bag-laden shoppers. All the major fashion chains (Topshop, H&M, Zara) and high street giants, plus John Lewis and Selfridges, ensure a constant flow of consumers. In between are smaller chains, gift stores, endless cafés and a vast food court, topped with a multi-screen cinema. The decor offers a mildly incongruous neo-classical theme, with sweeping marble halls, frolicking nymph murals and Romanesque busts surveying the retail frenzy.

Unicorn Grocery

89 Albany Road, Chorlton, M21 0BN (861 0010/www.unicorn-grocery.co.uk). Bus 84, 86, 270. **Open** 9.30am-7pm Tue-Fri; 9am-6pm Sat; 11am-5pm Sun.
A large grocery store selling everything the environmentally-concerned shopper could wish for. The produce

MANCHESTER BY AREA

is locally sourced, organic and/or GM free, and all household products can be guaranteed not to kill fish or turn squirrels radioactive. There's also a wide range of dairy-free, gluten-free and sugar-free items.

Nightlife

Iguana Bar

115-117 Manchester Road, Chorlton M21 9PG (881 9338/www.iguana bar.co.uk). **Open** 10am-midnight Mon-Thur, Sun; 10am-1am Fri, Sat.

This unpretentious, welcoming set-up has a penchant for vodka (there's over 50 varieties behind the bar), continental beers and live entertainment. A deli counter offers soup, panini, coffee and the like until 8pm, after which a more rock 'n' roll approach kicks in and live music and comedy become the main draw. Stop in for long-running weekly stand-up session Mirth on Mondays, or check the website for an eclectic roster of world music-orientated gigs.

Manchester Apollo

Stockport Road, Ardwick Green, M12 6AP (0870 380 0017/www.carling.com/ music). **Bus** 67, 192, 196/Ardwick rail. **Open** varies. **Admission** varies.

A staple of the Manchester gig circuit, just a short walk from Piccadilly, this former theatre turned mid-sized live music venue is packed nightly by music fans variously seeking hip hop, dance, rock and cheesy pop. Pay more for a civilised seat on the balcony, or grab a piece of the action on the dancefloor below. Also known as the Carling Apollo.

Pleasure

498 Wilmslow Road, Withington, M20 4AN (434 4300/www.pleasurelounge. co.uk). **Bus** 41, 42, 42a, 43, 47, 48, 140-143, 157, 178, 179/Burnage rail. **Open** 10am-midnight Mon-Thur, Sun; 10am-1am Fri, Sat.

Withington drinking den Pleasure ups the ante for local competition. Run by the owner of Oxford Road's now-closed Zumeba, the venue embodies the former club's easy atmosphere and decent programming, which includes pre-club warm-ups, plus relaxed jazz sessions on Sundays, an open mic Mondays for aspiring musicians and occasional comedy jams.

Rampant Lion

17 Anson Road, Victoria Park, M14 5BZ (248 0371). **Bus** 50, 130/ Levenshulme rail. **Open** noon-1am Mon-Thur; noon-2am Fri, Sat; noon-12.30am Sun.

A large, friendly drinking den with an under-utilised basement, the Rampant Lion was functioning as local boozer and student oddity until the team behind Cord (p91) and Centro (p100) moved in to sort things out. It now features cool club nights, gigs, occasional barbecues and more. It's a safe bet for a relaxing stop-off if you're passing and fancy a quick pint, but when there's an event on it becomes a destination proper, justifying the cab fare out of town.

XS

343 Wilmslow Road, Fallowfield, M14 6NW (257 2403/www.xsmalarky. co.uk). **Open** 11am-2am Mon-Thur, Sun; 11am-3am Fri, Sat.

This friendly pub, deep in student country, is most notable for being home to relaxed and enjoyable comedy caper XS Malarky – a weekly social compèred by highly regarded local comedian Toby Hadoke.

Arts & leisure

Belle Vue Greyhound Stadium

Kirkmanshulme Lane, Gorton, M18 7BA (0870 840 7550/www.lovethe dogs.co.uk). **Bus** 201, 203, 204/Belle Vue rail. **Open** 6pm Tue, Thur-Sat. **Admission** £5.50-£6, £4 11-16s, free under-11s.

Four race meetings a week, every week, featuring one of the world's fastest animals. Choose from trackside bellowing and fast food or the more refined option of three courses and polite cheering in the Grandstand restaurant.

Manchester United's 'theatre of dreams' p164

MANCHESTER BY AREA

Lancashire County Cricket Club

Talbot Road, Old Trafford, M16 0PX (0870 062 4000/Lodge 874 3333/ www.lccc.co.uk). Metrolink Old Trafford/ Bus 114, 252, 253, 254, 255, 256, 257, 263, 264. **Open** *Office* 9am-5pm Mon-Fri. Closed in winter.

The home of Lancashire County Cricket Club for 150 years (and Andrew 'Freddie' Flintoff for considerably less), the pavilion at Old Trafford is looking a little tatty, though a £30million modernisation programme is on the cards, which will include ground expansion. The Lodge, a 68-room hotel overlooking the pitch, provides a place to stay for die-hard fans, while a small museum (open on 1st XI and International match days) displays 200-years-worth of cricketing memorabilia.

Manchester United Football Club

Sir Matt Busby Way, Old Trafford, M16 0RA (0870 442 1999/www. manutd.com). Metrolink Old Trafford/ Bus 256, 263. **Open** *Museum* 9.30am-5pm daily. *Tour* 9.40am-4.30pm daily. **Admission** *Museum* £6; £4.25 reductions; £17.50 family ticket; free under-5s. *Museum & tour* £9.50; £6.50 reductions; £27 family ticket; free under-5s.

The stadium of the world's most famous football team isn't in the most glamorous of locations, but it nevertheless boasts the Premier League's largest capacity, recently expanded to 76,000. If you can't get your mitts on a matchday ticket (they're extremely hard to get hold of without a season ticket), console yourself with United's impressive museum. Kids can try and kick the ball as hard as Wayne Rooney (a high-tech machine measures maximum velocity – they'll have to top 77mph to beat United's star players), or trot down the players' tunnel as part of the popular behind-the-scenes tour (book in advance to avoid disappointment; tickets can be bought via the website).

Stockport

Stockport may be seen as a plainer, less fashionable sister to Manchester, but it still manages to hold its own. The vast borough is made up of eight districts and reaches from Manchester to the Peak District. Visitors can head out to **Mellor** and **Marple** for pubs and walks, **Bramhall** and **Lyme Park** (p169) for their historical houses or in to **Heaton Moor** for drinks and dinner. Stockport centre itself is a mix of high-street shops and meandering cobbled streets, with a splendid 15th-century market place and Victorian covered hall at the top of town. It's also home to the landmark brick viaduct, as painted by Lowry, and the UK's first (and only!) hat museum.

Sights & museums

Hatworks

Wellington Mill, Wellington Road South, Stockport, SK3 0EU (0845 833 0975/ www.hatworks.org.uk). Bus 42, 173, 192, 203/Stockport rail. **Open** 10am-5pm Mon-Fri; 1-5pm Sat, Sun, bank hols. Last entry 4pm. **Admission** free; £2 guided tour.

Proudly describing itself as 'the UK's only museum devoted solely to the hatting industry', Hatworks is a quaint experience, displaying machinery and memorabilia from local hatting factories (once the town's prime trade, hence Stockport County FC's nickname of the Hatters). A second floor is crammed with headwear donated by everyone from Vivienne Westwood to Fred Dibnah, plus there's an extensive family area where kids can play dress-up.

Staircase House

30-31 Market Place, Stockport, SK1 1ES (480 1460/www.staircase house.org.uk). Bus 42, 173, 192, 203/Stockport rail. **Open** noon-5pm Mon-Sat; 10am-5pm Sun, bank hols. **Admission** £3.50; free reductions; £12 family ticket.

A night at the Plaza

Stockport's art deco cinema is enjoying a new heyday.

Elegance isn't a word often associated with a night at the flicks, but patrons at the **Stockport Plaza** (p166) expect to step into another era, and to do so with a bit of class. From usherettes with doily headdresses to the Pathé newsreels played before the main feature, the Plaza delights in its position as a 1930s Super Cinema, a Grade-II listed building and a much-loved urban anachronism in the heart of Stockport.

Built in 1932, at the height of the Depression and during the switchover from silent movies to 'talkies', the Plaza served as something of an escape for people used to the hard life of a northern industrial town. From 1967 to 1999 the building was a Mecca bingo hall, but was converted back to a cinema by a charitable trust in 2000, and fully restored in 2005. Boasting a single screen with an impressive 1,200-seat capacity, the volunteer-staffed Plaza certainly knows its clientele: several recent screenings could have sold out three times over. When it's not screening films, the venue serves as a variety theatre showing classic plays from the 1940s and '50s, that appeal both to a nostalgic older crowd and young urbanites with a thing for Bette Davis.

And then there's the Compton Organ that's kept in Rolls Royce-condition so that the likes of Radio 2's Nigel Ogden can accompany the occasional silent movie double bills. Organ music also precedes regular classic movie screenings, and the house organist delivers a rousing rendition of the national anthem at the end of the night.

Located behind the tourist information office, and extensively restored following a major fire in 1995, Staircase House is a very modern presentation of the city's architectural history told through the surviving layers of this impressive building. Dating back to the 15th century, and continuously occupied until shortly after World War II, its rooms are filled with replica period furnishings and artefacts, most of which can be handled.

Stockport War Memorial & Art Gallery

Wellington Road South, SK3 8AB (474 4453/www.stockport.gov.uk). Bus 42, 173, 192, 203/Stockport rail. **Open** 11am-5pm Mon, Tue, Thur, Fri; 10am-5pm Sat. **Admission** free.

In contrast to the entrance's grand colonnaded steps, the gallery space that hosts a changing programme of art exhibitions consists of just a pair of drab, functional rooms. Beyond is a more impressive and imposing statue of Britannia, with a kneeling warrior beneath a beautiful glass-domed ceiling, surrounded by engraved lists of the fallen. Upstairs, the memorial hall acts as the main gallery.

Eating & drinking

Arden Arms

23 Millgate, Stockport, SK1 2LX (480 2185/www.arden-arms.co.uk). Bus 42, 173, 192, 203/Stockport rail. **Open** noon-11.45pm daily. **Pub.**

This traditional 19th-century coaching inn has won awards for its ale and ambience. The Arms has everything a good pub should – great food, friendly service, real fires for the winter and an alfresco area for the summer. The owners previously ran a restaurant and, on top of hearty lunches, do a blinding Sunday roast. Beer comes from the local Robinson's Brewery.

Swan with Two Necks

36 Princes Street, Stockport, SK1 1RY (480 2341). Bus 42, 173, 192, 203/Stockport rail. **Open** 11am-11pm daily. **Pub.**

Built in 1926, this is a long, narrow Robinson's pub, and one of several in Stockport town centre that have made it into CAMRA's *Inventory of Historic Pub Interiors* (the nearby Queen's Head is another). There's a snug, a vault and a comforting amount of wood and glass. The food is traditional pub grub, with huge portions followed by a small bill. You can sometimes smell the beer at the nearby Robinson's brewery.

Nightlife

Blue Cat Café

17 Shaw Road, Heaton Moor, Stockport, SK4 4AG (432 2117/www.bluecatcafe.co.uk). Bus 42a/Heaton Chapel rail. **Open** 7am-midnight daily.

Comedy and live music in the heart of the Heatons: the Blue Cat is a little enclave of city bohemia picked up and transplanted to the 'burbs. Established for nearly a decade, it proudly showcases the best new bands, both local and touring, most of which you can see without having to pay an admission fee. Past highlights include Johnny Marr and Viva Stereo. Sharing premises with the Blue Cat Recording Studio, and the creation in 2004 of the label Blue Cat Records, contributes to the muso appeal.

Arts & leisure

Sale Sharks

Edgeley Park, Hardcastle Road, Stockport, SK3 9DD (286 8926/www.salesharks.com). Bus 11, 28, 192, 309, 310, 368, 369, 371, X69/Stockport rail.

One of the oldest clubs in English Rugby history, currently playing their best-ever matches. Sale Sharks play at the home of Stockport County FC – a League Two side that offers a refreshing antidote to English football's over-priced Premiership.

Stockport Plaza

The Plaza, Mersey Square, Stockport, SK1 1SP (477 7779/www.stockportplaza.co.uk). Bus 42, 191, 192/Stockport rail.

See box p165.

Quarry Bank Mill p169

Days Out

The listings in this guidebook cover only the central portion of Greater Manchester. In this chapter, you'll find highlights of the wider urban area, along with trips that dip into the beautiful and accessible countryside that surrounds the city.

Alderley Edge

About 15 miles south of Manchester into the footballer belt, the plush little town of Alderley Edge is something of a magnet for the Cheshire set. The centre is full of boutiques, bijou restaurants and amusingly expensive charity shops; aim for the junction of the central London Road and Stevens Street for the most browsable. You can pass a happy hour indulging in material pursuits here, but what distinguishes Alderley Edge from any other wealthy satellite town is the primeval geological feature that gives

the town its name. Just over a mile away via the B5087, Macclesfield Road, the edge itself is a red sandstone escarpment 600 feet (185 metres) high, thought to be the result of a cataclysmic prehistoric flood event, and on a clear day you can see for miles across the Cheshire plain.

The land is owned by the National Trust and on certain days (call 01625 584412 for details) you can turn up for a fascinating guided walk that will point out the geological history as well as a wealth of intriguing features, including the site of a beacon planned to be used to alert the country to the arrival of the Spanish Armada, a hermit's refuge and the face of a wizard carved into the rock. This face is relatively recent, but does draw attention to the lore that formed the basis for Alan Garner's brilliant Edge-set 1960 children's novel *The Weirdstone of Brisingamen*.

Peel Tower, Ramsbottom p170

Take a refreshment break at the pleasant tearoom situated next to the car park; then, if you're driving, consider taking in Nether Alderley Mill (Congleton Road, Nether Alderley, SK10 4TW, 01625 527468, www.national-trust.org.uk, closed winter), a gem of an Elizabethan corn-mill, complete with informative guided tours and working water wheel, a mile south on the A34.

Getting there: Take the train from Manchester Piccadilly to Alderley Edge, or, by car, take the A34 direct from the city centre.

Lyme Park

Disley, Stockport, Cheshire, SK12 2NX (01663 762023/www.nationaltrust. org). **Open & admission** days & times vary; check website for details. This attractive country house on the threshold of the Peak District has much to recommend it, but owes its more recent fame to being the setting for Colin Firth's memorable appearance from the lake in the 1995 BBC adaptation of *Pride and Prejudice*. As well as that happy memory, visitors will be treated to roaming herds of red and fallow deer on the numerous country walks. If you're on foot, be aware that the park entrance is over a mile from the hall and buildings; a shuttle bus operates when the house is open, in the spring and summer.

Lyme Hall dates back to Tudor times and Tudor elements survive, although most of the present-day building dates from extravagant 18th-century conversions. It's surrounded by an elegant series of Victorian conservatories and gardens. All the usual National Trust facilities – café, knowledgeable guides, a shop – are present and correct, and there's also an adventure playground.

For a taste of the Peak District proper, you can nip across the Derbyshire border five miles away to the rambler-friendly village of Hayfield. It's something of a mecca for walkers, as one of the best access points to the rugged moorland and mountain of Kinder Scout, the historic site of the 1932 mass trespass that ultimately led to today's right to roam. Should Kinder prove a little too ambitious then the village of Little Hayfield is a mile away on paths and minor roads, or you could follow one of the paths on the Sett Valley trail (follow signs from Hayfield station car park or call in to the information centre on Station Road; 01663 746222).

For a meal try the Pack Horse (3-5 Market Street, SK22 2EP, 01663 740074, www.thepackhorsehayfield.co.uk), a handsome pub offering locally sourced meat dishes and good veggie options.

Getting there: Lyme Park is on the A6 12 miles south of Manchester. To reach Hayfield, continue on the A6, then go left on the A6015 once through Disley. Disley train station is half a mile from the park gates; the line (or a bus, or a mile's walk) also connects to New Mills, from where you can get a bus to Hayfield.

Quarry Bank Mill

Quarry Bank Road, Styal, Wilmslow, Cheshire, SK9 4LA (01625 527468/ www.quarrybankmill.org.uk). **Open** days & times vary; check website for details. **Admission** £8.50; £4.70 reductions.

One of the industrial jewels in the National Trust's crown, Quarry Bank Mill is an impressively preserved 18th-century mill building, the centre of a working colony established by founder Samuel Greg that was both socially and technologically revolutionary for its time. Set in a wooded country estate, it stands as a living portal to the past, as well as a pretty setting for rambles and picnics.

Approached down a hill, the vast red-brick building nestles next to the river (the first mill was powered by water wheel, a stunning example of which is still active). The north of England's damp climate was ideal for cotton processing – too dry, and the cotton wouldn't stretch – and the mill stands as a reminder of what made the region the industrial powerhouse it was. At the start of the walkthrough tour, museum interpreters in period dress show you early spinning techniques before taking you into halls of still-operative machinery – the deafening clatter of the demonstration is an experience in itself. In the neighbouring Apprentice House you can see where a significant body of orphaned children lived and worked.

A decent café provides meals and refreshments, before a walk around the surrounding Styal Country Estate follows the route of the man-made lakes and tributaries that powered the mill.

Ten minutes' walk away is Styal village. Originally an insignificant hamlet, this developed into a workers' colony when Greg established the mill, and today it remains mostly unaltered from the mid 19th century – the shop, school, chapel and cottages are intact remnants of this sprawling monument to the industrial revolution.

Getting there: By car, take the B5167 out of the city centre, then the B5166 to Quarry Bank Mill, a journey of about ten miles. Styal has a railway station but services (from Manchester Piccadilly) are infrequent.

Ramsbottom

The agreeable Victorian mill town of Ramsbottom, in the moorlands of north Manchester, was established in the early 19th century by Daniel and William Grant – who live on in fiction as Dickens' Cheeryble brothers in *Nicholas Nickleby*. The town sits nestled in the Irwell Valley below the looming Holcombe Hill and, while unremarkable for shopping (aside from the farmers' market on the second Sunday of every month), makes a good base for other activities. A good way to get there is on the East Lancs Steam railway (0161 764 7790, www.east-lancsrly.co.uk), which runs between Heywood, Bury and Rawtenstall at weekends.

Following Bridge Street up the hill brings you to the *Tilted Vase* sculpture in the marketplace, which is part of the 40-mile Irwell Sculpture Trail (www.irwellsculpturetrail.co.uk); a less ambitious hike is Holcombe Hill itself. Follow Carr Street and head uphill bearing to the left, past the Shoulder of Mutton pub (a decent stop for food or liquid refreshment; 01706 822001) and take the path of your choice. Once

ascended – a straightforward hour's walk for all levels (or there's a road for cheats with cars) – you will see the Peel Tower, a landmark for miles around. Built in 1852 in tribute to Sir Robert Peel, the 19th-century Prime Minister (born in nearby Bury) and founder of the modern police force, the tower is sometimes open at weekends (you'll know because the flag is raised, or you can call 0161 253 5899), its 150-step ascent offering an even more striking view than that already available.

Getting there: By road, take the M66 then the A676. On public transport, take the Metrolink to Bury, then the 472 or 475 bus (except Sunday).

Ashton-under-Lyne

Ashton is one of the less glamorous satellites orbiting the M60 ring road (to the east); but despite its lack of pizzazz, it contains a pair of undersung but quietly excellent museums that should ensure a gently memorable day out.

In the town centre, the Museum of the Manchesters (Ashton Town Hall, OL6 6DL, 0161 342 2254, closed Sun) commemorates the experiences and sacrifices of the Manchester Regiment, which was established in 1881 and associated with the town for many years. The Regiment is best known for the World War I poets who served with it, including Wilfred Owen. Among the regimental memorabilia, a recreation of a trench is a suitably sobering experience.

A mile away across the town centre, following first Stamford Street and then, after the roundabout, Park Parade, the Portland Basin Museum (Portland Place, Ashton-under-Lyne, 0161 343 2878, closed Mon) nudges up alongside the Ashton Canal, where hourly barge trips run on Sundays (except in winter; for details, check with the organisers on 0161 339 1332). The old warehouse is crammed full of artefacts from a century or so ago, and also has a lovingly recreated 1920s street.

Getting there: Take bus 216 or 219 from Manchester city centre, or drive there on the A635.

Essentials

Radisson Edwardian p177

Hotels

Manchester is in the middle of a genuine hotel shake-up. As more and more classy, modern names open their doors in the City Centre, the city's hoteliers have been forced to take a long, hard look at their properties and the quality of their accommodation services. The big news, in every sense, is the arrival of the **Hilton** in the Beetham Tower. The tallest residential building in the UK at the time of writing, the statement-making glass edifice is Manchester's newest landmark, with arguably the best hotel-bar in town.

The city has upped its game considerably in terms of the quality of accommodation on offer, with the three **Eclectic Collection** hotels – Great John Street, Eleven Didsbury Park and Didsbury House – providing some of the most stylish options in town. Money is being ploughed into hotels across the city, and many have received major facelifts, or at least substantial refurbishment (often by luxury chains such as Adobe, Arora, Q Hotels and the Principal Hotels group). And the majority of those that have not yet made improvements plan to do so in the forthcoming months. Previously failing premises have now been rejuvenated and even budget chains are making more of an effort to keep up with the local competition. This is all great news for visitors, who now have more interesting and varied options to choose from than ever before.

City Centre

Arora International

18-24 Princess Street, M1 4LY (236 8999/www.arorainternational.com). Metrolink St Peter's Square/City Centre buses/Piccadilly rail. **£££**.

Cliff Richard isn't a name you'd normally associate with cutting-edge design. Yet the holy rock 'n' roller is part-owner of one of the hippest hotels in the city. The Arora is a vision of contemporary cool, with sleek, modern rooms and funky furniture. (Four Cliff-themed rooms feature artworks and objects from the singer's personal collection.) A visit to the hotel bar and fine dining restaurant, Obsidian p69, is a must.

Britannia Manchester

35 Portland Street, M1 3LA (832 7073/www.britanniahotels.com). Metrolink Piccadilly Gardens/City Centre buses/Piccadilly rail. **££**.

The Britannia's main selling points are its location – right on Piccadilly Gardens – and its very reasonable rates. The ostentatious building and decor will not be to everyone's taste, but it's perfect for those who like a bit of faded grandeur, with a sweeping gold staircase and huge chandeliers. A refurbishment planned for 2007 should modernise things, but may also mean the loss of the fabulous flock wallpaper.

Great John Street Hotel

Great John Street, M3 4FD (831 3211/www.eclectic-hotel-collection.com). City Centre buses/Salford Central rail. **££££**.

Great John Street, an Eclectic Collection hotel, pulls out all the stops to deliver a truly luxurious boutique experience. Housed in an old Victorian school by the *Coronation Street* set, the hotel offers duplex suites only, each uniquely designed. Hand-carved furniture, roll-top baths and super-sexy fabrics and fittings lend the place a modern-vintage feel. The absence of a restaurant and guest parking is made up for by a butler's tray for breakfast, a chi-chi ground-floor bar and a rooftop hot tub.

SHORTLIST

Best new
- Hilton (p174)
- Hilton Chambers (p178)

Best for hipsters
- Arora (p173)
- Great John Street Hotel (p173)
- The Lowry (p179)
- Staying Cool (p176)

Best hotel bars
- Cloud 23 at the Hilton (p130)
- Tempus at the Palace (p177)

Hotels with heritage
- Midland Hotel (p174)
- Palace Hotel (p177)
- Radisson Edwardian (p177)

Cheap as chips
- Hatters (p177)
- New Union Hotel (p178)

Budget style
- Hilton Chambers (p178)
- The Ox (p178)

Best breakfast
- Malmaison (p174)
- Whitehouse Manor (p181)

Stellar restaurants
- Obsidian at Arora (p69)
- River Restaurant at the Lowry (p137)

Best suites
- Didsbury House Hotel (p181)
- Midland Hotel (p174)

Best spa
- The Lowry (p179)
- Radisson SAS (p179)

Location, location, location
- Britannia Manchester (p173)
- New Union Hotel (p178)
- Radisson SAS (p179)

Best traditional
- Abbey Lodge (p179)
- Etrop Grange (p179)

ESSENTIALS

Hilton

NEW *303 Deansgate, M3 4LQ*
(870 1600/www.hilton.co.uk). Metrolink
G-Mex/City Centre buses/Deansgate
rail. **£££.**

There may be a set of swanky apartments above, but for 23 impressive
floors the Beetham Tower belongs to
the Hilton, as witnessed by the unmiss-
able branding. Rooms are kitted out
with all the latest technology
(ergonomic work stations, laptop
access). Cloud 23 bar (p130), at the top,
is straight out of *Lost in Translation*.
The ground-floor Podium restaurant-
bar doesn't have the impressive views,
but does great food.

Jurys Inn

56 Great Bridgewater Street, M1 5LE
(953 8888/www.bookajurysinn.com).
Metrolink G-Mex/City Centre
buses/Deansgate rail. **££.**

Well placed for the Bridgewater Hall
(opposite), Manchester Central (aka G-
Mex) and Deansgate Locks, this pur-
pose-built Jurys offers fairly priced,
good-standard accommodation. The
bedrooms and communal areas have
been refurbished according to the inof-
fensive, generically modern brand spec.
Unique to this Jurys is the Inntro bar,
with plasma screen sport action. Ask
for a room at the front to watch the
Hallé musicians coming and going from
the back door of Bridgewater Hall.

Malmaison

Piccadilly, M1 3AQ (278 1000/
www.malmaison-manchester.com).
Metrolink Piccadilly/City Centre
rail/Metrolink Piccadilly. **£££.**

A favourite with visiting bands and
celebs, the Mal is a first choice for those
who like to think of themselves as pos-
sessors of style. The old Joshua Hoyle
textile mill recently received a £1.8 million facelift, introducing a dark-toned
red, brown and black colour scheme to
many of the suites. The star of the new
line-up is the seriously sexy Moulin
Rouge room; the freestanding bath in
the lounge takes around 30 minutes to
fill, such is its depth.

Manchester Marriott Victoria & Albert

Water Street, M3 4JQ (832 1188/
www.marriott.com). City Centre
buses/Salford Central rail. **£££.**

Originally a textile warehouse, this
Grade II-listed building now houses 148
hotel rooms, a conference centre and a
bar and restaurant. The corporate feel
is softened by exposed wooden beams,
bare brickwork and quirkily shaped
rooms, while photographic reminders
of former occupier Granada TV – now
based across the road (*Coronation
Street* actors can sometimes be found in
the bar here) – line the mezzanine
gallery off reception. Nice smellies.

Midland Hotel

Peter Street, M60 2DS (236 3333/
www.qhotels.co.uk). Metrolink St Peter's
Square/City Centre buses/Oxford Road
rail. **££££.**

This grand old dame of Manchester
hotels opened in 1905. It's had its fair
share of high-profile visitors over the
decades (Winston Churchill, Princess
Anne) and goes down in history as the
place where Charles Stewart Rolls and
Frederick Henry Royce met. After a
few years in the wilderness, the
Midland is back on glamorous form
after a massive £15 million makeover
by new owners Q Hotels. The feel is
modern classic throughout, from the
marble-floored reception to richly fur-
nished rooms.

Novotel Manchester Centre

*21 Dickinson Street, M1 4LX (235
2200/www.novotel.com). Metrolink
St Peter's Square/City Centre
buses/Oxford Road rail.* **£££.**

Describing itself as a 'new generation
Novotel', this hotel does have more to
offer than similarly branded accommodation in the city. The rooms may
be a set size, but effort has gone into
funking up the decor, and a good spa
and gym add to the appeal. There are
busy bars in the vicinity, but if an
evening in a Wetherspoons isn't your
bag, then head to nearby Chinatown.

The Ox p178

Serviced apartments

Staying Cool

Manchester city centre has been quick to take up the relatively recent phenomenon of serviced apartments and aparthotels. If you're keen to experience the city at your own pace, these could fit the bill, providing space to live, work and play as you choose. Most come with the kind of appliances and accessories you'd find (or dream of having) in your own home, and while breakfast isn't made for you, there are also no room service knocks on your door at 7am. And with spaces available in new, central residential developments, visitors now have the chance to make themselves at home in some of the most fashionable addresses in town.

The **Staying Cool** apartments (Clowes Street, M3 5NF, 835 1074, www.stayingcool.com) in the Edge development, off Blackfriars (with further options in Castlefield) show that self-catering accommodation doesn't have to mean toning down on luxury. The boutique apartments have Apple Mac entertainment centres, fresh fruit and a juicer to squish it in and good coffee in the cupboards.

Well located close to the Northern Quarter is the **Place**

Apartment Hotel (Ducie Street, M1 2TP, 778 7500, www.the placehotel.com). The spacious four-star accommodation has enough rooms to get lost in, plus DVD, satellite TV and CD players as standard. Being a converted grade-II warehouse means plenty of exposed brickwork and original features.

Manchester's most recently opened serviced apartments can be found on Shudehill. **Premier Apartments** (Icon 25, 64 Shudehill, M4 4AA, 236 8963, www.premierapartmentsmanchest er.com) offer open-plan living with a dining space, kitchen and lounge. And international chain Bridgestreet now havre snazzy **Atrium** (74 Princess Street, M1 6JD, 235 2000, www.atrium apartments.co.uk) apartments on the corner of Princess Street and Whitworth Street, while the Gallery on Blackfriars Street houses a number of modern, fully-equipped apartments by **Nomorehotels** (22-26 Blackfriars Street, M3 5JS, 0870 850 8514, www.nomorehotels. co.uk) with washing machines, dishwashers and great-looking marble bathrooms.

Palace Hotel

Oxford Street, M60 7HA (288 1111/ www.principal-hotels.com). Metrolink St Peter's Square/City Centre buses/ Oxford Road rail. **£££**.

This well-loved, characterful hotel, housed in the old Refuge Assurance Building (p115), was recently acquired by the prestigious Principal Hotels group, and received a £7 million facelift in 2005. The restored glass dome over the vast reception makes for an impressive entrance, while the new Tempus bar mixes original marble flooring and Victorian tiles with cool design. While there are 70 new, stylish bedrooms, the remaining 200 or so have yet to be re-vamped, but are charmingly traditional and boast majestic ceilings.

Princess on Portland

101 Portland Street, M1 6DF (236 5122/www.princessonportland.co.uk). Metrolink Market Street/City Centre buses/Piccadilly rail. **££**.

The Princess on Portland was originally a silk storehouse and was first converted into a hotel in 1982. More recently Best Western have stepped in to run the show, introducing 85 hotel rooms, a new restaurant and bar. Bedrooms are clean and contemporary, if somewhat corporate. The Modern European Brasserie on Portland (p105) is open to guests and the general public.

Queens Hotel

34 London Road, M1 2PF (236 1010). Metrolink Piccadilly/City Centre buses/Piccadilly rail. **£**.

The name and rainbow flag outside give you a clue to this hotel's orientation. Previously known as Hollywood International, it's kitsch and camp with an anything-goes attitude and open-all-hours policy. Black and white images of film icons adorn the red lobby, while the bar is pink in every sense. Some rooms are a little rough around the edges – but improvements are slowly being made, and the characterful and flamboyant guests make up for the tired decor.

Radisson Edwardian

Free Trade Hall, Peter Street, M2 5GP (835 9929/www.radissonedwardian. com). Metrolink St Peter's Square/City Centre buses/Oxford Road rail. **££££**.

Some may say that turning the Free Trade Hall into a hotel is criminal, but the Radisson has made real efforts to do so sympathetically, retaining many of the building's original features. A new extension houses 263 deluxe bedrooms, each with a king-size bed, lots of sleek technology and a marble bathroom. Suites are named after those who have performed or spoken at the hall, with Dylan and Fitzgerald making penthouse appearances, and Gladstone and Dickens patronising the meeting rooms.

Rosetti

107 Piccadilly, M1 2DB (247 7744). Metrolink Piccadilly Gardens/City Centre buses/Piccadilly rail. **£££**.

Abode Hotels have now acquired the Rosetti, which means change is on the horizon, with a refurbishment planned for summer 2007. The current quirky design is likely to be replaced with something safer and more neutral. The existing restaurant/bar will make way for a cocktail bar and branded MC café-bar on the ground floor, with a Champagne bar and restaurant in the basement below.

Northern Quarter

Hatters

50 Newton Street, M1 2EA (236 9500/ www.hattersgroup.com). Metrolink Piccadilly Gardens/City Centre buses/ Piccadilly rail. **£**.

A short walk from Piccadilly station, Hatters offers hostel accommodation for backpackers and budget travellers. Rooms and facilities are basic, but added extras like complimentary tea, coffee and toast and quality mattresses on the bunk beds make the stay more comfortable. An open kitchen and canteen area gives guests somewhere socialble to warm up their soup. Friendly and lively staff lead regular pub crawls and tours around the area.

ESSENTIALS

Hilton Chambers

Hilton Chambers

NEW *15 Hilton Street, M1 1JJ (236 4414/www.hattersgroup.com). Metrolink Piccadilly Gardens/City Centre buses/Piccadilly rail.* **£**.

The Northern Quarter has little in the way of decent rooms, so hurray for Hilton Chambers. Part of the Hatters group, the accommodation falls somewhere between hostel and small hotel, with a mix of private en suite double rooms and dorms. It retains an informal atmosphere, with barbecues on the decked courtyard in summer, 24-hour reception and helpful staff.

Castlefield

The Ox

71 Liverpool Road, M3 4NQ (839 7760/ www.theox.co.uk). Metrolink G-Mex/City Centre buses/Deansgate rail. **£**.

It's well known that this award-winning gastropub is the place for *Coronation Street* star watching. What's less well known is that it has nine comfortable rooms, each with its own funky style; the overall feel is retro-cool meets vintage chic. And within easy walking distance of the City Centre, the hotel is great value for money. All bedrooms are en suite and although breakfast isn't available, there are plenty of places nearby to grab a cappuccino. See also p131.

Gay Village

New Union Hotel

111 Princess Street, M1 6JB (228 1492/www.newunionhotel. com). Metrolink St Peter's Square/ City Centre buses/Oxford Road rail. **£**.

Pink, but not exclusively so, the New Union has a great position on the corner of Canal and Princess Streets. Ideal for travellers who prefer to spend money on having a good time while saving on accommodation. Groups are well catered for with triple and quad rooms. Karaoke takes place in the venue below.

Rembrandt

33 Sackville Street, M1 3LZ (236 1311/
www.rembrandtmanchester.com).
Metrolink Mosley Street/City Centre
buses/Piccadilly rail. **£**.

If you're after plush accommodation in
the city, don't visit the Rembrandt. But
if you want to be shown a lively time in
the centre of Manchester's Gay Village,
then this is the hotel for you. With a
popular and lively bar open until the
small hours, the pub-hotel is a well
known fixture on the gay circuit and
popular with a more mature crowd.
There are 20 well priced clean but basic
rooms, most with en suite bathrooms.
A bright breakfast room makes for an
agreeable morning coffee spot.

Manchester Airport

Etrop Grange

Thornley Lane, Manchester M90 4EG
(0870 609 6123/www.corushotels.com).
Buses 18, 18a, 19, 20, 43, 199, 200,
369, 379, TS18, TS21/Manchester
Airport rail. **££**.

At the other end of the airport accommodation scale to Radisson SAS (see
below), Etrop Grange is a traditional
English hotel of the pot pourri variety.
Built in 1780, the country house offers
64 bedrooms with flowery or tartan
designs. Choose from huge oak four
posters or polished iron bedsteads with
layers of bedding. A converted coach
house holds the restaurant, with its
candelabras and big white tablecloths.

Radisson SAS

Chicago Avenue, Manchester Airport,
M90 3RA (490 5000/www.radisson
sas.com). Buses 18, 18a, 19, 20,
43, 199, 200, 369, 379, TS18,
TS21/Manchester Airport rail. **£££**.

Manchester's most convenient airport
hotel option is directly linked with the
three terminals via a futuristic walk-
way, and is also connected to the railway into town. Shiny floors and
low-flying spot lighting make it feel
very 21st century, if rather airport-like.
Rooms are comfy and facilities good;
there's a relaxing health club, beauty
salon and pool, and for those in a rush,
an express laundry service and a
check-out and grab-and-run breakfast.

Salford

Holiday Inn Manchester West

Liverpool Street, M5 4LT (743 0080/
www.ichotelsgroup.com). Buses 25, 69,
71, 294/Salford Central rail. **££**.

A mid-range option in sunny Salford;
what the Holiday Inn lacks in character it makes up for in reliability. You
know what you're getting at this
straightforward chain – in this case, 82
modernlooking rooms and a newly
opened bar and restaurant. A recent
refurbishment has given the place a
clean, fresh feel.

Lowry

50 Dearmans Place, Chapel Wharf,
M3 5LH (827 4000/www.thelowry
hotel.com). City Centre buses/Salford
Central rail. **££££**.

The hotel of choice for visiting actors,
politicians and Premiership footballers,
the Lowry is Manchester's original
five-star hotel. The address may be
Salford, but it's located right on the
City Centre's edge, on the banks of the
murky River Irwell. Everything is as it
should be – huge, achingly hip rooms
with super-sized beds, original modern
art, discreet service and clued-up staff.
A swanky spa and the serene River
Restaurant (p137), run by champion
chef Eyck Zimmer, are further draws.

Out of the city

Abbey Lodge

501 Wilbraham Road, Chorlton, M21
0UJ (862 9266). Buses 16, 46, 47, 85,
85c, 86c, 168, 276. **£**.

A converted Victorian family home in
the heart of Bohemian Chorlton, the
Abbey exemplifies the perfect English
B&B. Pristinely kept and expertly run,
the place is decorated in a classical but
unfussy way. Bedrooms are of a good
size and are all en suite. There's no
communal morning room, but a

Abbey Lodge p179

bespoke breakfast tray is available. And with one of the finest delis in the area, the Unicorn, across the road, expect quality organic products.

Belmore Hotel

143 Brooklands Road, Sale, M33 3QU (973 2538). Metrolink Brooklands/ Buses 99, 266, 267, 268. **££**.
The Belmore restaurant has been getting first-rate reviews since its transformation by JW Lees in 2006 and with chef Carl Chapel (the Ivy, Juniper) on board. The hotel's 20 en-suite bedrooms have yet to reach the restaurant's decorative standards, but modernisation plans are afoot to tie in with the venue's new, fashionable theme. Work is expected to be completed by spring 2007.

Best Western Willowbank

Wilmslow Road, Fallowfield, M14 6AF (224 0461/www.bestwestern.co.uk). Buses 41, 42, 43, 44, 46, 47, 48, 142, 143, 145, 147, 157, 158/Train. **££**.
First, a warning. If you like modern and minimal design, this place isn't for you. The Willowbank is from the more-is-more school of style, with bedrooms busy enough to make you cross-eyed. If you can get past this, you'll find a pretty reliable hotel. It's also the only half-decent place that services the student area of Fallowfield, otherwise dominated by rundown B&Bs and tatty hotels.

Didsbury House Hotel

Didsbury Park, Didsbury, M20 5LJ (448 2200/www.eclectic-hotel-collection.com). Buses 23, 42/East Didsbury rail. **£££**.
The second great townhouse hotel in Eamon and Sally O'Laughlin's Eclectic Collection, just up the road from Eleven (see below), Didsbury House has the attractive look and style of its older sibling, with a few added extras. There are more rooms, with 27 en suites, including two stunning loft rooms complete with vaulted, beamed ceilings and double baths; the small but perfectly formed bar is as stylish as any in the City Centre, and there's a dry sauna.

Eleven Didsbury Park

Didsbury Park, Didsbury, M20 5LH (448 7711/www.eclectic-hotel-collection.com). Buses 23, 42/East Didsbury rail. **£££**.
Eleven Didsbury Park was the first suburban townhouse hotel to open in Manchester. It remains one of the city's best-loved destinations, and offers great rooms and calm, quiet surroundings in the trendy 'burbs. Interior design credit goes to Sally O'Laughlin, who has created an undeniably hip but welcoming hotel. The garden has a lovely decked area with white parasols and linen chairs, leading onto a manicured lawn.

Traveller's Retreat

3/4 Beechmount Road, Harpurhey, M9 5XS (205 2400). Buses 17, 17a, 52, 64, 123, 131, 163/Dean Lane rail. **££**.
OK, Harpurhey may not be the most glamorous of destinations, but it is well connected, being just a short bus ride from the City Centre. Hidden down a fairly uninspiring street off Rochdale Road, this hotel is a cheerful discovery. Originally two Victorian houses that have now been knocked through, the interestingly shaped rooms are all of a good size, and have large beds. Decor is modern with an African twist – a nod to the owner's Caribbean heritage.

Whitehouse Manor

New Road, Prestbury, Macclesfield SK10 4HP (01625 829 376). Buses 19, 19x/Macclesfield rail. **£££**.
Leafy land of footballers' wives and long gravel drives, Prestbury is 20 miles from Manchester, but worth the journey if your destination is the Whitehouse. The lovingly restored Georgian townhouse has eleven individually themed bedrooms, all with stunning bathrooms. These range from rooms with traditional four posters swathed in fabric, to more contemporary alternatives like the (literally) sparkling Crystal suite. Owner Ryland Wakeham is a trained chef, so breakfasts are something special. And just across the road is the Whitehouse Restaurant, where evening meals may be charged to guests' rooms.

Getting Around

Arriving & leaving

By air

Manchester Airport
489 3000/www.manchesterairport. co.uk. About 10 miles south of Manchester, junction 5 off M56.
The airport has three terminals, all of which are accessible by train, bus and coach. All transport runs into one interchange, which is open 24 hours a day, with links to the terminals via Skylink walkways.

Airport trains
Direct trains run to the airport from Piccadilly and take about 20 minutes. It is cheapest to buy two singles at £2.65 each (off-peak) rather than a return. Direct trains also run from Stockport every hour, again £2.65 for a cheap day single, which must be purchased before you get on the train. Visit www. nationalrail.co.uk or call 08547 484950 for exact departure times.

Airport buses
Local buses leave the City Centre every 30 minutes from early in the morning until late at night. **Stagecoach** operate the frequent 43 service between the centre and the airport which takes roughly an hour. The 199 bus is the fastest service from Stockport and takes about 20 minutes. To check timetables visit www.gmpte.co.uk.

Airport parking
There is ample car parking provided for all three terminals. The cheapest option is the **Shuttle carpark**, 15 minutes from the airport and accessible by a free bus. Discounted prices on the web start from £4 a day. Visit www.manchesterairport.co.uk.

There are also **Long Stay** carparks, **Premier** carparks and **Terminal** carparks that charge more accordingly.

By rail

Manchester Piccadilly is the main rail station in the City Centre and most trains stop here. **Victoria**, **Oxford Road** and **Deansgate** stations also service the centre. Smaller stations link Greater Manchester and the suburbs with the City Centre. For information on ticket prices call 08457 484950/www.nationalrail. co.uk. You can get timetable and price information and buy tickets for any train operator in the UK via www.trainline.co.uk. Or find your local station code at www.gmpte. co.uk and contact the GMPTE 24-hour automated service (228 0322) to see how your train is running.

The **Metrolink** (see p183) runs services to Piccadilly, Victoria and Deansgate (G-Mex).

By coach

National Express
Manchester Central (formerly Chorlton Street Coach Station), Chorlton Street, M1 (08705 80 80 80/www.national express.com).
Services to destinations around the UK.

Public transport

The **GMPTE** oversee all public transport. Most bus stations have a Travelshop that provides general travel and timetable information, as well as selling multi-journey tickets. The main Travelshop is in Piccadilly Gardens next to the Metrolink stop. Service and timetable information is also provided by **Traveline** on 0870 608 2608.

Travelcards

Saver tickets are available across the train, tram and bus networks. There are Day Saver tickets for each specific service but if you are planning to do a lot of travelling around then the System One off-peak Day Saver is the best value option. This allows you to travel on any bus, train and Metrolink between 9.30am and midnight any day of the week. The day ticket costs £7 and can be bought from bus drivers, at rail stations and Metrolink ticket machines.

Travelling with children

Under-fives travel free on both the buses and the Metrolink. On the train, two children are allowed to travel free with each full fare-paying adult. Children between five and 15 pay a concessionary fare on all transport but may need an Under 16 Card. There is no discount for students or children on the System One off-peak Day Saver and the full adult price of £7 will be charged.

Buses

Tickets can be bought from the driver on all buses, but they only take cash, so it's advisable to have the right change. **Stagecoach** and **First Manchester** are the main operators in the centre. Fares vary depending on journey length, but single tickets start at around £1 and go up to £3.80. A Stagecoach Day Saver costs £3 and a First Day Saver costs £3.30, but travel is limited to the bus company you bought the ticket on. Alternatively a System One Day Saver can be bought from the driver for £4 (£3.50 off-peak) and offers unlimited travel on any bus for the whole day.

Metroshuttle

This brilliant free City Centre bus service runs from Manchester Piccadilly and visitors can hop on

and off at stops all around the city. There are three circular lines, with routes covering Deansgate, King Street, Quay Street and Castlefield.

Night buses

Night buses are sometimes entertaining and often rowdy, but they do offer a cheap and generally safe alternative to getting a taxi home. Late services run from Piccadilly Gardens and other City Centre stops, but most only operate on a Friday and Saturday. Buses run regularly until around 3.30am (check www.gmpte.co.uk for timetables) and travel to Greater Manchester and the suburbs. Fares are generally £2.50 or less.

Trams

The **Metrolink**, or Met, as it's known, is a system of modern overground trams that run through the centre of Manchester and out to the suburbs, replacing many of the old smaller local train stations and services. It operates seven days a week, 365 days a year and is one of the most convenient and quickest ways to travel into the City Centre. Lines run from the centre out as far as Altrincham, Bury and Eccles and there are plans to extend the service out to Ashton-Under-Lyne, Rochdale and Oldham, Chorlton and Manchester Airport in the next few years. The network also provides links to some of the city's main leisure and tourist attractions.

Fares

Buy tickets from machines on the platform before boarding. Prices vary depending on journey length, but tickets should cost no more than £4.80 for a return at peak time.

Timetable

Services run every six minutes between Bury and Altrincham via the City Centre, and every 12 minutes between Eccles and

ESSENTIALS

Piccadilly. Trams operate from around 6am until roughly 11pm Monday to Thursday, and until midnight on Saturdays and 10pm on Sundays, although these times vary depending on the station. 'Off-peak' applies to trams running from 9.30am onwards Monday to Friday and all-day Saturday, Sunday and bank holidays.

Taxis

Hackney Cabs ('black cabs') are licensed by the local council and can be hailed down on the street or picked up at a taxi rank. Look out for cabs with their 'taxi' logo illuminated to show that they are free. There are many ranks around the City Centre, including Piccadilly Gardens, Piccadilly station, St Peter's Square and Albert Square. You can also book a black cab (for example Mantax, 230 3333) and some accept credit cards, but it is best to confirm this before you start your journey. Taxi fares increase after midnight.

Minicabs

Private Hire cabs are usually saloon vehicles and are generally cheaper than black cabs. They cannot be hailed on the street and it is illegal for them to pick up customers on the road. Drivers touting for business on the street are often unlicensed, expensive and potentially dangerous. Book minicabs in advance over the phone; find taxi numbers on 118 500. Legitimate drivers should display their licence in the car and a licence plate on the back of the vehicle.

Driving

Manchester City Centre has its fair share of one-way systems, but it is a relatively easy place to navigate and tourist attractions are well signed.

Parking

Always read the signs. City Centre traffic wardens aren't shy of slapping on tickets, wheel-clamps and even towing offending vehicles away. As a general guide, you cannot park on a single yellow line between 8am and 6pm Monday to Saturday. Never park on a double yellow line, in a loading bay or on a space marked for residents or the disabled unless you have the appropriate permit.

There is both on- street and off-street parking in the City Centre. On-street parking is often restricted to one, two or three hours maximum depending on where in town you are stopping. A ticket must be purchased from the machine on the pavement with tariffs starting at around 50p for 15 minutes. Parking on the road is free after 6pm and on Sundays. There are numerous **NCP** car parks (0870 606 7050/www.ncp.co.uk) around Manchester, many of which are 24-hour. These offer secure parking and charge around £2.50 for two hours.

Towed vehicles

Vehicles that are towed away are taken to the pound in Ardwick, which must be contacted to get your car back (234 4145). Proof of identity is needed – usually car keys and two other forms of ID. The current charge is £135. If the vehicle isn't claimed within 14 days, this increases to £165.

Vehicle hire

There are a number of companies in and around the city. **EasyCar** offers good rates, and has an office just by Piccadilly rail station. Visit www.easycar.com. Otherwise, try:
Avis 236 8874, www.avis.co.uk
Enterprise Rent-A-Car 708 8860, www.enterprise.com
Hertz 0870 846 0001, www.hertz.co.uk

Resources A-Z

Accident & emergency

City Centre and Greater Manchester hospitals with 24-hour Accident & Emergency departments are listed below. The UK number for police, fire and ambulance is **999**.

Booth Hall Children's Hospital
Charleston Road, Blackley, M9 7AE (795 7000) Bus 51, 62, 88, 88, 118, 162, 294/Moston rail.

Hope Hospital *Stott Lane, Salford, M6 8HD (789 7373). Metrolink Ladywell/Bus 10/M10, 25, 27, 33, 55, 63, 67, 68, 69, 70, 71, 100, 484/ Eccles rail.*

Manchester Royal Infirmary
Oxford Road, M13 9WL (276 1234). Bus 15, 16, 41-44, 46-48, 50, 53, 111, 113, 130, 140-143, 145, 147, 157, 191, 197/Oxford Road rail.

North Manchester General Hospital *Delauneys Road, Crumpsall, M8 5RB (795 4567). Bus 51, 52, 62, 88, 89, 115, 118, 149, 151, 154, 156, 162, 185, 294/Crumpsall rail.*

Credit card loss

American Express *01273 696933*
Diners Club *01252 513500*
MasterCard/Eurocard *0800 964767*
Switch *0870 600 0459*
Visa/Connect *0800 895082*

Customs

For allowances see
www.hmrc.gov.uk.

Disabled travellers

The majority of buses and trains have disabled access. Metrolink stations are equipped with ramps, lifts or escalators and most platforms have modified edges to help visually impaired travellers. The website www.manchester.gov.uk lists hotels, restaurants, attractions and shops in the city that comply with most access requirements. **Shopmobility** at the Arndale Centre provide mobility aids (839 51100), while **DIAL Trafford** (877 8546) and **Manchester Disabled People's Access Group** (273 5033) provide information for people with sensory impairment and physical disabilities respectively.

Electricity

The UK uses the standard European 220-240V, 50 cycle AC voltage via three-pin plugs.

Dental emergency

University Dental Hospital
Higher Cambridge Street, M15 6FH (275 6666/Out of hours 0845 6018529). Bus 15, 16, 41-44, 46-48, 53, 85, 86, 99, 101, 104, 108, 109, 111, 140-143, 145, 147, 157, 191, 197, 250, 253, 263, 290, 291/Oxford Road rail. **Open** 8.30am-5pm Mon-Fri; 10am-12.30pm Sat, Sun, bank hols (out of hours). A limited number of patients can be seen (on a first come, first served basis).

Embassies & consulates

Australian Consulate *Century House, St Peter's Square, M2 3ND (237 9440). Metrolink St Peter's Square/City Centre buses/Oxford Road rail.*

Residents of other English-speaking countries should, in the event of an emergency, contact the relevant embassy or consulate in London for advice or information:

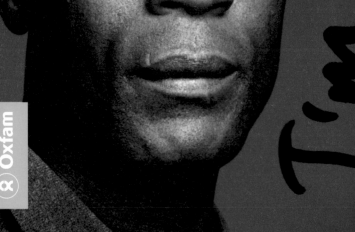

Chris, 40, London

Oxfam

I'm in

In fact, a child dies from hunger every five seconds. Saying *I'm in* means you're part of a growing movement that's fighting the injustice of poverty - in a way that works best for you. You can give money, work in one of our shops, join our campaign to urge politicians to do more, or simply give your name. Text 'TIMEOUT' and your name to 87099. We'll let you know how to help. We can do this. We *can* end poverty. Are you in?

I said 'I'm in' because it's the 21st Century and people still go without food. that's shameful

Let's end poverty together. Text 'TIMEOUT' and your name to 87099.

Standard text rates apply. Registered charity No.202918

American Embassy
020 7499 9000/www.usembassy.org.uk.
Canadian High Commission
7258 6600/www.canada.org.uk.
Irish Embassy *020 7235 2171/*
www.dfa.ie.
New Zealand High Commission
020 7930 8422/www.nzembassy.com.
South African High Commission
020 7451 7299/www.southafrica
house.com.

Internet

There are a reasonable number of
internet cafés and points in and
around Manchester. The majority
of public libraries have terminals
and many hotels and bars are
installing Wi-Fi (for which there
is often a user-fee). Visit www.
wi-fihotspotlist.com for a list of
local providers or try:

easyInternet Café

*8 St Ann's Square, M2 7HA (832 1122).
Metrolink St Peter's Square/City Centre
buses/Victoria rail.* **Open** 8am-10pm
Mon-Fri; 9am-9pm Sat, Sun.

Pure Space Café Bar
(wireless)

*11-13 New Wakefield Street, M1 5NP
(236 4899/www.pure
spacecafebar.co.uk). Metrolink St Peter's
Square/City Centre buses/Oxford Road
rail.* **Open** noon-1am Mon-Thur, Sun;
noon-3am Fri, Sat.

Suburb (wireless)

*63 Deansgate, M3 2BW (832 3642/
www.suburbstore.com). Metrolink
Victoria/City Centre buses/Victoria
rail.* **Open** 9am-6pm Mon-Sat.

Opening hours

Banks 9am-4.30pm (some close
at 3.30pm, some 5.30pm) Mon-Fri;
sometimes also Saturday mornings.
Offices Normally 9am to 5pm
Mon-Fri.
Shops 10am-6pm Mon-Fri; but
many stores now open until 8pm.
Most shops in the City Centre

are open on Sunday, either from
11am to 5pm or noon to 6pm.

Pharmacies

Britain's best-known pharmacy
chain is **Boots**, with branches in
the City Centre and most of the
surrounding town centres. The
main branch in Manchester is on
Market Street, open until 8pm.
There are no 24-hour pharmacies
in Manchester, but a handful are
open late. **A&A Pharmacy** (58
Wilmslow Road, Rusholme, 224
8501) is open until 10pm and is
just a few minutes out of the City
Centre on the 42 bus.

Police stations

Call **999** in an emergency and ask
for the police or call 872 5050 at all
other times. The main police station
is on Bootle Street, but all suburbs
are served by a local neighbourhood
station. Call Directory Enquiries
for details (118 118/500/888) or
visit the Greater Manchester Police
website at www.gmp.police.uk.
Bootle Street Police Station
*Bootle Street, Manchester, M2 5GU
(856 3221/856 8696). Metrolink St
Peter's Square/City Centre buses/
Oxford Road rail.*

Postal services

Post offices are usually open 9am to
5.30pm Monday to Friday and 9am
to noon Saturday.
Manchester Post Office *26 Spring
Gardens, M2 1BB (0845 722 3344).
Metrolink Market Street/City Centre
buses/Piccadilly rail.*

Smoking

From summer 2007 there will be
no smoking in any public places
in England, including bars,
restaurants and stations.

ESSENTIALS

Telephones

The dialling code for Manchester, Greater Manchester, Salford and Stockport is 0161. If you're dialing from outside the UK, dial your international access code, then the UK code, 44, then the full number omitting the first 0 from the code. To dial abroad from the UK first dial 00, then the country code.

US mobile phones only operate in the UK if they have tri- or quad-band facility.

Public phones

Public payphones take coins or credit cards. The minimum cost is 20p. International calling cards offering bargain minutes via a freephone number are widely available.

Time

Manchester operates on Greenwich Mean Time (GMT), which is five hours ahead of North American Eastern Standard Time. In spring, the UK puts its clocks forward by one hour to British Summer Time. In autumn, clocks go back by one hour to GMT.

Safety

Manchester is generally a safe city to visit. Visitors should remain vigilant in crowded areas – buses, busy streets, train stations – for petty criminals. Keep your valuables in your hotel room or safe and make sure the cash and cards you carry are tucked away in your bag.

Tipping

Tip in taxis, minicabs, restaurants, hotels, hairdressers and some bars (not pubs). Ten per cent is normal; note that some restaurants add on a service charge of up to 15 per cent.

Tickets

The main venues in Manchester sell their tickets through third parties. (Note that there's normally a booking fee involved.) **Ticketmaster** (www.ticket master.co.uk, 0870 5344 4444) and **Ticketweb** (0870 534 4444) have tickets for the major theatres and venues in the centre. **Live Nation** (www.livenation.co.uk) also represent a good number of venues. Small, independent places generally sell tickets from their own box office or through promoters.

Tourist information

Manchester's main tourist office is by St Peter's Square, and offers a wide variety of information on accommodation, sights and more general details on Manchester and the surrounding suburbs. Stockport and Salford have their own centres.

Manchester Tourist Information *Town Hall Extensions, Lloyd Street, M60 2LA (0871 222 8223/www. manchester.gov.uk). Metrolink St Peter's Square/City Centre buses/Oxford Road rail.*

Stockport Tourist Information *Staircase House 30/31 Market Place Stockport SK1 1ES (474 4444/ www.staircasehouse.org). Stockport Bus Station buses/Stockport rail.*

Salford Information Centre Lowry *Pier 8, Salford Quays, M50 3AZ (848 8601/www.destinationsalford. com). Metrolink Harbour City/Bus 69, 290, 291.*

Visas

EU citizens do not require a visa to visit the UK; citizens of the USA, Canada, Australia, South Africa and New Zealand need only a passport for tourist visits. Check current status on www.ukvisas. gov.uk well before you travel.

Index

Sights & Areas

ESSENTIALS

Eating & Drinking

a

Abdul's p115
Abergeldie Café p90
Ape & Apple p65
A Place Called Common p90
Arden Arms p166
Asian Fusion p154

b

Bar 38 p66
Barburrito p104
Beech p154
Bluu p91
Brasserie on Portland p105
Briton's Protection p66

c

Café Jem&I p154
Choice Bar & Restaurant p131
Circus Tavern p105
Cloud 23 p131
Corbieres p66
Cord p91
Crescent p134
Crown & Kettle p91

d

Dimitri's p131
Dry Bar p91
Duke's 92 p131

e

Earth Café p91
EastZEast p105
Establishment p66
Evuna p67

f

French p67

g

Gaucho Grill p67
Greens p154
Grill On The Alley p67

h

Hare & Hounds p67
Harry Ramsden's p132
Hunter's BBQ p91

i

Isinglass p154

j

Jai Kathmandu p157
Juniper p157

k

Katsouris Deli p67
King's Arms p135
Knott, The p132
Koreana p68
Kro 2 p119

l

Lamb Hotel p143
Lass O'Gowrie p119
Le Mont p68
Lime Tree p157
Lounge Ten p68
Luso p69

m

Manto p106
Marble Arch Inn p144
Marble Beer House p157
Market Restaurant p92
Metropolitan p157

n

Northern Quarter Restaurant & Bar p92

o

Obsidian p69
Odd p92
Ox, The p132
Old Wellington Inn p69
Olive Lounge & Bistro p144

p

Pacific p106
Palmiro p157
Petra Restaurant p157
Peveril of the Peak p119
Pure Space p119

r

Red Chilli p106
Red Lion p157
Revolution p119
River Restaurant p135
Room p69
Royal Oak p158

s

Sam's Chop House p69
Shlurp p71
Simply Heathcotes p71
Sinclair's Oyster Bar p71
Slattery p144
Soup Kitchen p92
Stock p71
Swan with Two Necks p166

t

Tampopo p71
Taurus p106
Temple of Convenience p119
Teppanyaki p106
That Café p158
This & That p92
Tribeca p109
Trof p158

y

Yang Sing p109

ESSENTIALS

ESSENTIALS

Manchester Visitor Information Centre
St Peter Square, Manchester, M60 2LA
+44 (0)871 222 8223

Mon-Sat 10.00am-5.30pm
Sun 10.30am-4.30pm